COMPUTER BOOK SERIES FROM IDG

Quicken For DOS For Dummies

MW00396568

Some cool date-editing tricks

If the selection cursor is on a date field, you can do this:

Press	What happens
+	Adds 1 day to the date shown
-	Subtracts 1 day from the date shown
y	Changes the date to the first date in the year
r	Changes the date to the last date in the year
m	Changes the date to the first date in the month
h	Changes the date to the last date in the month
t	Changes the date to the current date

Five Ways to Yelp for Help

Press this key or key combination	To do this...
F1	Displays a screeful of context sensitive help information.
Ctrl-F1	Displays a list of topics covered in on-line help.
Ctrl-F7	Displays more information in the Qcard pop-up message box.
Ctrl-F8	Shrinks and unshrinks the Qcard pop-up message box.
Ctrl-F9	Removes and redisplays the Qcard pop-up message box.

Three things that every Quicken user should do

1. Use the Retirement Planner to estimate when and how you can retire.

2. Create a category list that makes it easy to track your spending and tax deductions.

3. Use the Reconcile command to balance bank accounts each month with only a few minutes of effort.

Displaying Menus with a Keystroke

F2	Displays the Print/Acct menu
F3	Displays the Edit menu
F4	Displays the Shortcuts menu
F5	Displays the Reports menu (if you're on the Register or Write Checks screens)
F6	Displays the Activities menu

. . . For Dummies: #1 Computer Book Series for Beginners

Quicken For DOS For Dummies

Cheat Sheet

Twenty Sneaky Shortcuts for Busy People

You can use these keyboard shortcuts. (If you need to press two keys simultaneously, such as the Ctrl key and the C letter key, I'll describe the key combination as Ctrl-D, OK?)

Use this key	Quicken does this
Esc	Cancels what I'm doing.
Enter	Moves to the next whatever the next field, the next step, the next screen . . . . :
Tab	Moves cursor to the next field.
Shift-Tab	Moves cursor to the previous field.
F10	Continue (as in "Carry on, Quicken . . . let's move to the next step").
Ctrl-C	Displays that list of categories and accounts so that I can select one.
+	Adds 1 day to this date (this only works if the cursor is in a date field).
-	Subtracts 1 day from this date (again, it only works if the cursor is in the date field).
Ctrl-Backspace	Erases the field the cursor is on.
Ctrl-O	Displays the calculators so that I can do some 'rithmetic
Ctrl-P	Prints a register when the register screen shows.
Ctrl-A	Displays the Select Account to Use screen.
Ctrl-S	Displays the Split Transaction screen.
Ctrl-D	Deletes the selected transaction.
Ctrl-V	Voids the selected transaction.
Ctrl-K	Displays the financial calendar.
Ctrl-Z	Reprints the last report (yes, again).
Alt-Z	Produces a quick report.
Ctrl-Ins	Copies the selected transaction.
Shift-Ins	Pastes the copied transaction into the selected row.

. . . For Dummies: #1 Computer Book Series for Beginners

QUICKEN FOR DOS FOR DUMMIES™

QUICKEN FOR DOS FOR DUMMIES™

by Stephen L. Nelson

IDG BOOKS

IDG Books Worldwide, Inc.
An International Data Group Company

San Mateo, California ✦ Indianapolis, Indiana ✦ Boston, Massachusetts

Quicken For DOS For Dummies

Published by
IDG Books Worldwide, Inc.
An International Data Group Company
155 Bovet Road, Suite 310
San Mateo, CA 94402

Library of Congress Catalog Card No.: 93-78747

ISBN: 1-56884-006-3

Printed in the United States of America

10 9 8 7 6 5 4 3 2 1

Distributed in the United States by IDG Books Worldwide, Inc.

Distributed in Canada by Macmillan of Canada, a Division of Canada Publishing Corporation; by Computer and Technical Books in Miami, Florida, for South America and the Caribbean; by Longman Singapore in Singapore, Malaysia, Thailand, and Korea; by Toppan Co. Ltd. in Japan; by Asia Computerworld in Hong Kong; by Woodslane Pty. Ltd. in Australia and New Zealand; and by Transword Publishers Ltd. in the U.K. and Europe.

For information on where to purchase IDG Books outside the U.S., contact Christina Turner at 415-312-0633.

For information on translations, contact Marc Jeffrey Mikulich, Foreign Rights Manager, at IDG Books Worldwide; FAX NUMBER 415-358-1260.

For sales inquiries and special prices for bulk quantities, write to the address above or call IDG Books Worldwide at 415-312-0650.

 is a trademark of IDG Books Worldwide, Inc.

COMPUTER
BOOK SERIES
FROM IDG

About the Author

This is the person Steve wishes he were: A tall, dark handsome type who served in MI5 with British Intelligence and then transferred to the Central Intelligence Agency after becoming a citizen of this country.,

This is the person who Steve really is: A tall, blonde, handsome, dull, boring CPA type with two girls, a wife, no pets, and a master's degree in finance. Steve happily moved from main frame computers to personal computers when they appeared on the scene. He has been working with Quicken for seven years (or many, many moons).

Steve has no hobbies or interests except watching TV (since someone stole his ski equipment and he quit Tae Kwon Do last year).

By the way, Steve is a bestselling author on the Quicken product and has written over 30 computer books.

About IDG Books Worldwide

Welcome to the world of IDG Books Worldwide.

IDG Books Worldwide, Inc., is a division of International Data Group, the world's largest publisher of computer-related information and the leading global provider of information services on information technology. IDG publishes over 194 computer publications in 62 countries. Forty million people read one or more IDG publications each month.

If you use personal computers, IDG Books is committed to publishing quality books that meet your needs. We rely on our extensive network of publications, including such leading periodicals as *Macworld*, *InfoWorld*, *PC World*, *Computerworld*, *Publish*, *Network World*, and *SunWorld*, to help us make informed and timely decisions in creating useful computer books that meet your needs.

Every IDG book strives to bring extra value and skill-building instruction to the reader. Our books are written by experts, with the backing of IDG periodicals, and with careful thought devoted to issues such as audience, interior design, use of icons, and illustrations. Our editorial staff is a careful mix of high-tech journalists and experienced book people. Our close contact with the makers of computer products helps ensure accuracy and thorough coverage. Our heavy use of personal computers at every step in production means we can deliver books in the most timely manner.

We are delivering books of high quality at competitive prices on topics customers want. At IDG, we believe in quality, and we have been delivering quality for over 25 years. You'll find no better book on a subject than an IDG book.

John Kilcullen
President and C.E.O.
IDG Books Worldwide, Inc.

IDG Books Worldwide, Inc. is a division of International Data Group. The officers are Patrick J. McGovern, Founder and Board Chairman; Walter Boyd, President. International Data Group's publications include: **ARGENTINA's** Computerworld Argentina, InfoWorld Argentina; **ASIA's** Computerworld Hong Kong, PC World Hong Kong, Computerworld Southeast Asia, PC World Singapore, Computerworld Malaysia, PC World Malaysia; **AUSTRALIA's** Computerworld Australia, Australian PC World, Australian Macworld, Network World, Reseller, IDG Sources; **AUSTRIA's** Computerwelt Oesterreich, PC Test; **BRAZIL's** Computerworld, Mundo IBM, Mundo Unix, PC World, Publish; **BULGARIA's** Computerworld Bulgaria, Ediworld, PC & Mac World Bulgaria; **CANADA's** Direct Access, Graduate Computerworld, InfoCanada, Network World Canada; **CHILE's** Computerworld, Informatica; **COLOMBIA's** Computerworld Columbia; **CZECH REPUBLIC's** Computerworld, Elektronika, PC World; **DENMARK's** CAD/CAM WORLD, Communications World, Computerworld Danmark, LOTUS World, Macintosh Produktkatalog, Macworld Danmark, PC World Danmark, PC World Produktguide, Windows World; **EQUADOR's** PC World; **EGYPT's** Computerworld (CW) Middle East, PC World Middle East; **FINLAND's** MikroPC, Tietoviikko, Tietoverkko; **FRANCE's** Distributique, GOLDEN MAC, InfoPC, Languages & Systems, Le Guide du Monde Informatique, Le Monde Informatique, Telecoms & Reseaux; **GERMANY's** Computerwoche, Computerwoche Focus, Computerwoche Extra, Computerwoche Karriere, Information Management, Macwelt, Netzwelt, PC Welt, PC Woche, Publish, Unit; **HUNGARY's** Alaplap, Computerworld SZT, PC World; **INDIA's** Computers & Communications; **ISRAEL's** Computerworld Israel, PC World Israel; **ITALY's** Computerworld Italia, Lotus Magazine, Macworld Italia, Networking Italia, PC World Italia; **JAPAN's** Computerworld Japan, Macworld Japan, SunWorld Japan, Windows World; **KENYA's** East African Computer News; **KOREA's** Computerworld Korea, Macworld Korea, PC World Korea; **MEXICO's** Compu Edicion, Compu Manufactura, Computacion/Punto de Venta, Computerworld Mexico, Macworld, Mundo Unix, PC World, Windows; **THE NETHERLAND'S** Computer! Totaal, LAN Magazine, MacWorld; **NEW ZEALAND's** Computer Listings, Computerworld New Zealand, New Zealand PC World; **NIGERIA's** PC World Africa; **NORWAY's** Computerworld Norge, C/World, Lotusworld Norge, Macworld Norge, Networld, PC World Ekspress, PC World Norge, PC World's Product Guide, Publish World, Student Data, Unix World, Windowsworld, IDG Direct Response; **PANAMA's** PC World; **PERU's** Computerworld Peru, PC World; **PEOPLES REPUBLIC OF CHINA's** China Computerworld, PC World China, Electronics International, China Network World; **IDG HIGH TECH BEIJING's** New Product World; **IDG SHENZHEN's** Computer News Digest; **PHILLIPPINES'** Computerworld, PC World; **POLAND's** Computerworld Poland, PC World/Komputer; **PORTUGAL's** Cerebro/PC World, Correio Informatico/Computerworld, MacIn; **ROMANIA's** PC World; **RUSSIA's** Computerworld-Moscow, Mir-PC, Sety; **SLOVENIA's** Monitor Magazine; **SOUTH AFRICA's** Computing S.A.; **SPAIN's** Amiga World, Computerworld Espana, Communicaciones World, Macworld Espana, NeXTWORLD, PC World Espana, Publish, Sunworld; **SWEDEN's** Attack, ComputerSweden, Corporate Computing, Lokala Natverk/LAN, Lotus World, MAC&PC, Macworld, Mikrodatorn, PC World, Publishing & Design (CAP), DataIngenjoren, Maxi Data, Windows World; **SWITZERLAND's** Computerworld Schweiz, Macworld Schweiz, PC & Workstation; **TAIWAN's** Computerworld Taiwan, Global Computer Express, PC World Taiwan; **THAILAND's** Thai Computerworld; **TURKEY's** Computerworld Monitor, Macworld Turkiye, PC World Turkiye; **UNITED KINGDOM's** Lotus Magazine, Macworld, Sunworld; **UNITED STATES'** AmigaWorld, Cable in the Classroom, CD Review, CIO, Computerworld, Desktop Video World, DOS Resource Guide, Electronic News, Federal Computer Week, Federal Integrator, GamePro, IDG Books, InfoWorld, InfoWorld Direct, Laser Event, Macworld, Multimedia World, Network World, NeXTWORLD, PC Games, PC Letter, PC World Publish, Sumeria, SunWorld, SWATPro, Video Event; **VENEZUELA's** Computerworld Venezuela, MicroComputerworld Venezuela; **VIETNAM's** PC World Vietnam

 The text in this book is printed on recycled paper.

Acknowledgments

Hey, reader — A lot of people spent a lot of time working on this book to make Quicken easier for you. You should know who these people are in case you ever meet them in the produce section of the local grocery store squeezing cantaloupe.

They are: Marta Partington, Shawn MacLaren, Pam Mourouzis, Barbara Potter and Judy Brunetti. Thanks also to the production staff of Beth Baker, Cindy Phipps, Tony Augsburger, Drew Moore, Mary Breidenbach, and Valery Bourke.

(The publisher would like to give special thanks to Patrick J. McGovern, without whom this book would not have been possible.)

Credits

Publisher David Solomon	**Project Editor** Marta Justak Partington
Managing Editor Mary Bednarek	**Editors** Shawn MacLaren Pamela Mourouzis Judy Brunetti
Acquisitions Editor Janna Custer	
Production Manager Beth Jenkins	**Technical Reviewer** Alan Gray
Senior Editors Sandra Blackthorn Diane Graves Steele	**Production Staff** Tony Augsburger Valery Bourke Mary Breidenbach Sherry Gomoll Drew Moore Gina Scott
Production Coordinator Cindy L. Phipps	
Acquisitions Assistant Megg Bonar	**Proofreader** Kathleen Prata
Editorial Assistant Patricia R. Reynolds	**Indexer** Joan Dickey
	Book Design University Graphics

Say What You Think!

Listen up, all you readers of IDG's international bestsellers: the one — the only — absolutely world-famous *...For Dummies* books! It's time for you to take advantage of a new, direct pipeline to the authors and editors of IDG Books Worldwide.

In between putting the finishing touches on the next round of *...For Dummies* books, the authors and editors of IDG Books Worldwide like to sit around and mull over what their readers have to say. And we know that you readers always say what you think.

So here's your chance. We'd really like your input for future printings and editions of this book — and ideas for future *...For Dummies* titles as well. Tell us what you liked (and didn't like) about this book. How about the chapters you found most useful — or most funny? And since we know you're not a bit shy, what about the chapters you think can be improved?

Just to show you how much we appreciate your input, we'll add you to our Dummies Database/Fan Club and keep you up to date on the latest *...For Dummies* books, news, cartoons, calendars, and more!

Please send your name, address, and phone number, as well as your comments, questions, and suggestions, to our very own *...For Dummies* coordinator at the following address:

...For Dummies Coordinator
IDG Books Worldwide
3250 North Post Road, Suite 140
Indianapolis, IN 46226

IDG BOOKS

(Yes, Virginia, there really is a *...For Dummies* coordinator. We are not making this up.)

Please mention the name of this book in your comments.

Thanks for your input!

Contents at a Glance

Introduction 1

PART I: Zen, Quicken, and the Big Picture 7

Chapter 1: Start Here 9
Chapter 2: An Introduction to the Big Picture 21
Chapter 3: Maximum Fun, Maximum Profits 37

PART II: The Absolute Basics 49

Chapter 4: Checkbook on a Computer 51
Chapter 5: Printing 101 69
Chapter 6: Perfect Balance 91
Chapter 7: Housekeeping 103
Chapter 8: Calculators, Smalculators 121

PART III: Home Appliances 141

Chapter 9: Credit Cards (and Debit Cards, too) 143
Chapter 10: Other People's Money 159
Chapter 11: Investments in a Nutshell 175

PART IV: Serious Business 205

Chapter 12: Payroll 207
Chapter 13: Customer Receivables 225
Chapter 14: Vendor Payables 235

PART V: The Parts of Tens 241

Chapter 15: Ten Questions I'm Frequently Asked about Quicken 243
Chapter 16: Ten Tips for Bookkeepers Who Use Quicken 249
Chapter 17: Ten Tips (More or Less) for Business Owners 257
Chapter 18: Ten Things You Should Do If You're Audited 261
Chapter 19: Ten Things I Blew Off (and My Excuses) 265
Chapter 20: Ten Magic Tricks You Can Try 271

Appendix A: Installation 277

Appendix B: Glossary of Business and Financial Terms 283

Index 299

Cartoons at a Glance
By Richard Tennant

page 141

page 49

page 241

page 120

page 174

page 7

page 205

page 234

page 248

page 36

Table of Contents

● ●

Introduction 1

  About This Book 1

  About the Author 1

  How to Use This Book 2

  What You Can Safely Ignore 2

  What You Should Not Ignore (Unless You're a Masochist) 3

  Three Foolish Assumptions 3

  How This Book Is Organized 4

    Part I: Zen, Quicken, and the Big Picture 4

    Part II: The Absolute Basics 4

    Part III: Home Finances 4

    Part IV: Serious Business 4

    Part V: The Part of Tens 5

    Appendix 5

    Conventions Used in This Book 5

  Special Icons 6

  Where to Next? 6

Part I: Zen, Quicken, and The Big Picture 7

  Chapter 1: Start Here 9

    Starting Quicken 9

    Setting Up a Categories List and Bank Account 10

    The ABCs of Using Quicken (a.k.a. Bonehead Quicken) 14

      Quicken, I command thee 14

      Entering stuff into a screen 16

    A Desperate Yelp for Help 19

    Exiting Quicken 20

  Chapter 2: An Introduction to the Big Picture 21

    Boiling Quicken Down to Its Essence 21

      Tracking tax deductions 22

      Monitoring spending 22

      Printing checks 23

      Tracking bank accounts, credit cards, and other stuff 23

    Setting Up Additional Accounts 23

      Setting up an additional bank account 24

      Hey, Quicken, I want to use that account! 26

Whipping Your Category Lists into Shape 26
    Subcategories . . . Yikes, what are they? 30
    Three tips on categorization 31
    Ch-ch-changing a category list 32
Do You Need a Little Class? 35

Chapter 3: Maximum Fun, Maximum Profits **37**
Should You Even Bother? 37
Serious Advice about Your Secret Plan 38
    Home secret plans 38
    Business secret plans 38
    Two things that goof up secret plans 39
Setting Up a Secret Plan 41
    Getting to the Set Up Budgets screen 41
    Entering budgeted amounts the simple way 42
    Entering budgeted amounts the fast way 44
    When you finish entering your budget 46
    Using the other budgeting commands 46

Part II: The Absolute Basics *49*

Chapter 4: Checkbook on a Computer **51**
Finding Your Checkbook 51
Recording Checks 52
    Entering a check in the register 52
    Changing checks you've already entered 54
    A kooky and clever little thing called QuickFill 55
Recording Deposits 56
    Entering a deposit in the register 56
    Changing a deposit you've already entered 58
Recording Account Transfers 58
    Entering an account transfer 58
    The other half of the transfer 60
    Changing a transfer you've already entered 60
Splitting Hairs 61
    Splitting checks 61
    Splitting deposits and transfers 63
Deleting and Voiding Transactions 63
The Big Register Phenomenon 64
    Moving around in a big register 65
    Finding that darn transaction 65

Chapter 5: Printing 101 69

Printing Checks 69
  Collecting check information 69
  What if you make a mistake entering a check? 72
  Printing a check you've entered 72
  A few words about check printing 77
  What if you discover a mistake after you've printed a check? 78
Printing a Check Register 78
Printing Good Ol' Reports 80
  Just the facts (of printing), ma'am 81
  Reviewing the standard reports 83
  The Other command in the Reports menu 85
  The printing dog-and-pony show 87
Charts Only Look Tricky 88

Chapter 6: Perfect Balance 91

Selecting the Account You Want to Balance 91
Balancing a Bank Account 92
  Telling Quicken, "Hey, man, I want to balance an account" 92
  Telling Quicken what the bank says 93
  Explaining the difference between your records and the bank's ... 94
Ten Things You Should Do If Your Account Doesn't Balance 99
  Verify that you're working with the right account 99
  Look for transactions that you forgot to record 99
  Look for backward transactions 100
  Look for a transaction that's equal to half the difference 100
  Look for a transaction that's equal to the difference 100
  Check for transposed numbers 100
  Get someone else to look over your statement and reconciliation 101
  Look out for multiple errors 101
  Try again next month (and maybe the month after) 101
  Get in your car, drive to the bank, and beg for help 102

Chapter 7: Housekeeping 103

Backing Up Is Hard to Do 103
  Backing up the quick-and-dirty way 103
  When and how often should you back up? 105
  If you lose your data and you did back up 106
  If you lose your data and you didn't back up 108
Files, Files, and More Files 109
  Setting up an additional file 109
  Shrinking files 111
Tweaking Quicken 114
  Automatic backup reminders 114
  Color you beautiful 115
  Using and abusing passwords 117

Chapter 8: Calculators, Schmalculators **121**

Using the Quicken Calculator 121
    Getting started with the calculator 121
    A cool calculator trick 123
    Putting the calculator away 124
    For mouse users only 124
Noodling Around with Your Investments 124
    Using the Investment Planning calculator 124
    How to become a millionaire 126
The Often Unbearable Burden of Debt 127
    Using the Loan Calculator to calculate payments 127
    Using the Refinance Calculator 130
Using the Retirement Planning Calculator 133
    The dilemma in a nutshell 133
    Making retirement planning calculations 134
    If you're now bummed out about retirement 136
    Playing retirement roulette 137
Planning for the Cost of College 137
    Using the College Planning calculator 137
    If you're now bummed out about college costs 139

Part III: Home Finances **141**

Chapter 9: Credit Cards (and Debit Cards, Too) **143**

Should You Even Bother? 143
Setting Up a Credit Card Account 144
    Adding a credit card account 144
    Selecting a credit card account so that you can use it 147
Entering Credit Card Transactions 147
    A whirlwind tour of the credit card register 148
    Recording a credit card charge 148
    Changing charges you've already entered 149
    Paying credit card bills 150
    That crazy reconciliation trick 151
    Paying the bill as part of the reconciliation 156
So What About Debit Cards? 157
The IntelliCharge Hoopla 157

Chapter 10: Other People's Money **159**

Should You Bother to Track Your Debts? 159
What Should I Do First? 160
Delivering a Pound of Flesh (a.k.a. Making a Payment) 161
    Describing the payment principal and interest 162
    Recording a loan payment 167
    Handling mortgage escrow accounts 168

Fixing Your Principal-Interest Breakdown 172
    Mending your evil ways 172
    You think this adjustment business is kooky? 173

Chapter 11: Investments in a Nutshell **175**
Should You Bother? 175
    Are your investments tax-deferred? 176
    Are you a mutual fund fanatic? 176
    Some investors don't need Quicken 176
    Many investors do need Quicken 177
Tracking a Mutual Fund 177
    Setting up a mutual fund investment account 177
    Recording your initial investment 180
    Buying near 185
    Recording your profits 188
    Selling dear 189
    Slightly tricky mutual fund transactions 190
Tracking a Brokerage Account 191
    Setting up a brokerage account 192
    Setting up security lists 192
    Working with cash 194
    Some other not-so-tricky transactions 198
Updating Securities Prices 201
Some Quick Reminders 202
    Adjusting your errors away 202
    Reports 203
The Path Not Taken 203
    Viewing a portfolio 203
    Recording transactions 204
    Portfolio tools 204

Part IV: Serious Business *205*

Chapter 12: Payroll **207**
Setting Up Payroll 207
    Preparing Quicken to handle payroll 207
    Getting the tax stuff right 209
Paying Someone for a Job Well Done 209
    Calculating gross wages 209
    All that deduction stuff 210
    Determining net wages 212
    Other taxes and deductions 212
    Recording a payroll check 212
Making Tax Deposits 215
Filing Quarterly Payroll Tax Returns 217

Those Pesky Annual Returns and Wage Statements 219
Doing the State Payroll Taxes Thing 219
Hey, When Is Payday? 220
     Remembering payday 220
     Reviewing the calendar 223
     Calendar Notes is sort of cool 224

Chapter 13: Customer Receivables 225

Setting Up Shop 225
Recording Customer Invoices 227
Recording Customer Payments 229
Tracking What Your Customers Owe 230

Chapter 14: Vendor Payables 235

Describing Vendor Payables (a.k.a. Your Unpaid Bills) 235
Tracking Vendor Payables 236
A Minor Problem about How Quicken Handles Payables 237
Meet a New Friend Named Billminder 238
     Turning Bill on 239
     Making Bill work 240

Part V: The Part of Tens *241*

Chapter 15: Ten Questions I'm Frequently Asked about Quicken 243

Does Quicken Work for a Corporation? 243
Does Quicken Work for a Partnership? 244
Can I Use Quicken for More than One Business? 244
What Kind of Business Shouldn't Use Quicken? 245
Can I Use Quicken Retroactively? 246
Can I Do Payroll with Quicken? 246
Can I Prepare Invoices with Quicken? 246
Can I Import Data from My Old Accounting System? 247
What Do You Think of Quicken? 247

Chapter 16: Ten Tips for Bookkeepers Who Use Quicken 249

Tricks for Learning Quicken if You're New on the Job 249
Learning the Basics 250
     Turning a computer on 250
     Starting Quicken 250
     Learning Quicken 251
Cross-Reference and File Source Documents 251
Always Categorize 251
Reconcile Promptly 252

Things You Should Do Every Month 252
Things You Should Do Every Year 253
About Debits and Credits (if You're Used to Them) 254
Converting to Quicken 254
Income Tax Evasion 255
Segregating Payroll Tax Money 255

Chapter 17: Ten Tips (More or Less)for Business Owners 257

Sign All Your Own Checks 257
Don't Sign a Check the Wrong Way 258
Review Canceled Checks Before Your Bookkeeper Does 258
How to Pick a Bookkeeper if You Use Quicken.............................258
Get Smart about Passwords 259
Cash-Basis Accounting Doesn't Work for All Businesses 259
When to Switch to Accrual-Basis Accounting................................259
What to Do if Quicken Doesn't Work for Your Business 260
Keep Things Simple 260

Chapter 18: Ten Things You Should Do If You're Audited 261

Leave Quicken at Home 261
Print Summary Reports for Tax Deductions 262
Collect All Source Documents 262
Call a Tax Attorney if the Agent Is "Special" 263
Don't Volunteer Information 263
Consider Using a Pinch Hitter 263
Understand Everything on Your Return 264
Be Friendly 264
Don't Worry 264
Don't Lie 264

Chapter 19: Ten Things I Blew Off (and My Excuses) 265

Electronic Payments with Checkfree..266
Exporting Tax Information 266
Memorized Transactions and Memorized Transaction Groups ...267
Command Line Parameters 267
Custom Reports 267
Quicken's Assistants 268
The Printer Settings Command 268
The Transaction Settings Command 268
The Check & Reports Settings Command 269
Savings Goals Accounts 269
If You're Not Impressed with My Excuses 269

Chapter 20: Ten Quicken Magic Tricks (More or Less) 271

Recording Checks That You Cash 271
Indicating That Money in an
   Account Is Set Aside 272
Splitting with Percentages 273
Date Field Editing Magic 273
Tracking Petty Cash and Mad Money 274
   Adding a cash account 274
   Tracking cash inflows and outflows 275
The Power of DOS 276

**Appendix A: How to Install Quicken in
Eleven Easy Steps If You're Really Busy** 277

Appendix B: Glossary of Business and Financial Terms 283

Index *299*

Reader Response Card .... *back of book*

Introduction

· ·

You aren't a dummy, of course. But here's the deal. You shouldn't have to be some sort of techno-geek or financial wizard to manage your financial affairs on a PC. You have other things to do, places to go, people to meet. And that's where *Quicken For DOS For Dummies* comes in.

In the pages that follow, I'll give you the straight scoop on how to use Quicken for DOS, without a lot of extra baggage, goofy tangential information, or misguided advice.

About This Book

This book isn't meant to be read cover to cover like some Robert Ludlum page turner. Rather, it's organized into tiny, no sweat descriptions of how you should do the things you need to do.

If you're the sort of person who just doesn't feel right not reading a book cover to cover, you can, of course, go ahead and read this thing from front to back. I can only recommend this approach, however, for people who have already checked the TV listings. There may, after all, be a "Rockford Files" rerun on.

About the Author

If you're going to spend your time reading what I have to say, you deserve to know what my qualifications are.

I have an undergraduate degree in accounting and a master's degree in finance and accounting. I am also a certified public accountant (CPA).

I've spent most of the last ten years helping businesses set up computerized financial management systems. I started with Arthur Andersen & Co., which is one of the world's largest public accounting and systems consulting firms. More recently, I've been working as a sole proprietor. When I wasn't doing financial systems work, I served as the controller of a small, 50-person software computer company.

Oh, yeah, one other thing. I've used Quicken for my business and for my personal record keeping for several years.

None of this makes me sound like the world's most exciting guy, of course. I doubt you'll invite me to your next dinner party. Hey, I can deal with that.

But knowing a little something about me may give you a bit more confidence in applying the stuff I write about. All joking aside, we're talking about something that's extremely important: *your money.*

How to Use This Book

I've always enjoyed reading encyclopedias. You could flip open, say, the E volume, look up *Elephants,* and then learn just about everything you needed to know about elephants for a fifth-grade report: where elephants lived, how much they weighed, and why they ate so much.

You won't read anything about elephants here. But you should be able to use this book like you use an encyclopedia. If you want to learn about something, look through the table of contents or the index and find the topic — *check printing,* for example. Then flip to the correct chapter or page and read as much as you need or enjoy. No muss. No fuss.

If there's anything else you want to learn about, of course, repeat the process.

What You Can Safely Ignore

Sometimes I provide step-by-step descriptions of tasks. I feel bad that I had to do this (but, hey, ya gotta learn somehow). So to make things easier for you, I describe the tasks using bold text. That way you know exactly what you're supposed to do. I also provide a more detailed explanation in regular text. You can skip the regular text that accompanies the step-by-step descriptions if you already understand the process.

Here's an example that shows what I mean:

1. **Press Enter.**

   Find the key that's labeled *Enter* or *Return.* Extend your index finger so that it rests gently on the Enter key. In one sure, fluid motion, press the Enter key with your index finger. Then release your finger.

OK, that's kind of an extreme example. I never actually go into that much detail. But you get the idea. If you know how to press Enter, you can just do that and not read further. If you need help, read the details.

Is there anything else you can skip? Let me see now. . . . You can skip the Technical sidebars, too. The information I stick in these sidebars is really only here for those of you who like that kind of stuff.

For that matter, I guess you can safely ignore the stuff in the Tip sidebars, too. But if you enjoy trying things another way, go ahead and read the Tips.

What You Should Not Ignore (Unless You're a Masochist)

Don't skip the Warning sidebars. (They're the ones flagged with the picture of the nineteenth century bomb.) They describe things you really shouldn't do.

Out of respect for you, I don't put in sidebar stuff like, "Don't smoke." You're an adult. You can make your own lifestyle decisions.

I reserve the Warning sidebars for more urgent and immediate dangers — things akin to "Don't smoke while you're filling your car with gasoline."

Three Foolish Assumptions

I assume just three things:

- You have a PC with a hard disk.
- You know how to turn the computer on.
- You want to use Quicken.

By the way, if you haven't already installed Quicken and need help, refer to Appendix A.

How This Book Is Organized

This book is organized into five, mostly coherent parts.

Part I: Zen, Quicken, and the Big Picture

Part I covers some upfront stuff you need to take care of. I promise that this isn't a waste of your time. I just want to make sure that you get off on the right foot.

Part II: The Absolute Basics

The second part of *Quicken for DOS For Dummies* explains the core knowledge that you need to keep a personal or business checkbook with Quicken: using the checkbook, printing, balancing your bank accounts, and using the Quicken calculators.

Some of this stuff isn't very exciting compared to MTV (especially Cindy Crawford's "House of Style"), but I try to make things fun.

Part III: Home Finances

Part III talks about using Quicken at home to manage and monitor things like credit cards, loans, mutual funds, stocks and bonds. If you don't ever get this far — hey, that's cool.

If you do get this far, you'll find that Quicken provides some tools that eliminate not only the drudgery of keeping a checkbook, but also the drudgery of most other financial burdens.

While we're on the subject, I also want to categorically deny that Part III contains any secret messages if you read it backwards.

Part IV: Serious Business

If you're pulling your hair out because you're using Quicken in a business, stop — at least for now — and read Part IV. It tells you about preparing payroll, tracking the amounts that customers owe you, and other wildly exciting stuff.

Part V: The Part of Tens

Gravity isn't just a good idea, it's the law.

By tradition, the same is true for this part of a . . . *For Dummies* book. "The Part of Tens" provides a collection of ten-something lists: ten things you should do if you get audited, ten things you should do if you own a business, ten things to do when you next visit Acapulco — oops, sorry about that last one. Wrong book.

Appendix

It's an unwritten rule that computer books have appendixes. This book has two: Appendix A tells you how to install Quicken. Appendix B is a glossary of key financial and Quicken terms.

Conventions Used in This Book

To make the best use of your time and energy, you should know about the following conventions used in this book:

- ✔ When I want you to type something, such as **Hydraulics screamed as the pilot lowered the landing gear,** I put it in bold letters. When I want you to type something that's short and uncomplicated, like **Jennifer,** it still appears in bold. By the way, the case of the stuff you type doesn't matter. If I tell you to type **Jennifer,** you can type **JENNIFER.** Or you can follow e. e. cumming's lead and type **jennifer.**

- ✔ Whenever I describe a message or information that you see on- screen, I present it as

  ```
  Surprise! This is a message on-screen.
  ```

- ✔ You can select menus and dialog boxes and choose commands with the mouse or keyboard. To use the mouse, just click the item you want. To use the keyboard, press Alt to activate the menu and then the bold letter in the menu, dialog box, or command. ("Activate" is just a computer buzzword that means, basically, "Dude, display a menu.") You don't need to activate a menu, therefore, if it's already displayed. For example, the letter *F* in the main menu command **F**ile Activities is in bold type. When the main menu is displayed, you can choose the File Activities command by pressing F. The letter *E* in **E**dit menu is in bold type but the Edit menu doesn't get activated unless you press Alt to activate the menu bar.

Special Icons

Like many computer books, this book uses icons, or little pictures, to flag things that don't quite fit into the flow of things. ...*For Dummies* books use a standard set of icons that flag little digressions:

 This icon points out nerdy technical material that you may want to skip (or read, if you're feeling particularly bright).

 Whee, here's a shortcut to make your life easier.

 This icon is just a friendly reminder to do something.

 And this icon is a friendly reminder *not* to do something . . . or else.

Where to Next?

If you're just getting started, flip the page and start reading the first chapter. If you have a special question, check the table of contents or index to find out where I talk about whatever it is that's giving you problems.

Part I
Zen, Quicken, and
The Big Picture

"THE IMAGE IS GETTING CLEARER NOW...I CAN ALMOST SEE IT...YES! THERE IT IS—THE GLITCH IS IN A FAULTY CELL REFERENCE IN THE FOOTBALL POOL SPREADSHEET."

In this part...

When you go to a movie theater, there are some prerequisites for making the show truly enjoyable. And I'm not referring to the presence of Sharon Stone or Arnold Schwarzennegger. Purchasing a bucket of popcorn is essential, for example. One should also think strategically both about seating and about soda size. And one may even have items of a, well, personal nature to take care of — like visiting the little boy's or girl's room.

I mention all this for one simple reason. To make getting started with Quicken as easy and fun as possible, there are some prerequisites, too. And this first part of *Quicken For DOS For Dummies* — Zen, Quicken, and the Big Picture — talks about these sorts of things.

Chapter 1
Start Here

In This Chapter

▶ Starting Quicken

▶ Setting up a bank account

▶ Using menus and commands

▶ Entering stuff into a screen

▶ Getting help

▶ Exiting Quicken

Starting Quicken

After you install Quicken (see Appendix A), it's a snap to start. Just press **q** or **Q** at the DOS prompt. The case doesn't matter. Remember, the DOS prompt looks like

```
C:\>
```

When you start Quicken for the very first time, you see a screen like the one shown in Figure 1-1. This is the Quicken Main Menu — the jumping-off point for all the things you do in Quicken.

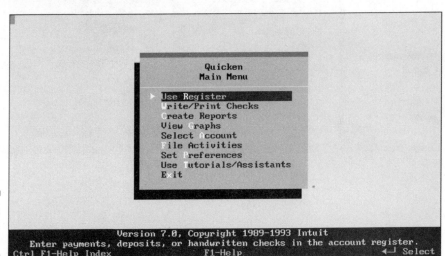

Version 7.0, Copyright 1989-1993 Intuit

Enter payments, deposits, or handwritten checks in the account register.

Ctrl F1-Help Index   F1-Help   ◄┘ Select

Figure 1-1:
The Quicken
Main Menu.

Setting Up a Categories List and Bank Account

Quicken is a checkbook-on-a-computer program. You use it to track the money that flows into and out of your checking account, and the money you've still got in your bank account after all those deposits and withdrawals. But first you have to set up a bank account on the computer. In fact, you won't be able to do anything with Quicken until you establish this bank account.

To set up your bank account, follow these steps:

1. **Find your checkbook.**

   Check your purse, your jacket, your desk, your briefcase. (It'll be in the last place you look.)

2. **Press Enter to choose the Use Register command from the Main Menu (see Figure 1-1).**

   Normally, choosing the Use **R**egister command tells Quicken that you're ready to describe some checks you've written on a bank account or some deposits you've made. But Quicken's no dummy. It knows you haven't even set up a bank account. So it displays the Standard Categories screen (see Figure 1-2).

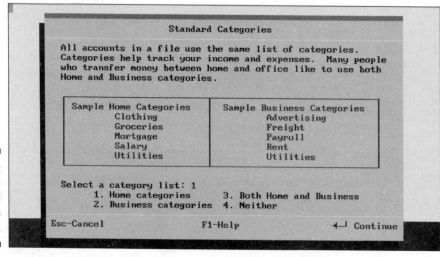

Figure 1-2:
The
Standard
Categories
screen.

See that pop-up message on the Standard Categories screen? Quicken supplies pop-up messages, called Qcards, so that you know what goes where. Unfortunately, these babies create an awkward problem for me, your humble author and new friend. If I leave the Qcards showing, they obscure some part of the screen. So I press Ctrl-F9 to remove them; that's why they don't appear in the figures that follow. (If you don't want the Qcards displayed on your screen, you can press Ctrl-F9, too. If you change your mind, and you want to see them later, just press Ctrl-F9 again.) You also can press Ctrl-F8 to shrink and unshrink the Qcard message. (Experiment to see how this works.) And you can press Ctrl-F7 to see related information.

3. Indicate which categories list you want.

Press 1 to track home finances. Press 2 to track business finances. Press 3 for both purposes. (Don't press 4 because it makes for a bunch of work later.)

4. Tell Quicken that you want to set up a bank account.

After you indicate which categories list you want, Quicken asks what kind of account you want to set up, using the screen shown in Figure 1-3. Move the *cursor* — it's that little flashing underline — to the Choose An Account Type question and press 1. If the Choose An Account Type question already shows a 1, hey, you're home free.

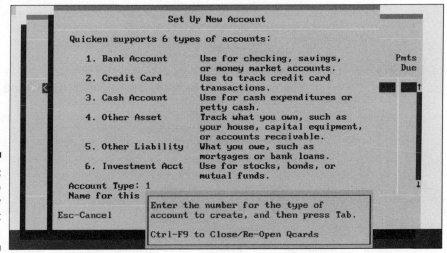

Figure 1-3:
The Set Up
New
Account
screen.

Using your bank statement balance as your account balance

The folks at Quicken really want you to use your bank statement balance as your account balance. This works best they've found. Make a note. If you use the bank statement balance, you need to (after you understand how the register works) enter all the transactions your register shows that weren't included in the bank state-

ment balance because they hadn't yet cleared the bank. I'm serious about this "make a note" business. You really should take one of those yellow sticky things, jot a note like "Add uncleared transactions," and then stick it on your monitor. I'll remind you again about this in Chapter 4.

5. Tell Quicken the name you want to use for the account.

Press Tab to move the cursor to the Name For This Account question and then type a name. You can be as general or as specific as you want, using up to 15 characters. I give my accounts incredibly clever, wildly precise names, such as *checking*.

6. Press Enter.

Quicken displays another new screen, which asks for your checking account balance and the date for which the balance is correct (see Figure 1-4).

7. Enter the account balance.

For example, if you have 4 dollars and 16 cents (sigh) in your checking account, type **4.16**. You don't need to type the dollar sign. You *do* need to type the decimal point so that you can indicate cents.

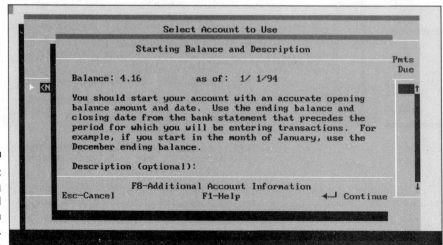

Figure 1-4:
The Starting
Balance and
Description
screen.

A menu activation alternative

You don't have to use the Alt and letter key combination to activate a pull-down menu on the Register screen. You also can use function keys as follows:

📌 F2 pulls down the **P**rint/Acct menu.

📌 F3 pulls down the **E**dit menu.

📌 F4 pulls down the **S**hortcuts menu.

📌 F5 pulls down the **R**eports menu.

📌 F6 pulls down the **A**ctivities menu.

The ability to pull down menus with a function key goes back to the old days of Quicken, which predated the popular graphical user interfaces and their penchant for Alt-key combinations.

8. **Enter the date from which you want Quicken to begin keeping your financial records.**

   Press Tab to move the cursor to the Date field. Then enter the date using the MM/DD/YY format. For example, if the date is January 1, 1994, type **1/1/94** (see tip at the end of this section). You can use the + and - signs to increase or decrease the date.

9. **Press Enter (yes, again).**

   Quicken displays the Select Account to Use screen (see Figure 1-5).

10. **Use the up- and down-arrow keys to highlight the new account you just created.**

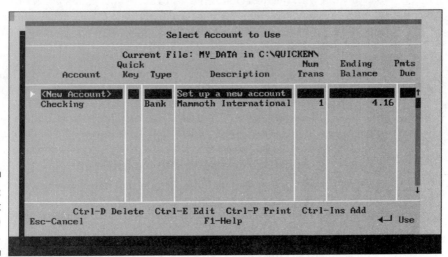

Figure 1-5:
Select
Account to
Use screen.

11. Press Enter (and I promise this is the last time).

Quicken displays the Register screen. You're done.

Some of the most valuable things you can do with Quicken require a full year of financial information. Because it doesn't take that long to enter checking transactions — even a whole year's worth — use January 1 as the starting date and, therefore, use the January 1 account balance as the starting balance.

The ABCs of Using Quicken (a.k.a. Bonehead Quicken)

Life with Quicken is easier if you start by learning the basics — for example, what menus and commands are, how you choose them, and how you enter information into the screens that Quicken displays.

Quicken, I command thee

In Quicken, you use commands to tell Quicken what you want it to do. Rather than just display a lengthy list of dozens and dozens of commands, Quicken uses menus to list and organize commands. The Quicken Main Menu is the first command grouping. Its first two commands provide direct paths, or routes, to two of Quicken's most useful and most frequently used screens, the Register and the Write Checks screen. The other main menu commands list additional menus of commands. The File Activities menu, for example, lists commands you use to work with the files Quicken uses to store your financial records. It's that simple. The Quicken Main Menu, for example, lists the main categories. When you pick a category, or Main Menu item, Quicken usually displays another list of menu items.

The items listed on a menu are called *commands.* I don't know why. Maybe it's because you usually (although not always) choose an item listed on a menu to "command" the software to do something: "Quicken, I command thee to print this report," for example. Or "Quicken, I command thee to erase this bit of information." You have a bunch of different ways to issue these commands.

Choosing a Main Menu command with the keyboard

You can choose a command with the keyboard in one of two ways.

Look closely at the menu in Figure 1-1: in each menu command; one of the letters is bold. The *R* in the Use **R**egister command is bold. The *W* in the **W**rite/ Print Checks command is bold. The *C* in the **C**reate Reports command is bold. If you can't see the bold type in the figure, look at the actual Quicken Main Menu on your screen.

You can choose a command on the visible menu by pressing the bold letter of the menu command. With the Main Menu displayed, for example, press R to choose the Use **R**egister command. Go ahead. Be bold. Try it. Voilà, the Register screen appears, containing the bank account you set up earlier in the chapter . By the way, these keyboard selection keys are called *hot keys*.

Choosing other commands with the keyboard

Some screens, like the Register screen shown in Figure 1-6, also display menus across the top of the screen. This row of menus is called a *menu bar*. (Sounds like a place where menus from all walks of life go after work for a drink and friendly conversation, doesn't it?)

When a screen includes a menu bar, you need to activate the menu bar to choose one of its menus. To activate a menu bar with the keyboard, press one of the Alt keys (you should have two on your keyboard), which are usually positioned at either end of the spacebar. Ah, the *spacebar* — the intergalactic cocktail lounge where astronauts and aliens mingle.

After you activate the menu bar by pressing Alt, choose the pull-down menu you want by pressing the hot key. For example, to display the **P**rint/Acct menu, press Alt-P (see Figure 1-6).

To choose a menu command on a pull-down menu, press the command's hot key. If the **P**rint/Acct menu is displayed, for example, press P to choose the Print Register command.

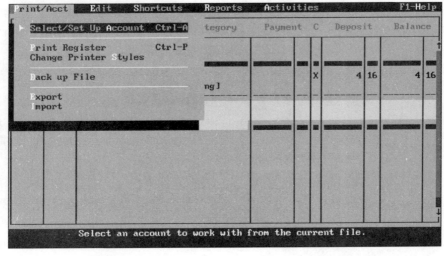

Figure 1-6: The Register screen showing the Print/Acct menu.

Unchoosing commands with the keyboard

To unchoose (bless you!) a command with the keyboard, press the Esc (Escape) key. For example, if you press Esc after pulling down a menu, Quicken removes the pull-down menu — in other words, you *escape* from the original command. If you press Esc after choosing a menu command that displays a screen, Quicken removes the screen — again, you escape from the original command.

Using the arrow keys to choose commands

You also can choose commands on a menu by using the up- and down-arrow keys. To do this, press the up- or down-arrow key to highlight the command you want to choose. Then press Enter. (This procedure isn't hard. If you think that it sounds complicated, try it.)

If you love them meeces to pieces, read this

You also can use your mouse (if you have one) to choose and unchoose commands.

To select a Main Menu command, for example, move the mouse so the *mouse pointer* (the on-screen square that moves as you move the mouse) rests on the command's name. Then press the mouse's left button. This action is called *clicking* the mouse. Clever, huh?

To select a menu in the menu bar, click the menu name. To choose a command on a pull-down menu, click on the command's name.

To unchoose a command, click the mouse's right button. If you want to remove the selected pull-down menu from the menu bar, click the right button. If you want to remove a screen, click the right button.

Entering stuff into a screen

When you get right down to it, Quicken is really just a record-keeping system. You enter information (what computer geeks like to call *data*), and Quicken stores the information for you.

To enter information into Quicken, simply fill in the blanks (or *fields*) that appear on a Quicken screen. If you've worked with other computer software before, you probably already know how to do this.

If you haven't, however, choose the **Write/Print Checks** command from the Main Menu. (If the Register screen is still displayed, press Esc to remove it and redisplay the Main Menu.) Quicken displays the Write Checks screen (see Figure 1-7), in which you fill in the blanks to print a check. (I talk more about the Write Checks screen in Chapter 5.)

Why not name fields pastures?

The input blanks you fill in on a screen are called *fields.* Fields isn't really a very good name, although everybody uses it. Why not call fields "input blanks," for example? Well, here's the short explanation: The bits of information you enter into the input blanks get stored on your hard disk in things called *fields;* these fields get grouped together into *records.* (All the fields you enter into the Write Checks screen get stored in a single record.) Records that store the same sort of information (such as checks you want to print) then get stored together in a *file.*

Sticking stuff into a field

To enter information into a field, move the cursor to the field and type. In Figure 1-7, the cursor (an underline) is on the Date field. It's very difficult to see. In fact, it's impossible to see. Little blinking underlines don't show up very well in book figures.

But back to the chase. If the cursor is on the Date field and you want to enter the date, just start typing.

Different fields collect different types of information. Some fields let you enter just about anything: letters, numbers, goofy symbols, and so on. Some fields don't. The Date field, for example, only wants entries that look like numeric dates: 4/8/94 (for April 8, 1994) or 12/27/95 (for December 27, 1995). The Amount field wants entries that look like check amounts.

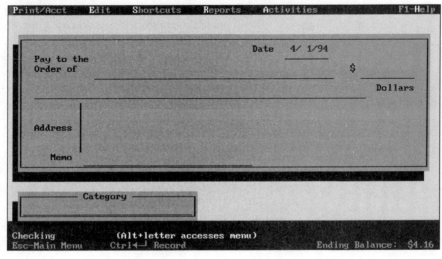

Figure 1-7: The Write Checks screen.

I talk more about which fields accept which kinds of information when I discuss how to use specific screens for information collection. See Chapter 4 for more about the Register screen. See Chapter 5 for more about the Write Checks screen.

Hopping from field to field

To enter information into another field, you need to move the cursor to that field. Here are the ways you can move from field to field:

- Press Tab to move to the next field.
- Press Shift-Tab to move to the preceding field.
- Press Enter to move to the next field.
- Click a field with the mouse.

Hopping around in a field

What if you type in the wrong information? Well, you can move the cursor in the field to change the information you originally typed. Here are the ways you can do this:

- Press the right-arrow key to move the cursor one character ahead.
- Press the left-arrow key to move the cursor one character back.
- Press the Home key to move the cursor to the first character in the field.
- Press the End key to move the cursor to the last character in the field.

Oops! I entered the wrong information

What if you enter some incorrect information — say you misspell a name, for example. No problem. First, move the cursor to the field containing the wrong information.

If the information is easy to retype, move the cursor to the first character in the field. Simultaneously, press the Ctrl and Backspace keys. (This action erases the field.) Then type the new, correct information.

Sometimes you don't need to retype the entire chunk of information. Suppose, for example, that while entering information into the Payee field, you misspell "Rodgers Electrical Supply Warehouse" as "Rogers Electrical Supply Warehouse." In other words, you leave out the *d* in Rodgers.

To fix this sort of mistake, move the cursor so that it's just before the character where you want to insert additional characters. Type the character or characters you want to insert. Note that Quicken inserts what you type at the correct cursor location.

Sometimes you won't want to insert characters, though. Say you misspell "Rogers" as "Fogers," for example. To replace a single character, move the cursor to the incorrect character — the *F* in Fogers, for example. Press the Insert key. Quicken replaces the underline with a blinking square. (*Blinking* is not an expletive. The cursor really does blink.)

In a weird twist, pressing Insert tells Quicken that you don't want to insert characters. Now you can just replace the incorrect character by typing over it with the correct character. Press the Insert key again if you want Quicken to insert characters when you type them.

You can tell whether Quicken will insert characters into a field or type over characters in a field by looking at the cursor. A square means Quicken will insert. A blinking underline means Quicken will type over.

A Desperate Yelp for Help

If you get into trouble while you're running Quicken, press F1 to get help. (Note that F1 is usually the software equivalent of a scream for help.)

If you press F1 while the Quicken Main Menu is displayed — say you're thinking, "What in the world is this thing?" — Quicken displays a screen containing information about the Main Menu (see Figure 1-8).

Usually, there is more than a single screen of information. And that's where two new friends can help: the PgDn and PgUp keys. Use PgDn and PgUp to go back and forth through the Help screen.

Any time you see a word or phrase on a Help screen that uses black letters, you can move the cursor to the word or phrase just like you move the cursor to any screen field. Then you can press Enter to learn more about that word or phrase. (This trick is kind of cool, don't you think?)

Want to know another cool Help trick? When you press Ctrl-F1, Quicken displays an alphabetic list of all its Help topics. To learn more about a topic, select the topic and press Enter.

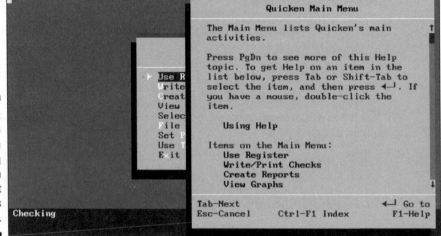

Figure 1-8:
The Help
screen
containing
information
about
Quicken's
Main Menu.

Exiting Quicken

To exit Quicken, you need the Quicken Main Menu (see Figure 1-1). At the Main
Menu, press X. (Remember, because the *x* in the word E**x**it is in bold, it is a hot
key.) Or use the up- and down-arrow keys to highlight the E**x**it option and then
press Enter.

If the Quicken Main Menu isn't displayed, press the Esc key until you see the
Main Menu. (Remember that Esc unchooses commands.) Then choose the E**x**it
command.

Don't exit Quicken by turning off your computer. This action may not cause
serious problems because Quicken is continually saving your data onto the
hard disk. But it is bad form — akin to eating the last potato chip or leaving the
gas tank empty in your spouse's car.

If you exit Quicken the wrong way — by turning off or resetting your computer
— the index file Quicken uses to organize your financial records gets, well,
wasted. Quicken will rebuild when you restart, but this process takes a few
seconds.

If you're just getting started, flip the page and start reading the next chapter,
"An Introduction to the Big Picture." If you have a special question, check the
table of contents or index to find out where I talk about whatever is causing you
problems.

Chapter 2
An Introduction to the Big Picture

In This Chapter

▶ Boiling Quicken down to its essence

▶ Setting up additional bank accounts

▶ Adding categories

▶ Removing categories

▶ Modifying categories

▶ Understanding classes

*B*efore you spend a bunch of time and money on Quicken, you need to understand the big picture.

You need to know what Quicken can do. You need to know what you actually want to do. And, as a practical matter, you need to know how to tell Quicken what you want it to do.

Boiling Quicken Down to Its Essence

When you boil Quicken down to its essence, the program does four things.

✓ It lets you track your tax deductions. Quicken makes preparing your personal or business tax return easier for you or your poor accountant, Cratchit.

✓ It lets you monitor your income and expenses, either on-screen or with printed reports. This stuff usually is great fodder for discussions about the family finances.

✓ It lets you print checks. This device is mostly a timesaver, but it is also darn handy for people with illegible handwriting.

✓ It lets you track your assets (such as bank accounts, investments, and real estate) and your debts (such as home mortgage principal, car loan balances, and credit card balances).

You can do some or all these things with Quicken. If you don't want to do any of these things, read the book anyway. I guarantee you'll learn something. (Besides, I get 43 cents every time someone buys this book — which will make me a millionaire when I'm 304-years-old.)

Tracking tax deductions

To track tax deductions, list the deductions you want to track. To make this list, pull out last year's tax return and note which deductions you claimed. (There's a darn good chance that last year's deductions will be the deductions you want to claim this year.)

With Quicken, you use *categories* to track your tax deductions. Later in this chapter, I'll talk about Quicken's categories.

Monitoring spending

At our house, we (my wife, Sue, and I) use Quicken's *categories* (is the suspense building?) to monitor what we spend on life's mundane little necessities: groceries, clothing, the telephone, and so on.

Your list of spending categories, by the way, shouldn't be an exhaustive list of superfine pigeonholes like "Friday night Mexican dinners," "Fast food lunches," and so on. To track your spending for eating out, a one-word category like "Meals" or "Grub" is easier.

In fact (I'm going to go out on a limb), you can probably get away with half a dozen categories or less:

- ✔ Household items (food, toiletries, cleaning supplies)
- ✔ Car
- ✔ Rent (or mortgage payments)
- ✔ Entertainment and vacation
- ✔ Clothing
- ✔ Work expenses

If you want, of course, you can expand this list. Heck, you can include dozens and dozens of categories. Based on my experience, though, I think you only need a handful.

Printing checks

Why would you want Quicken to print your checks? For one thing, Quicken is really fast if you have a great deal of checks to print. Second, Quicken makes your checks look neat and professional.

Of course, computer check forms aren't cheap; they definitely cost more than checks you write by hand.

By the way, I've "checked" around. Although you can order Quicken check forms from other sources (like your local office supplies store), the check forms cost the same if you order from Intuit (the maker of Quicken).

Here's a piece of advice for business owners: get a check form with the remittance advice. A remittance advice is a little slip of paper attached to the check form; you use a remittance advice to describe why you wrote a particular check. I talk more about this in Chapter 5.

Tracking bank accounts, credit cards, and other stuff

First, decide which bank accounts and credit cards you want to track. In most cases, you'll want to track all bank accounts and any credit cards on which you carry a balance.

You also may want to track other assets (the things you own, such as investments, cars, a house) and liabilities (the things you owe, such as margin loans from your broker, car loans, a mortgage).

Shoot, I suppose you could even track what your neighbor owns — or at least the things you especially covet. I'm not sure that this is a very good idea, however. Hmmm. Maybe you should track just those things that your neighbor owns but you've borrowed.

Setting Up Additional Accounts

When you start Quicken for the first time, you set up a bank account (see Chapter 1). If you want to track another bank account — for example, a savings account — you need to set it up, too.

Setting up an additional bank account

To set up another bank account, give the account a name and then its balance as of a set date:

1. **Choose the Select Account command.**

   With the Quicken Main Menu displayed, use the arrow keys to highlight the Select Account command. Then press Enter. Quicken displays the Select Account to Use screen, as shown in Figure 2-1.

There's another way to get to the Select Account to Use screen. If the Register screen or Write Checks screen is displayed, the **P**rint/Acct menu (which appears on both screen's menu bars) also lists the Select Account command. When you choose this command, Quicken displays the Select Account to Use screen.

2. **Choose the <New Account> option.**

   Use the arrow keys to highlight the <New Account> option on the Select Account to Use screen. Then press Enter. Quicken displays the Set Up New Account screen, as shown in Figure 2-2.

3. **Tell Quicken that you want to set up a bank account.**

   Move the cursor to the Account Type field and press 1. I discuss the other account types later in the book. If the suspense is just killing you: Chapter 9 describes how to set up and use credit card accounts. Chapter 10 describes how to set up and use liability accounts. Chapter 11 describes how to set up and use investment accounts. And Chapter 13 describes how to set up and use other assets accounts.

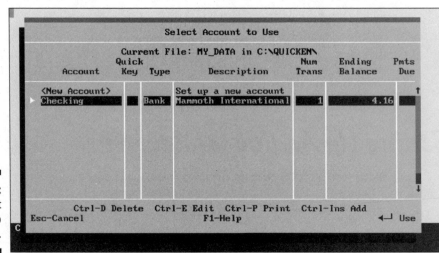

Figure 2-1:
The Select
Account to
Use screen.

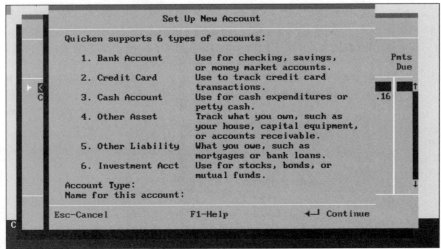

Figure 2-2:
The Set Up
New
Account
screen.

4. Name the account.

Move the cursor to the Name For This Account field and enter a name. You
can type anything you want, including the name of your first girlfriend or
boyfriend, the town you grew up in, or something else really irrelevant.
Most people, though, use the name to identify the account. You might
name a checking account, for example, *Checking.* However, remember that
you can't give two accounts the same name. Each account name must be
specific enough to identify that account for you and Quicken.

5. Press Enter.

Quicken displays the Starting Balance and Description screen, as shown in
Figure 2-3.

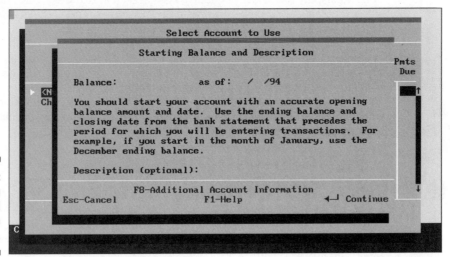

Figure 2-3:
The Starting
Balance and
Description
screen.

6. Enter the bank account balance.

Move the cursor to the Balance field and enter the balance amount. (The folks at Intuit, by the way, really want you to use the number from your bank statement. If you have terrible financial records — say you haven't reconciled your account since Ronald Reagan left office — this idea is probably good advice. If you maintain accurate financial records, go ahead and use your check register balance.)

7. Enter the account balance date.

Move the cursor to the Date field and enter the exact date on which you plan to start keeping records for the account with Quicken. Type the two-digit month number, the two-digit day number, and the two-digit year number. To enter January 1, 1994, for example, type **1/1/94.**

8. (Optional) Enter the account description.

Move the cursor to the Description field and enter whatever you want. The description is optional — in other words, Quicken doesn't need it. The description is purely for your benefit. Kind of a nice touch, huh?

9. Press Enter.

Quicken redisplays the Select Account to Use screen, which now lists the new account you just created.

Hey, Quicken, I want to use that account!

In Quicken, you can work with only one account at a time. To tell Quicken which account you want to work with, use the Select Account to Use screen (see Figure 2-1).

You can display the Select Account To Use screen in two ways. Starting from either the Register screen or the Write Checks screen, choose Select/Set Up Account from the **P**rint/Acct menu. Or you can choose Select **A**ccount from the Quicken Main Menu.

After you display the Select Account to Use screen, use the arrow keys to highlight the account you want; then press Enter. Quicken selects the account and displays either the Register screen or the Write Checks screen so that you can begin recording transactions. (To read more about entering checking account transactions, see Chapter 4.)

Whipping Your Category Lists into Shape

When you set up Quicken (see Chapter 1), you tell Quicken to use either the predefined home categories, the predefined business categories, or both the home and business categories.

The predefined categories lists may be what you want. Then again, they may not be what you want. Table 2-1 shows the home categories list, and Table 2-2 shows the business categories list. If you tell Quicken to use both the home and business categories, your category list combines the categories shown in Table 2-1 and those shown in Table 2-2.

Take a minute to look through the lists. If you find categories you don't need, cross them off the list. You can delete them in a minute. If you need categories you don't see, add them to the list. You can add them in about two minutes.

Remember, it's pretty simple to determine whether you need a category. You need a Quicken category

✔ To track an income or spending item for income tax purposes

✔ To track an income or spending item because you want to know how much you really spend (for example, renting VCR tapes)

✔ To track an income or spending item that you want to budget

Table 2-1	The Predefined Home Categories
Categories	**Descriptions**
Income Categories	
Bonus	Bonus Income
CPP	Canadian Pension Plan
Div Income	Dividend Income
Gift Received	Gift Received
Int Inc	Interest Income
Invest Inc	Investment Income
Old Age Pension	Old Age Pension
Other Inc	Other Income
Salary	Salary Income
Expense Categories	
Auto	Automobile Expenses
Fuel	Auto Fuel
Loan	Auto Loan Payment
Service	Auto Service
Bank Chrg	Bank Charge

(continued)

Table 2-1 *(continued)*

Categories	Descriptions
Charity	Charitable Donations
Cash	Cash Contribution
Non-cash	Non-cash Contribution
Child Care	Child-Care Expense
Christmas	Christmas Expense
Clothing	Clothing
Dining	Dining Out
Dues	Dues
Education	Education
Entertain	Entertainment
Gifts	Gift Expense
Groceries	Groceries
GST	Goods and Services Tax
Home Rpair	Home Repair & Maintenance
Household	Household Miscellaneous Expenses
Housing	Housing
Insurance	Insurance
Int Exp	Interest Expense
Invest Exp	Investment Expense
Medical	Medical & Dental
Doctor	Doctor & Dental Visits
Medicine	Medicine & Drugs
Misc	Miscellaneous
Mort Int	Mortgage Interest Expenses
Other Exp	Other Expenses
PST	Provincial Sales Tax
Recreation	Recreation Expense
RRSP	Reg Retirement Savings Plan
Subscriptions	Subscriptions
Supplies	Supplies

Categories	Description
Tax	Taxes
Fed	Federal Tax
Medicare	Medicare Tax
Other	Miscellaneous Taxes
Prop	Property Tax
Soc Sec	Social Security Tax
State	State Tax
Tax Spouse	Spouse's Taxes
Fed	Federal Tax
Medicare	Medicare Tax
Soc Sec	Social Security Tax
State	State Tax
Telephone	Telephone Expense
UIC	Unemployment Insurance Commission
Utilities	Water, Gas & Electric
Gas & Electric	Gas & Electric
Water	Water

Table 2-2	The Predefined Business Categories
Categories	**Descriptions**
Income Categories	
Gr Sales	Gross Sales
Other Inc	Other Income
Rent Income	Rent Income
Expense Categories	
Ads	Advertising
Bus. Insurance	Insurance (not health)
Bus. Utilities	Water, Gas, Electric
Business Tax	Taxes & Licenses
Car	Car & Truck

(continued)

Table 2-2 *(continued)*

Categories	Descriptions
Commission	Commissions
Freight	Freight
Int Paid	Interest Paid
L&P Fees	Legal & Professional Fees
Late Fees	Late Payment Fees
Meals & Entertn	Meals & Entertainment
Office	Office Expenses
Rent on Equip	Rent — Vehicle, Machinery Equipment
Rent Paid	Rent Paid
Repairs	Repairs
Returns	Returns & Allowances
Supplies, Bus.	Supplies
Travel	Travel Expenses
Wages	Wages & Job Credits

Subcategories . . . Yikes, what are they?

In this book, I try to simplify Quicken for you. To achieve this goal, I tell you which features you can ignore if you're feeling overwhelmed. For example, I think you can ignore subcategories.

"Subcategories," you say, "Yikes, what are they?"

Subcategories are categories within categories. The Taxes category (under Expense Categories) in Table 2-1, for example, has six subcategories: Fed (Federal Tax), Medicare (Medicare Tax), Other (Miscellaneous Taxes), Prop (Property Tax), Soc Sec (Social Security Tax), and State (State Tax).

When you use subcategories, you can tag a transaction that pays taxes as paying specific types of taxes such as federal income tax, medicare tax, and social security tax). When you want to see how you've spent your money, Quicken summarizes your spending both by category and, within a category, by subcategory. On a Quicken report, you may see the following detail:

Taxes

Federal Tax	900
Medicare Tax	100
Social Security Tax	700
Total Taxes	1700

Subcategories are useful. But they make working with Quicken a little more complicated and a little more difficult. As a practical matter, you usually don't use subcategories. If you want to track a spending category, it really belongs on your list as a full-fledged category.

Because I don't think you should mess with subcategories, I'm not going to talk about them in more detail.

If you want to use Quicken's subcategories, don't delete the subcategories shown in Table 2-1. If you don't want to use Quicken's subcategories, go ahead and delete them.

Three tips on categorization

I have just three tips for categorizing:

1. **Cross off any category you won't use.**

   If you're Jewish or Muslim, for example, delete the Christmas gift category. If you're Canadian, get rid of the U.S. tax categories. Extra, unneeded categories just clutter your list. (In fact, I think you should have just a handful of categories — the fewer to deal with, the better.)

2. **Don't be afraid to lump similar spending categories together.**

   If you pay water, natural gas, electricity, and sewer, for example, why not use a single Utilities category? (If you pay different utility companies for your water, natural gas, electricity, and sewer, you still can see what you spent on a single utility. For example, you can see what you spent on electricity by looking at how much you paid the electric company.)

3. **Be sure that you categorize anything that may be a tax deduction.**

   Categorize medical and dental expenses, state and local income taxes, real estate taxes, property taxes, home mortgage interest and points, investment interest, charitable contributions, casualty and theft losses, moving expenses, unreimbursed employee expenses, and all vague miscellaneous deductions. (By the way, the preceding is the complete list of itemized deductions at the time this book was written.)

Ch-ch-changing a category list

OK, you should be ready to fix any category list problems. Basically, you can do three things: add categories, remove categories, and change category names and descriptions.

Adding categories

Adding categories is a snap. Here's what you do:

1. **Display the Register screen or the Write Checks screen.**

   Choose the Use **R**egister command or the **W**rite/Print Checks command from Quicken's Main Menu.

2. **Select the Shortcuts menu.**

   You can do this, for example, by choosing Alt-S (see Figure 2-4).

3. **Choose the Categorize Transfer List.**

   Press C. Quicken displays the Category and Transfer List screen (see Figure 2-5), which lists the categories available and the accounts you've set up.

4. **Select the <New Category> option.**

   Press Home and then Enter. Quicken displays the Set Up Category screen (see Figure 2-6). Use this screen to set up the new category.

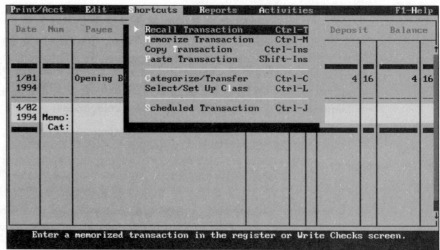

Figure 2-4:
The
Shortcuts
menu.

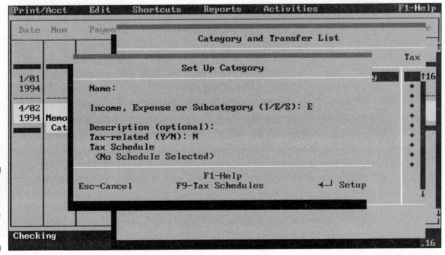

```
Print/Acct    Edit    Shortcuts    Reports    Activities              F1-Help
 Date   Num    Payee                                                         e
                          Category and Transfer List

                  Category/Transfer   Type        Description         Tax

  1/01        Openin    Invest Inc      Inc    Investment Income       ◆ ↑16
  1994                  Old Age Pension  Inc    Old Age Pension        ◆
                        Other Inc       Inc    Other Income           ◆
  4/02                  Salary          Inc    Salary Income          ◆
  1994  Memo:         ► Auto            Expns  Automobile Expenses
        Cat:            Fuel            Sub    Auto Fuel
                        Loan            Sub    Auto Loan Payment
                        Service         Sub    Auto Service
                        Bank Chrg       Expns  Bank Charge
                        Charity         Expns  Charitable Donations    ◆
                        Cash            Sub    Cash Contributions      ◆
                        Non-Cash        Sub    Non-Cash Contributions  ◆
                        Childcare       Expns  Childcare Expense       ↓

                  Ctrl-D Delete   Ctrl-E Edit   Ctrl-P Print  Ctrl-Ins Add
                  Esc-Cancel          F1-Help      F8-Move        ↵  Use
 Checking
                                                                        .16
```

Figure 2-5:
The Category
and Transfer
List screen.

5. Enter a short name for the category.

Move the cursor to the Name field and enter a name. Although you can use up to 15 characters, enter the shortest name possible that clearly identifies the category. (You enter category names when you enter transactions into the register; shorter names take less time to type. Of course, if you don't have anything better to do, go ahead and use long and easy-to-misspell category names.)

```
Print/Acct    Edit    Shortcuts    Reports    Activities              F1-Help
 Date   Num    Payee                                                         e
                          Category and Transfer List

                                                                    Tax
                              Set Up Category
  1/01                                                      y        ↑16
  1994         Name:                                                ◆

  4/02         Income, Expense or Subcategory (I/E/S): E            ◆
  1994  Memo                                                        ◆
        Cat    Description (optional):                              ◆
               Tax-related (Y/N): N                                 ◆
               Tax Schedule                                         ◆
                <No Schedule Selected>                              ◆

                              F1-Help
               Esc-Cancel   F9-Tax Schedules        ↵ Setup        ↓
```

Figure 2-6:
The Set Up
Category
screen.

```
 Checking                                                          ◆ .16
```

6. Indicate whether the category is an income or expense category.

Move the cursor to the Income, Expense, Or Subcategory field and type **I** or **E.**

7. Enter a description for the category.

Move the cursor to the Description field, and then describe the category. (If you don't record a description, Quicken uses the category name on reports that show the category.)

8. Indicate whether the category is a tax deduction.

Move the cursor to the Tax-related field, and then press Y for yes or N for no.

Use the Tax Schedule field to tell Quicken which federal income schedule or form it should export information to. You don't need to enter this bit of information yet. In fact, I think it's rarely worth the effort.

9. Add the category to the category list.

If the cursor is on the Tax-related field, press Enter. Or press F10 when the cursor is on any field. Quicken adds the new category to the Category and Transfer List screen (see Figure 2-5). The list includes the name, type (Income, Expense, or Sub), description, and a diamond symbol (indicating whether a category is tax-related).

Removing categories

Removing categories takes only a couple of keystrokes. With the Category and Transfer List screen displayed, use the arrow keys or click the category to highlight the category you want to remove. Then press Ctrl-D.

Quicken displays a message asking you to confirm your decision. If you want to remove the selected category, press Enter. If not, press Esc.

Changing category names and descriptions

You can change a category's name, type (I, E, or S), description, and tax-related status if you discover that you made a mistake — such as misspelling a word in the description.

Display the Category and Transfer List screen. Then use the arrow keys (or click the category) to highlight the category you want to change. Then press Ctrl-E.

Quicken displays the Edit Category screen (see Figure 2-7), whose fields contain the selected category's information: name, type, description, and tax-related status.

Move the cursor to the field with the erroneous entry and correct your mistake. If you want to curse softly because you erred in the first place, go ahead. Then press F10 to save your changes.

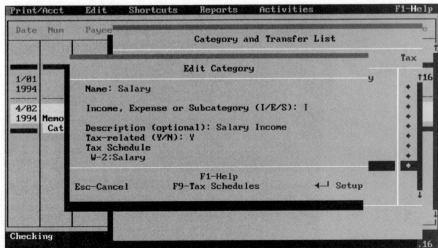

Figure 2-7:
The Edit
Category
screen.

Do You Need a Little Class?

Categories aren't the only way to summarize your financial records. Quicken provides a second tool called *classes*.

I use classes — with good success — to track the *types* of gross income and expenses (writing, consulting, teaching, and so on) that my business produces and incurs. But I have mixed feelings about classes.

Classes present a couple problems. First, you can't budget by classes. (Before you say, "But, Steve, I don't want to budget," please read the next chapter.) Second, you must remember to tag transactions with their classes. (In comparison, Quicken reminds you to include a category.)

In fact, I don't think you should worry about classes until you get really comfortable with Quicken's categories and until you want a way to organize your financial information across categories.

And since I don't think you should trouble yourself with classes, I'm not going to describe how to use them.

If you're serious about using categories, read the next chapter.

If you're not serious about using categories, if you're muttering "typical accountant" under your breath, skip ahead to Chapter 4, which explains how to keep your checkbook on your computer.

The 5th Wave

By Rich Tennant

"OH SURE, $1.8 MILLION DOLLARS SEEMS LIKE ALOT RIGHT NOW, BUT WHAT ABOUT RANDY? WHAT ABOUT HIS FUTURE? THINK WHAT A COMPUTER LIKE THIS WILL DO FOR HIS S.A.T. SCORE SOMEDAY."

Chapter 3
Maximum Fun, Maximum Profits

· ·

In This Chapter

▶ Tips for personal budgets

▶ Tips for business budgets

▶ Setting up a budget manually

▶ Setting up a budget automatically

▶ Printing a budget

· ·

*B*udgets aren't financial handcuffs. Budgets are plans that outline how people should spend their money to achieve the most fun or how businesses should spend their money to make the most profit.

Should You Even Bother?

A budget is just a list of the ways you earn and spend money.

If you create a good, workable categories list, you're on the verge of devising a solid budget. (All you need to do is specify how much you earn in each income category and how much you spend in each expense category.)

Does everybody need a budget? No, of course not. Maybe you're already having a bunch of fun at home with your money. (You lucky dog!) Maybe you make money so effortlessly in your business that there's really no reason to plan your income and expenses. (And what business are you in?)

For everyone else, though, a budget improves your chances of getting where you want to go financially. In fact, so it doesn't sound as sinister, I call a budget a *secret plan.*

Serious Advice about Your Secret Plan

Before I describe how to outline your secret plan, I want to provide you with a few tips.

Home secret plans

You can do four things to help ensure that your secret plan works:

- Plan your income and expenses as a family. When planning your secret plan, two heads invariably work better than one. What's more, a family budget — oops, I mean secret plan — should reflect the priorities and feelings of everyone who has to live by the plan. Don't use a secret plan to minimize what your spouse spends on clothing or on long-distance telephone calls to relatives in the old country. You need to resolve the clothing and long-distance issues before you finalize the plan anyway. (That'll be $75 for the marriage counseling session.)

- Include some cushion in your plan. In other words, don't budget to spend every available dollar. If you plan from the start to spend every dollar you make, you'll have to fight the mother of all financial battles: paying for unexpected expenses when you don't have the money. (You know the sorts of things I mean: car repairs, medical expenses, or that cocktail dress or tuxedo you absolutely must have.)

- Regularly compare your actual income and expenses to your planned income and expenses. I think that this tip is the most important; it's also where Quicken helps you the most. As long as you use Quicken to record what you receive and spend, you can print reports that show what you planned and what actually occurred.

- Adjust the plan as necessary. When you have problems with your secret plan, you know it's time to make adjustments — spending less time on the phone to Aunt Juanita in Puerto Rico, for example.

Business secret plans

The preceding list of tips applies to business planning as well. But I have a special tip for small businesses that use Quicken. (I'm going to write very quietly now so that no one hears. . . .)

Is there anyone else in the room? No? OK, here's the tip: go to the library, ask for the Robert Morris & Associates Survey, and check how other businesses like yours spend money.

This survey is too cool. Robert Morris & Associates surveys bank lending officers and then publishes a summary of the information that these bankers receive from their customers. For example, you can look up the percentage of sales that the average tavern spends on beer and peanuts.

Plan to spend an hour or so at the library. It takes a while to get used to the way the Robert Morris & Associates Survey displays information. For example, you won't see a line on the tavern page labeled *beer and peanuts*. It'll be called *cost of goods sold* or some similarly vague accounting term. (Got to love accountants, huh?)

Remember to make a few notes so that you can use the information to plan your own business financial affairs better.

Two things that goof up secret plans

Because we're talking about you-know-whats, let me touch on a couple things that really goof up your plans: windfalls and monster changes.

The problems with windfalls

The boss steps into your office, smiles, and then gives you the good news. You're getting a $5,000 bonus. *Yippee*, you think. On the outside, of course, you maintain your dignity. You act grateful but not effusive.

You call your husband. Bob (that's your husband) says that he'll pick up a bottle of wine on the way home to celebrate.

As you drive home, you conclude that you can use the $5,000 as a down payment for that family van you've been eyeing. You figure that after you combine your bonus with the usual trade-in, the payments will be a manageable $200 a month.

On his way home, meanwhile, Bob buys those $800 golf clubs he's been coveting for three years. Then, feeling slightly guilty, he buys you the $600 set.

You may laugh at this scenario, but suppose that it really happens. Furthermore, pretend that you still buy the van. In the end, you've spent $6,400 and you've signed up to pay $200 monthly for the next 11 years.

Here's the problem: your bonus check won't be $5,000. You're probably going to pay roughly $1,500 in federal income taxes, $400 in social security and medicare taxes, and then even some state income taxes. (Gotta love the government!)

Other money may be taken out for forced savings plans — like a 401(k) plan — or for charitable giving. After all is said and done, you get maybe half the bonus in cash.

Let's see now. You have $2,500 in cold hard cash in your hands, but (with Bob's help), you've already spent $6,400 *and* signed up to make $200-a-month payments.

In a nutshell, windfalls create two big problems: you never get the entire windfall — though it's easy to spend as if you will. In addition, most people use windfalls for big purchases that ratchet up their living expenses. Cars. Boats. Houses.

My advice is simple:

- ✔ Don't spend a windfall until you hold the check in your hand. (Even better, wait six months or so. Then Bob can think about whether he really needs those new golf clubs.)
- ✔ Don't spend a windfall on something that increases your monthly living expenses without redoing your budget.

The problem with monster income changes

If your income changes radically, planning becomes really hard.

Suppose that your income doubles. One day you're cruising along making $35,000, and the next you're suddenly making $70,000. (Congratulations, by the way.)

Should you find yourself in this position, however, you may discover that $70,000 isn't as much money as you might think.

Go ahead and laugh. But if your income doubles, your income taxes more than quadruple.

It's a great myth that the rich don't pay much in income taxes. If you make $30,000 a year, you probably pay about $1500 in federal income taxes. If you make $200,000, you pay about $45,000. So a sevenfold increase in income results in a thirtyfold increase in income taxes. I mention this not to get you agitated over whether it's fair to make the rich pay more, but so that you can plan better if you experience any monster income changes.

Another thing — I know it sounds crazy, but I think you may find it hard to spend $70,000 wisely if you've been making a great deal less. If you make some big purchases, like cars and boats and houses, you not only burn a lot of cash, but you also ratchet up your monthly living expenses.

Zen and monster income changes

A philosophical digression, please. Except for the necessary creature comforts — cozy places to live, adequate food, and comfortable clothes — I don't think that material wealth affects the quality of our lives.

I don't mean to minimize the challenge involved in raising a family of four on $14,000 a year. But I really don't think those who make $300,000 a year have better lives than those who make $30,000.

Sure, they spend more money. They buy more stuff. They buy more expensive stuff. But they don't live better. They don't have better marriages. Their kids don't love them more. They don't have better friends or more considerate neighbors.

Deep down, you already know this. I know that you do.

Monster income changes the other way are even more difficult. If you've been making $70,000 a year and then your salary drops to $35,000, for example, it's going to hurt. And probably more than you think.

Taste in stores and hobbies, for example, usually matches income level. Make $35,000 and you think in terms of $5 and $10 purchases. Make $70,000 a year and you think in terms of $10 and $20 purchases. But if your income drops from $70,000 to $35,000, you may find yourself making $20 purchases that you really can't afford.

What should you do? If you experience a monster income change, redo your secret plan.

Setting Up a Secret Plan

Enough metaphysical stuff. It's time to set up your budget — er, I mean, secret plan.

Getting to the Set Up Budgets screen

To set up a budget, access the Set Up Budgets screen:

1. **Display either the Register screen or the Write/Print Checks screen.**

   From the Main Menu, choose the Use **R**egister or **W**rite/Print Checks command. You can try talking to your computer, like Scotty does on "Star Trek." But this approach doesn't work unless you have one of those voice command recognition things.

2. **Choose the Set Up Budgets command.**

   From the Activities menu, choose the Set Up Budgets command. Quicken displays the Set Up Budgets screen shown in Figure 3-1.

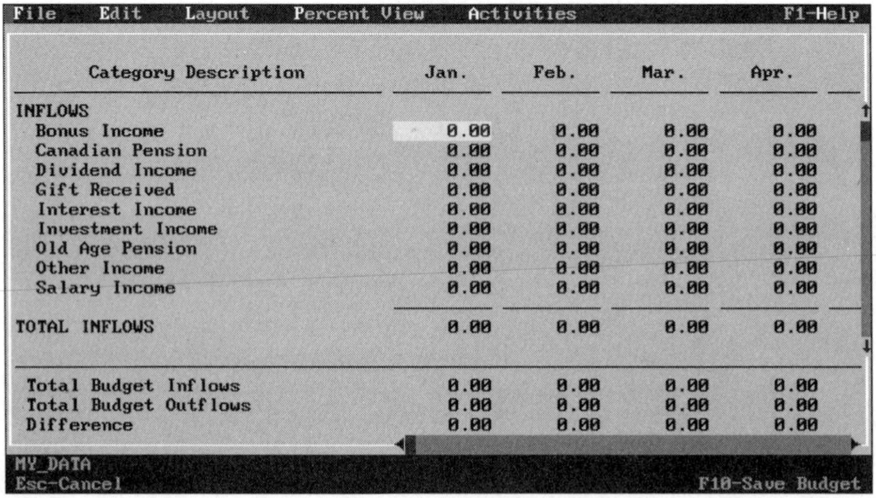

Figure 3-1:
The Set Up Budgets screen.

```
 File     Edit     Layout    Percent View    Activities                    F1-Help

        Category Description        Jan.       Feb.       Mar.       Apr.

 INFLOWS
    Bonus Income                    0.00       0.00       0.00       0.00
    Canadian Pension                0.00       0.00       0.00       0.00
    Dividend Income                 0.00       0.00       0.00       0.00
    Gift Received                   0.00       0.00       0.00       0.00
    Interest Income                 0.00       0.00       0.00       0.00
    Investment Income               0.00       0.00       0.00       0.00
    Old Age Pension                 0.00       0.00       0.00       0.00
    Other Income                    0.00       0.00       0.00       0.00
    Salary Income                   0.00       0.00       0.00       0.00

 TOTAL INFLOWS                      0.00       0.00       0.00       0.00


 Total Budget  Inflows             0.00       0.00       0.00       0.00
 Total Budget Outflows             0.00       0.00       0.00       0.00
 Difference                        0.00       0.00       0.00       0.00

 MY_DATA
 Esc-Cancel                                               F10-Save Budget
```

This screen isn't very complicated. The income and expense categories that you've created appear down the screen's left edge. Quicken also lists subtotals for any categories with subcategories (if you have them) for the total inflows and outflows.

The new menu bar has menus with useful commands for setting up budgets. (I describe only the most useful commands, steering clear of those that you'll probably never need.)

Entering budgeted amounts the simple way

Here's the two-step way to enter budgeted amounts (not to be confused with the Texas Two-Step):

1. **Select the amount you want to budget.**

   Highlight the amount using the arrow keys or clicking.

2. **Enter the budgeted amount.**

   Type the amount that you've budgeted. And press Enter.

If this process doesn't make sense, don't feel bad. Just try it — it's really easy.

Just for fun, pretend that you're budgeting your salary and that you've just received a humongous raise.

Here's an example: to enter the January Salary Income as $3,000, move the highlight square to the January Salary Income field. (Remember, fields aren't the things with rabbits. Well, they are, of course. But on-screen fields are the input blanks.) Then type **3000** and press Enter.

Quicken updates any subtotals and grand totals that use the Salary Income amount. (The Total Inflows subtotal is just below the Salary Income row; the Total Budget Inflows subtotal is at the bottom of the screen.) Figure 3-2 shows the new Set Up Budget screen.

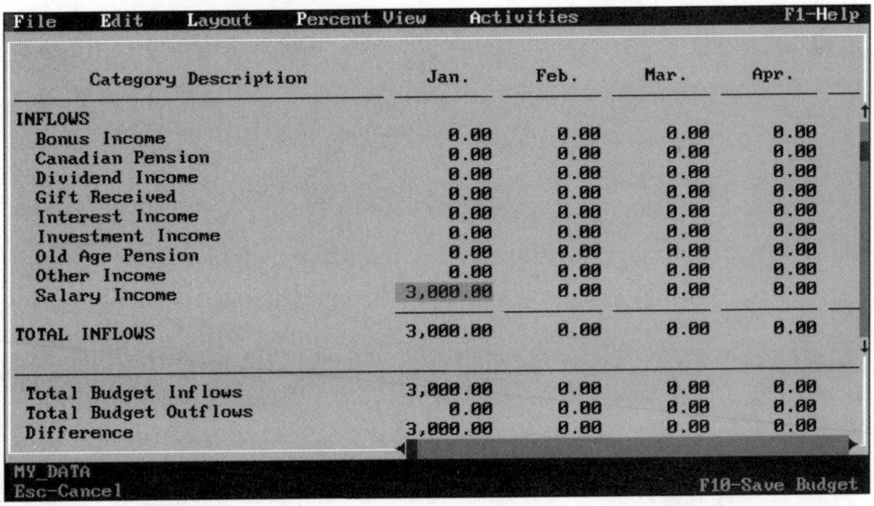

```
 File    Edit    Layout    Percent View    Activities              F1-Help

        Category Description        Jan.      Feb.      Mar.      Apr.

 INFLOWS
    Bonus Income                     0.00      0.00      0.00      0.00
    Canadian Pension                 0.00      0.00      0.00      0.00
    Dividend Income                  0.00      0.00      0.00      0.00
    Gift Received                    0.00      0.00      0.00      0.00
    Interest Income                  0.00      0.00      0.00      0.00
    Investment Income                0.00      0.00      0.00      0.00
    Old Age Pension                  0.00      0.00      0.00      0.00
    Other Income                     0.00      0.00      0.00      0.00
    Salary Income                3,000.00      0.00      0.00      0.00

 TOTAL INFLOWS                   3,000.00      0.00      0.00      0.00


    Total Budget Inflows         3,000.00      0.00      0.00      0.00
    Total Budget Outflows            0.00      0.00      0.00      0.00
    Difference                   3,000.00      0.00      0.00      0.00

 MY_DATA
 Esc-Cancel                                              F10-Save Budget
```

Figure 3-2: The Set Up Budget screen showing January income.

To see the other months, scroll the screen to the right. To see the categories that aren't at the top of the list, scroll the screen down. You can scroll two ways:

Keyboard: To scroll the screen to the right, press Tab. To scroll the screen back or to the left, press Shift-Tab. To scroll the screen up and down, press PgUp and PgDn. Guess which does what? Quicken also scrolls the screen if you use the arrow keys to select an amount that doesn't appear on-screen — such as by pressing the Right arrow when the cursor is already on the farthest right column or the Down arrow when the cursor is already on the bottom row.

Mouse: You also can use the vertical and horizontal scroll bars. Just drag the square scroll bar marker in the direction you want to scroll. You also can click the arrows at either end of the scroll bars, or you can click the scroll bars themselves (the scroll bar marker moves toward the place where you clicked).

But you can't scroll everything. For example, the column headings showing the categories don't scroll, and neither do the rows showing the months, total budget inflows, and total budget outflows. Quicken leaves them on-screen so that you can tell which row is which and how things are going: good, bad, or ugly.

Entering budgeted amounts the fast way

It figures, doesn't it? There's the simple way, and then there's the fast way, and "never the twain shall meet."

When monthly budgeted amounts are the same all year

First, enter the first month's figures. (Highlight a field, type a number, and press Enter. If you want to whistle while you work, go ahead.)

After you've entered the first month's figures, select the Edit menu by pressing Alt-E. Then choose the Fill Columns command. Quicken takes your January budget numbers and copies them to February, March, April, and so on through the rest of the year. Pretty cool, huh?

When budgeted amounts are the same as last year's

If you used Quicken for record keeping during the preceding year, you can copy the amounts from last year and use them as part or all of the current year's budget. To do so, select the Edit menu by pressing Alt-E. Then choose the AutoCreate All command or the AutoCreate Row command.

Which command is which? Good question, my friend. Use AutoCreate All when you want to budget each category for the current year based on figures from the preceding year. Use AutoCreate Row when you want to budget the high-lighted row.

No matter which AutoCreate command you choose, Quicken displays the Automatically Create Budget screen (see Figure 3-3), which lets you tell Quicken what it should copy from last year and where in the current year it should paste the information.

Here's how to use the AutoCreate All and AutoCreate Row commands:

1. **Indicate which months you want to copy.**

   Use the Copy From and Through fields to indicate which months' actual category totals should be copied from the previous year. If you want to copy the entire year of 1994, for example, type **1/94** and **12/94**.

2. Tell Quicken where to paste the copied actual category totals.

Type the month number in the Place Budget Starting in Month field. January is month 1, February is month 2, and so on.

3. Indicate whether Quicken should round the actual category totals.

Want to round the actual category totals? No problem. Press 1 to tell Quicken it shouldn't round, 2 to round to the nearest $1, 3 to the nearest $10, and 4 to the nearest $100.

4. (Optional) Use category averages.

To use the average actual spending in a category for the months identified in the Copy From and Through fields, move the cursor to the Use Average for Period field and press Y.

5. (Optional) Filter by class.

This step doesn't keep out the riffraff. If you've been using classes, you can select the classes on which you want your new budget to be based. If you want to filter by class, move the cursor to the Filter by Class field and then press Y. If you don't want to filter by class, leave the field set to N.

6. (Optional) Inflate or deflate last year's amounts.

You know the old budgeting trick where someone says, "Shoot, I'll just take last year's amounts and inflate them by, oh, 3 percent." Well, you can do the same thing with Quicken. Move the cursor to the New Budget Is % of Actual Transaction Data field. Then tell Quicken by what percentage it should increase the preceding year's figures to create the new year's figures.

7. Clap your hands twice and press Enter.

Quicken uses the information that you enter on the Automatically Create Budget screen to fill in the Set Up Budget screen. If you decide to filter by class, Quicken now displays a screen that lets you select the classes you want to include. I didn't include a picture of the screen because I assume that you aren't using classes. (Incidentally, you don't really need to clap your hands.)

Don't worry too much about this class business. Sure, it's kind of a cool tool. But if you're just getting started, you don't need things that complicate your life.

When a single category's monthly budget is the same all year

Enter the first month's budget figure. Press Alt-E to select the Edit menu. Then choose the Fill Right command. Quicken takes the budget number from the highlighted category and copies it to the other months.

```
 File    Edit    Layout    Percent View    Activities              F1-Help


      Category Description              Jan.       Feb.       Mar.     Apr.

 INFLOWS
    Bonus Inco┌──────────── Automatically Create Budget ──────────┐   0.00
    Canada Pen│                                                   │   0.00
    Dividend I│  Copy from:  1/94 through: 12/94                  │   0.00
    Gift Recei│  Place budget starting in month: 1                │   0.00
    Gross Sale│  Round values to nearest: 1                       │   0.00
    Interest I│      1. None              3. $10                  │   0.00
    Investment│      2. $1                4. $100                 │   0.00
    Old Age Pe│  Use average for period (Y/N): N                  │   0.00
    Other Inco│  Filter by class (Y/N): N                         │   0.00
    Rent Incom│  New budget is 100% of actual transaction data    │   0.00
    Salary Inc│                                                   │   0.00
              │  Esc-Cancel        F1-Help        ←┘ Continue ────┘
    Total Budge                                           0        0.00
    Total Budget Outflows              0.00       0.00       0.00     0.00
    Difference                      3,000.00       0.00       0.00     0.00
 MY_DATA                                          ◄
 Esc-Cancel                                                 F10-Save Budget
```

Figure 3-3:
The
Automatically
Create
Budget
screen.

For example, if your rent runs $500 a month from January through June and then $600 through December, enter **500** in the January Rent field and use the Fill Right command to copy 500 to February, March, and so on through December. Then enter **600** in the July Rent field and use the Fill Right command to copy it (supplanting the original 500) to August, September, and so on through December.

When you finish entering your budget

When you finish entering your budget — that is, your secret plan — either the simple way or fast way, press Esc. Quicken, concerned that you've worked so hard, asks whether you want to save your work (see Figure 3-4). You do, so highlight the Save Changes To Budget option and then press Enter.

In Chapter 5, I explain how to print reports, including a report that compares your actual spending with (ugh) your budget. Stay tuned.

Using the other budgeting commands

If you choose the File, Edit, or Layout commands, you'll realize that I haven't described all the commands available. (I describe the Activities menu commands, which appear on many screens, in later chapters.)

```
 File    Edit    Layout    Percent View    Activities              F1-Help

       Category Description         Jan.      Feb.      Mar.      Apr.

 INFLOWS
    Bonus Income                    0.00      0.00      0.00      0.00
    Canada Pension Plan             0.00      0.00      0.00      0.00
    Dividend Income                                     0.00      0.00
    Gift Received        Budget Has Been Modified       0.00      0.00
    Gross Sales                                         0.00      0.00
    Interest Income   1. Save changes to budget MY_DATA 0.00      0.00
    Investment Inco   2. Discard changes                0.00      0.00
    Old Age Pension                                     0.00      0.00
    Other Income      Esc-Cancel    F1-Help    ←┘ Select 0.00     0.00
    Rent Income                                         0.00      0.00
    Salary Income                                       0.00      0.00

    Total Budget Inflows          3,000.00    0.00      0.00      0.00
    Total Budget Outflows             0.00    0.00      0.00      0.00
    Difference                    3,000.00    0.00      0.00      0.00

 MY_DATA
 Esc-Cancel                                              F10-Save Budget
```

Figure 3-4:
The "Budget
Has Been
Modified"
message.

You don't need to know what these other commands do. But if you're interested, here's the low-down:

- ✔ **File Print Budgets** lets you print a copy of the budget after you create it. After you learn how to print in Chapter 5, using this command is as easy as rolling off a log.

- ✔ **File Save Budget As** lets you save the budget information shown on the Set Up Budgets screen in a separate file. When you choose this command, you need to supply a name for your budget: Mary, Phil, Jerome, or whatever.

- ✔ **File Load Budget** lets you retrieve a budget saved previously. When you choose this command, you need to tell Quicken the budget's name.

- ✔ **File Backup Budgets** lets you copy your budgets to a floppy disk — if you used the File Save Budget As command.

- ✔ **File Restore Budgets** copies backed-up budgets from a floppy disk back to your computer's hard disk.

- ✔ **Edit Inflate/Deflate Budget** changes your budget by some percentage. If you really want to irritate your spouse, for example, you can arbitrarily multiply your budget by 90 percent — thereby cutting every budgeted income and expense item by 10 percent.

- ✔ **Edit Two Weeks** lets you break down a specific monthly budget figure into two-week budget figures. Select the monthly budget figure you want to break down before you choose this command.

- ✔ **Edit Clear Budget** erases what you've already entered. Be careful with this command.

- ✔ **Edit Budget Subcats** tells Quicken whether you want to budget by subcategory. If the Budget By Subcategory switch is on, a check mark appears in front of the menu command. Turn the switch off by choosing the command. (If the switch is off — there's no check mark — you can turn subcategory budgeting on by choosing the command.)

- ✔ **Edit Budget Transfers** tells Quicken whether you want to budget account transfers. I talk about account transfers in the next chapter. Like the Budget Subcat command, this command is a switch.

- ✔ **Layout Months** tells Quicken that you want to budget by the month. You don't need to use this command unless you've used one of the other Layout menu commands, because Quicken budgets by the month unless you tell it to do otherwise.

- ✔ **Layout Quarters** tells Quicken that you want to budget by the quarter. If you flip-flop between months, quarters, and years, Quicken automatically converts the budget figures for you.

- ✔ **Layout Years** tells Quicken that you're a big picture person (or business) and want to budget by the year.

- ✔ **Layout Hide Cents** tells Quicken that you don't want to see the cents.

- ✔ **Percent View Normal View** is the usual way of doing things. When you view the budget using Normal View, Quicken shows the numbers you actually entered. Quicken displays things in Normal View because it's the only view that allows you to enter numbers.

- ✔ **Percent View by Income Total** lets you view the budgeted income and expense items as percentages of the total income. You can see what percentage of your total income you're spending on housing, for example.

- ✔ **Percent View by Expense Total** lets you view the budgeted income and expense items as percentages of the total expense, sort of like the By Income Total view.

- ✔ **Percent View by Respective Total,** a hybrid of the By Income Total and By Expense Total commands, lets you view income items as percentages of the total income and expense items as percentages of the total expenses.

In all four of the views you can toggle between percent view and the amount view by pressing F9.

Part II
The Absolute Basics

The 5th Wave   By Rich Tennant

PORTRAIT OF A CYBERHOLIC

CYBERHOLICS SPEND HOURS BALANCING THEIR CHECKBOOKS ON A COMPUTER, WHEN THEY COULD DO IT IN MINUTES WITH A PEN AND CALCULATOR.

In this part...

*O*K, you're ready for the show to start. Which is good. This next part — The Absolute Basics — covers all the nitty gritty details of using Quicken to keep your personal and business financial records.

If you're just starting to use the Quicken program or you've just come from Part I, you'll find the stuff covered here dang important, dare I say, essential to using Quicken even in the most basic way.

Chapter 4
Checkbook on a Computer

. . . .

In This Chapter

▶ Recording checks

▶ Recording deposits

▶ Recording transfers

▶ Splitting categories

▶ Voiding and deleting transactions

▶ Working with large registers

. . . .

This is it: the big time. You're finally going to use Quicken to enter checks, deposits, and transfers. I think you'll be amazed how simple these tasks are. Along the way, I also explain some of the neat tools that Quicken provides for making these tasks easier, faster, and more precise.

Finding Your Checkbook

To enter checkbook transactions, use the Register screen. To get to the Register screen from Quicken's Main Menu, choose the Use **R**egister command. Quicken displays the Register screen shown in Figure 4-1. The first account lists the starting balance you specified when setting up the account. Figure 4-1, for example, shows a starting balance of $4.16. Bummer.

By the way, if you've set up more than one account, the Register shows the account you last used. If this isn't the one you want to work with, choose the Select/Set Up **A**ccount to Use command from the **P**rint/Acct menu, highlight the account you want with the arrow keys, and press Enter.

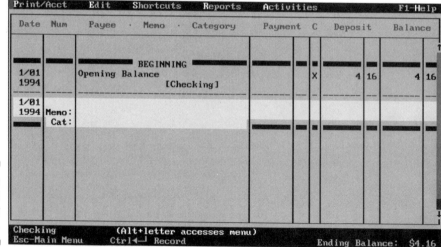

Figure 4-1:
The
Register
screen.

If you're not in the Quicken Main Menu and you see a menu bar that includes an Activities menu, press Alt-A to activate the menu and then choose the **R**egister command to get to the Register screen.

Recording Checks

You can enter checks by using either the Register screen (described in this chapter) or the Write Checks screen (described in the next chapter). Use the Register screen for checks you don't want to print by using Quicken, and use the Write Checks screen to enter checks you do want to print by using Quicken. (This rule isn't ironclad, but it does make things easier.)

Entering a check in the register

To enter a check in the Register screen, simply describe to whom you wrote the check and how much you paid.

Suppose that you wrote a check to the cable television company for $25.50 to pay for your monthly cable service. Follow these steps to record the check:

1. Enter the check date.

Type the date in the Date field using the MM/DD format. Enter January 1, 1994, for example, as **1/1**. Because Quicken retrieves the current year from the clock inside your computer, you usually don't have to enter the year.

You can adjust the date in any date field using the + and - keys. The + key adds one day to the current date; the - key subtracts one day from the current date. When I describe how to record a deposit, I'll tell you about another way to enter the date.

2. Enter the check number.

Type the check number in the Num field. If the preceding transaction was a check, Quicken fills the Num field with its guess as to the new check number — one more than the preceding check number. If this guess is right, leave it in place. If it's wrong, replace Quicken's guess with the correct number. You can use the + and - keys to adjust the check number one number at a time.

3. Name the payee.

Move the cursor to the Payee field and enter the name of the person or business to whom you wrote the check. If the cable company name is Movies Galore, for example, type **Movies Galore** in the Payee field.

4. Enter the check amount.

Enter the check amount in the Payment field. You don't have to type the dollar sign, but you do have to include the decimal point. For this example, type **25.50**.

5. (Optional) Include a memo description.

Identify why you wrote the check in the Memo field. You might identify the cable payment as the February payment, for example. Businesses should use this field to identify the invoice paid by entering the invoice number.

6. Designate a category.

Type the name of the category that should be used to summarize this check in the Category field. The payment to your cable company might be categorized under Utilities. If you're not a superfast typist, Quicken will probably guess which category you're entering before you finish typing. For example, if you type **Ut,** Quicken fills in the rest of the word *Utilities* for you. I talk about this feature, called *QuickFill,* in the next section.

You don't have to remember category names. If you forget the category names that you've set up — which may happen often until you've worked with Quicken for a while — you can display the Category and Transfer List screen. Highlight the correct category by using either the arrow keys or the mouse, and then press Enter.

To display the Category and Transfer List screen, you can either activate the Shortcuts menu and choose the Categorize and Transfer List command or press Ctrl-C. Quicken also displays this screen when you enter a category name that does not appear on the list. Quicken displays a message box telling you that it can't figure out what the heck you entered. The message box asks whether you want to add the new category name to your category list (press 1 to do so) or see the Category and Transfer List screen (press 2). If you have questions about the Category and Transfer List screen, refer to Chapter 2.

7. Press Enter.

This action tells Quicken that you want to record the transaction in the register. Quicken — timid because you two haven't worked together for very long — displays a message box that asks you whether it's OK to record the transaction. Press Enter again. Quicken beeps merrily, calculates the new account balance, and moves the cursor to the next field in the register. If you don't want to record the transaction because you realize that you made an error, press 2, indicating "Yikes! I goofed!" Fix the incorrect fields, move the cursor back to the Category field, and then press Enter twice.

Figure 4-2 shows the cable company check recorded in the register. By the way, Quicken codes the new balance in the Balance field in red to indicate that you've overdrawn your account. You know what that means — overdraft charges.

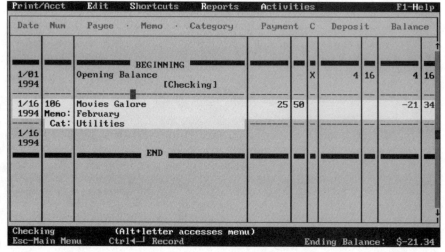

Figure 4-2:
The check register after you record your check to the cable company.

Print/Acct	Edit	Shortcuts	Reports	Activities		F1-Help

Date	Num	Payee · Memo · Category	Payment	C	Deposit	Balance
		BEGINNING				
1/01 1994		Opening Balance [Checking]		X	4 16	4 16
1/16 1994	106 Memo: Cat:	Movies Galore February Utilities	25 50			−21 34
1/16 1994						
		END				

Checking   (Alt+letter accesses menu)
Esc-Main Menu   Ctrl◄┘ Record   Ending Balance: $-21.34

Remember, if you used your bank statement to determine your beginning balance, you need to enter each of the checks and deposits that do not show as cleared on your bank statement.

Changing checks you've already entered

Making changes is easy. Just use the arrow keys to highlight the check transaction you want to change. Use Tab and Shift-Tab to move the cursor to the field you want to change. (Or you can click the field with the mouse.) Then make your correction.

A kooky and clever little thing called QuickFill

Quicken has a funny quirk: if it can guess what you're typing in a field, it fills in the rest of the field for you. I already mentioned how this feature works for category names. But it gets even better.

For example, the second time you use a Payee name, Quicken recognizes it and figures, "Hey, there's probably stuff from the last Movies Galore transaction that should be the same for this transaction." So Quicken uses the first transaction's information to fill in the current transaction's fields: payee, amount, memo, and category.

Although QuickFill may sound dumb at first, it is a real time-saver. For example, you probably pay Movies Galore the same amount every month. The complete payee name is certainly the same, and the category should be the same, too. When Quicken fills in these fields with the previous month's information, it saves you time and effort.

QuickFill doesn't do everything for you, however. You still need to enter the date and check number. And, of course, if Quicken QuickFills a field with the wrong information, you must correct the wrong information.

Memorized transactions and copied transactions

Two other Quicken features — *memorized transactions* and *copied transactions* — are basically obsolete now that QuickFill exists. But because you may have heard about these tools, I'll quickly describe how they work.

A memorized transaction is simply a transaction that you've stored in a special list. To store the transaction, highlight it in the register and then choose the Memorize Transaction command from the Shortcuts menu.

When you want to use one of the memorized transactions, choose the Recall Transaction command from the Shortcuts menu to display a list of the previously memorized transactions. Then select the one you want to reuse.

Copied transactions work a little differently. To copy a transaction, highlight the transaction you want to copy and then choose the Copy Transaction command from the Shortcuts menu. Quicken copies the transaction to a temporary storage area.

To use the copied transaction information, highlight an empty row in the register, choose Paste Transaction from the Shortcuts menu, and then edit the newly pasted information.

Both memorized transactions and copied transactions are handy tools. If you're feeling a little overwhelmed, however, don't spin your wheels trying to get up to speed with them. QuickFill almost always does the job for you.

Recording Deposits

Recording a deposit works almost the same as recording a check, except you enter the deposit amount in the Deposit field rather than the check amount in the Payment field.

Entering a deposit in the register

Suppose that you receive $100 from Aunt Enid for your birthday. Here's how to record this deposit in the register:

1. **Enter the deposit date.**

   Type the date in the Date field using the MM/DD format. Enter January 16, 1994, for example, as **1/16.** As with check dates, you only have to enter the year if the current year number (which Quicken retrieves from your computer's internal clock) is wrong.

You can adjust the date using the + and - keys. The + key adds one day to the current date; the - key subtracts one day from the current date.

You also can use the Calendar command, which appears in the Activities menu, to enter a date. When you choose this command, Quicken displays a calendar screen. Move the cursor to the day you want to select and then press F9. The Calendar command isn't all that exciting, but it's new to Quicken 7. So you may want to check it out — at least once — to see whether you like it.

2. **(Optional) Enter the deposit number if the bank supplies one.**

   Are you the meticulous type? Then go ahead and move the cursor to the Num field and type the deposit number.

3. **Name the person from whom you received the deposit.**

   In this case, type **Aunt Enid** in the Payee field.

4. **Enter the deposit amount.**

   Type **100** in the Deposit field. Don't include the dollar sign or any other punctuation. If Aunt Enid sweats money and sometimes hands out $1,000, for example, you enter the deposit amount as 1000 — not as 1,000 or $1,000.

5. **(Optional) Enter a memo description.**

   Describe the reason for the deposit in the Memo field. You might label the money from Aunt Enid **Birthday Gift**, for example. If you deposit a customer's check in a business account, use this field to identify the customer's invoice number.

6. Enter the category.

You know how this stuff works: type the name of the category that summa-rizes this deposit in the Category field. For example, Aunt Enid's check might be described as **Gift Received** (an income category on the standard home category list). A customer deposit could be categorized as **Gr Sales**, an abbreviation for Gross Sales.

To see a list of categories, press Ctrl-C to display the Category and Transfer List screen. Or choose the **C**ategorize And Transfer command from the **S**hortcuts menu.

7. Press Enter.

This action tells Quicken that you want to record the transaction in your register. When Quicken asks you whether it's OK to record the transac-tion, press Enter again.

If you made an error when recording the deposit, press 2 when Quicken asks whether you want to record the transaction to indicate that you want to return to the transaction. Fix the error, move the cursor back to the Category field, and press Enter twice.

Figure 4-3 shows the check register after you record Aunt Enid's thoughtful gift. Your account is no longer overdrawn — way to go! But before you read any further, maybe you should call Aunt Enid and thank her.

```
 Print/Acct     Edit      Shortcuts      Reports    Activities              F1-Help

 Date   Num     Payee  ·  Memo  ·  Category    Payment  C    Deposit    Balance


                          BEGINNING
 1/01           Opening Balance                         X      4 16        4 16
 1994                        [Checking]

 1/16  106      Movies Galore               25 50                        -21 34
 1994           February       Utilities

 1/16           Aunt Enid                                    100 00       78 66
 1994  Memo:    Birthday gift
       Cat:     Gift Received
 1/16
 1994
                          END

 Checking              (Alt+letter accesses menu)
 Esc-Main Menu      Ctrl◄─┘ Record                  Ending Balance:  $78.66
```

Figure 4-3: The check register after you record the deposit from Aunt Enid.

Changing a deposit you've already entered

No big surprise here — this process works just like changing a check. First, use the arrow keys to highlight the deposit. Press Tab and Shift-Tab to move the cursor to the field you want to change. (You can also click the field with the mouse.) Then make your corrections.

Recording Account Transfers

Account transfers are transactions in which you move money from one account — such as your savings account — to another account — such as your checking account. (If you have one of those combined savings and checking accounts, you probably do this sort of thing all the time.)

Quicken makes account transfers quick work — as long as you've already set up both accounts. (If you don't have the second account set up, you need to do so first. If you don't know how, flip back to Chapter 2.)

Entering an account transfer

Buckle up. I'm going to go through the steps for recording an account transfer really fast. (For the most part, recording an account transfer works the same way as recording a check or deposit.)

Suppose that you want to record the transfer of $50 from your checking account to your savings account. (You may want to do so to make sure that you have enough money to purchase a nice gift for Aunt Enid.) Here's what you need to do:

1. **Enter the transfer date.**

   Enter the date on which you moved the money from one account to the other in the Date field.

2. **(Optional) Enter the transfer number.**

   Move the cursor and pound away at your keyboard.

3. **Enter a description of the transaction.**

   Use the Payee field to describe the transfer — for example, you might type **For Aunt Enid's Next Gift**.

4. **Enter the transfer amount.**

   Indicate amounts transferred out of an account in the Payment field. Enter amounts transferred into an account in the Deposit field.

5. (Optional) Enter a memo description.

If necessary, include more information about the transaction in the Memo field.

6. Designate the other account.

Enter as the category the account to which or from which money is being transferred. (This step is the only tricky part.) Move the cursor to the Category field and type the name of the account. To see the Category and Transfer List screen, press Ctrl-C. To see the account names — account names are listed at the bottom of the screen — press End.

7. Press Enter.

This action tells Quicken that you want to record the transfer transaction in your register. When Quicken asks you if it's OK to record the transaction, press Enter again.

If you make an error when recording the transfer, press 2 when Quicken asks whether you want to record the transaction to indicate that you want to return to the transaction. Fix the error, move the cursor back to the Category field, and press Enter twice.

Figure 4-4 shows the check register after you transfer money from your checking account to your savings account. Now you can purchase something nice for Aunt Enid's next birthday — maybe that new Def Leppard CD.

```
 Print/Acct    Edit    Shortcuts    Reports    Activities            F1-Help

  Date   Num    Payee  ·  Memo  ·  Category   Payment  C   Deposit    Balance


 ▬▬▬          ▬▬▬ BEGINNING ▬▬▬                    ▬
  1/01        Opening Balance                    X      4 16        4 16
  1994                        [Checking]
 ▬▬
  1/16  106   Movies Galore               25 50                   -21 34
  1994        February       Utilities
 ▬▬
  1/16        Aunt Enid                                 100 00      78 66
  1994        Birthday gift   Gift Received
 ▬▬
  1/19        For Aunt Enid's next gift   50 00                     28 66
  1994  Memo: Def Leppard CD?
        Cat: [Savings]
 ▬▬
  1/19
  1994
             ▬▬▬ END ▬▬▬

 Checking              (Alt+letter accesses menu)
 Esc-Main Menu    Ctrl◄┘ Record              Ending Balance:  $28.66
```

Figure 4-4:
The check register after you enter the transfer transaction.

Take a look at the Category field. Notice that Quicken uses the [and] symbols to identify the Category field entry as an account and not as an income or expense category.

The other half of the transfer

Here's the cool thing about transfer transactions: Quicken automatically records the other half of the transfer for you. Figure 4-4 shows a $50 reduction in the checking account due to the transfer. Quicken uses this information to record a $50 increase in the savings account. Automatically. Biddabam. Biddaboom.

To see the other half of a transfer transaction, highlight the transfer transaction. Then select the Edit menu and choose the Go To Transfer command. (You can select the Edit menu and choose the Go To Transfer command at the same time by pressing Ctrl-X.) Quicken displays the other account's register (see Figure 4-5).

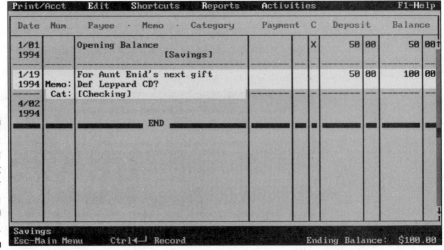

Figure 4-5:
The savings account register showing the $50 increase.

Changing a transfer you've already entered

Predictably, this process works just like changing a check or a deposit. First, highlight the transfer. Then press Tab and Shift-Tab to move the cursor to the field you want to change. Make your correction, move the cursor back to the Category field, press Enter twice, and then go to lunch.

Splitting Hairs

Here's a Quicken riddle for you: how do you categorize a check that pays for more than one type of expense? For example, suppose that you trot down to the grocery store and pick up $10 of groceries (which should be categorized as a Groceries expense) and $10 of motor oil (which should be categorized as an Auto expense). You categorize this transaction by using a *split category*.

When you're ready to categorize the check, choose the Split Transaction command from the Edit menu (or press Ctrl-S). Quicken displays the Split Transaction screen, as shown in Figure 4-6.

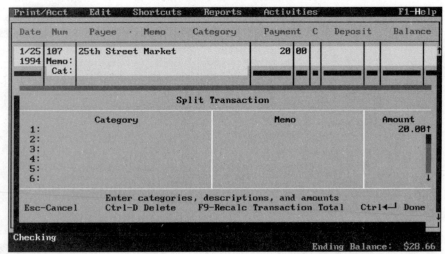

Figure 4-6:
The Split
Transaction
screen.

Splitting checks

To categorize a $20 check to the grocery store that includes $10 for groceries and $10 for motor oil

1. **Enter the first category name in the first Category field.**

   Type the category name **Groceries**. (Remember, you can display the Category and Transfer List screen by pressing Ctrl-C.)

2. **(Optional) Enter a memo description for the first categorized portion of the check.**

   Move the cursor to the first Memo field and type your description. (You might list the food you bought: peanuts, grapefruit juice, and ice cream. Lots of ice cream.)

3. Enter the amount spent for the first category.

Input the amount in the first Amount field. If the first category is Groceries and you spent $10 on food, type **10**.

4. Repeat steps 1, 2, and 3 for each spending category.

Because you spent another $10 on motor oil, for example, type **Auto** in the second Category field. Include a memo description of the expenditure (such as motor oil) in the second Memo field. Move the cursor to the second Amount field and enter the amount spent — for this example, type **10**.

Figure 4-7 shows a completed Split Transaction screen. You can split a transaction into as many as 30 pieces. Use the PgUp and PgDn keys to scroll through the list of split amounts. Or use the mouse to click the vertical scroll bar.

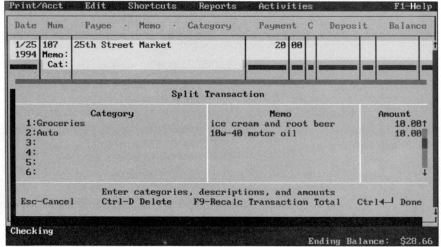

Figure 4-7:
The completed Split Transaction screen.

5. Verify that all spending has been categorized.

If necessary, either add a category or delete the split transaction line that's uncategorized. (To delete a split transaction line, move the cursor to one of the fields in the line and press Ctrl-D.)

6. Record the split by pressing Ctrl-Enter.

When the Split Transaction screen is complete — you've completely and correctly categorized all the parts of the transaction — press Ctrl-Enter. Quicken displays the Register screen again. When you select the split transaction, the Category field shows the word Split to identify the transaction as split.

Splitting the difference

Quicken assumes that the transaction amount you enter in the Register screen agrees with the total of the individual split transaction amounts you enter in the Split Transaction screen.

If you're not sure whether the total of the split transaction amounts equals the payment or deposit amount, your best bet is *not* to enter the amount in the register. Instead, enter the individual split transaction amounts in the Split Transaction screen. When you leave the Split Transaction screen by pressing Ctrl-Enter, Quicken totals your individual split amounts. If the total is positive, the program plugs into the Deposit field. If the total is negative, the program plugs it into the Payment field.

If you've already entered either a payment or deposit amount but are not sure that the split transaction amounts agree with what you entered, you have another option. Press F9 to tell Quicken to match the payment or deposit amount on the Register screen to the individual split transaction amounts total. I call this method the "I don't care if it's a round hole, I want to pound this square peg into it" approach. But, all F9 really does is to calculate the split transaction line amounts total and plug this total into the Payment or Deposit field.

Quicken always shows any difference between the Register screen amount and the split transaction amounts in the last split transaction line.

Splitting deposits and transfers

Are you wondering whether you can split deposits and transfers? Well, you can. In fact, you split deposits and transfers like you split categories in a check transaction. The basic trick is to use the Split Transaction screen to list each category name and amount.

You also can mix and match categories and transfers on the Split Transaction screen (this approach is quite common in a business setting). Some splits can be categories and some can be account transfers. For more information — as to why and when you would want to do this — flip forward to Chapter 12.

Deleting and Voiding Transactions

You can delete and void register transactions using the **Edit** menu's **Delete Transaction** and **Void Transaction** commands.

Using either command is a snap. Just highlight the transaction you want to delete or void and then choose the appropriate command. Quicken supplies a message box asking you to confirm your decision (see Figure 4-8). Press 1 if you want to zap the transaction. Press 2 if you fear you've made a terrible mistake.

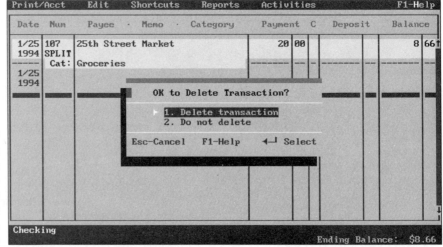

Figure 4-8:
The OK To
Delete
Transaction
message
box.

Use the **V**oid Transaction command when you void a check. Quicken leaves voided transactions in the register, but it marks them as void and erases the payment or deposit amount. So, by using the **V**oid Transaction command, you keep a record of voided or canceled transactions.

Use the **D**elete Transaction command to remove a transaction from your register completely.

When you void a transaction, Quicken does three things: it sticks the word Void at the front of the Payee field, it marks the transaction as cleared, and it erases the Payment or Deposit field. So far, so good. But if you happen to fill in the Payment or Deposit field later, Quicken uses that payment or deposit amount to adjust the account balance — though Quicken still shows the transaction as voided. I keep thinking the folks at Intuit will fix this bug, but they haven't yet. Just make sure that you don't edit transactions after you void them. If you do, it's all too easy to foul up your account balance.

The Big Register Phenomenon

If you start entering a bunch of checks, deposits, and transfers in your register, your register soon contain hundreds and even thousands of transactions. You can still use the tools and techniques discussed in the previous sections to work with one of these big registers. Nevertheless, the following sections help you deal with (drum roll, please) the big register phenomenon.

Moving around in a big register

Use the PgDn and PgUp keys to scroll through your register one screen of transactions at a time.

Use the Home key to jump to the first transaction in a register. Just move the cursor to the Date field and press Home.

You can use the End key to jump to the last transaction in a register. Can you guess how? Move the cursor to the Category field and press End.

To move to the next transaction entered on a specific date, choose the Go To Date command from the Edit menu. When prompted by Quicken, enter the date in MM/DD/YY fashion. Enter April 8, 1993, for example, as **4/8/93**. Quicken highlights the first transaction it finds on the specified date.

Finding that darn transaction

Looking for a particular check, deposit, or transfer? No problem. The Edit menu's Find command provides a handy method for finding that elusive transaction. Here's what you do:

1. **Choose Find from the Edit menu.**

   Select the Edit menu and choose Find. Quicken displays the Transaction to Find screen, as shown in Figure 4-9. Use this screen to describe the transaction you want to find; give as much detail as possible.

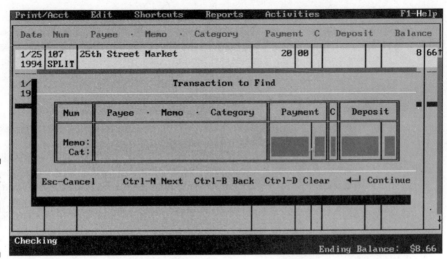

Figure 4-9: The Transaction to Find screen.

2. Enter the transaction number.

If you know the transaction number, move the cursor to the Num field and input the transaction number.

3. Name the payee.

If you know the contents of the Payee field, type the payee name in the Payee field. If you only know a part of the name, enter the characters you do know followed by two periods. For example, if you want to find a transaction for which Aunt Enid is the payee, but you're not sure that you entered anything more than **Aunt**, type **Aunt..** in the Payee field. (See the sidebar entitled "Search Criteria 'R' Us" for more information on wildcard letters.)

4. Enter the transaction amount.

If the transaction is a check and you know the amount, input the amount in the Payment field. If the transaction is a deposit and you know the amount, input the amount in the Deposit field.

5. Enter the memo description.

If you know the transaction's memo description, enter the memo description in the Memo field. If you know only a piece of the memo, enter what you do know followed by two periods. To find a memo description that starts with the word Gift, for example, type **Gift..** in the Memo field.

6. Enter the category.

If you know the transaction's category, move the cursor to the Cat field and type the category name or the account name.

If you make a mistake describing some piece of the transaction you want to find, move the cursor to that field and press Ctrl-Backspace to erase what's in the field. If you've made a bunch of mistakes and need to start from scratch, throw your hands up in the air, scream, and then press Ctrl-D to erase all fields.

7. Let the search begin.

When you've described as much of the transaction as you can, press Ctrl-B to begin looking backward from the selected transaction. Or press Ctrl-N to begin looking forward. (The selected transaction is the transaction that was highlighted when you chose the **Find** command from the **Edit** menu.)

If Quicken finds a transaction that looks like the one you've described, it pages through the register and highlights the transaction. Remember that Quicken uses *all* the information you enter to find the transaction. So for Quicken to find a transaction, the transaction's fields must match all the information you entered.

Look at it another way. If you tell Quicken to find a $100 check from Aunt Enid, Quicken only looks for $100 checks from Aunt Enid. It won't find a $100 check from Uncle Ob, and it won't find a $50 check from Aunt Enid. (Fields that are blank on the Transaction To Find screen aren't used in the search, by the way.)

Search Criteria 'R' Us

You can get pretty tricky when specifying the look of a transaction you want to find. Quicken lets you use three special characters to determine the Payee, Memo, and Category search criteria.

Use two periods (..) to represent a single character or string of characters. If you specify the Payee search argument as **..Aunt..**, Quicken finds any transaction that includes the word Aunt in the Payee field: Aunt Enid, Aunt Jemima, Uncle Ob and Aunt Eustace, and so on. (Case *does* matter, by the way — *aunt* isn't the same thing as *Aunt*.)

Use the question mark (?) to represent a single character. If you specify the Memo search argument as **Ju?**, Quicken finds transactions with the memos of Jul and Jun.

The tilde character (~) says, "Not!" (Just for the record, the folks at Intuit thought of this long before Wayne and Garth.) For example, if you specify the Payee search argument as **~..Aunt..**, Quicken finds any transaction that doesn't contain the word Aunt in the Payee field.

Chapter 5
Printing 101

In This Chapter

- ▶ Collecting the information you need to print a check
- ▶ Fixing mistakes
- ▶ Printing checks
- ▶ Printing registers
- ▶ Printing reports
- ▶ Using the Reports menu commands
- ▶ QuickZooming report totals
- ▶ Sharing information with a spreadsheet or word processor
- ▶ Editing and rearranging report information
- ▶ Creating charts

Printing Checks

Printing checks in Quicken is, well, quick. You collect the information you want to print, press a couple keys, and tell Quicken how to identify the checks. Sounds simple enough, right?

Collecting check information

To write a check, you collect information for the actual check form and record the printed check in your register.

Before you do anything, make sure that the active account is the one on which you want to write the check. To access the correct account, choose the Select Account command from the Main Menu. After Quicken displays the Select Account to Use screen, highlight the account you want and then press Enter.

To collect the information you need to print a check, take these steps:

1. **Display the Write Checks screen.**

   Either choose the **Write/Print Checks** command from the Main Menu or choose the **Write Checks** command from the **Activities** menu. Figure 5-1 shows the Write Checks screen.

2. **Enter the check date.**

   Move the cursor to the Date field and then enter the date on which you plan to print the check (probably today's date). Remember to type the date in MM/DD/YY fashion — enter April 8, 1994, as **4/8/94.** Also remember that you don't have to enter the year unless you want to refer to a year other than the current one. (Refer to Chapter 4 if this stuff doesn't sound familiar.)

3. **Enter the name of the person you're paying.**

   Move the cursor to the Pay to the Order Of field and type. If you want to write a check to me, for example, type **Steve Nelson**. (Feel free to do so. If you send me a check, I'll even cash it as a sort of public service.)

4. **Enter the amount of the check.**

   Type the amount in the $ field. (If you're sending a check to me, be sure that you make the amount nominal — for sure, not more than five or ten dollars.) When you press Enter to move the cursor to the next field, Quicken spells out the amount on the line under the payee name.

5. **Enter the payee's address.**

   If you're going to mail the check in a window envelope, move the cursor to the Address field. Then type the address of the person or business you're paying.

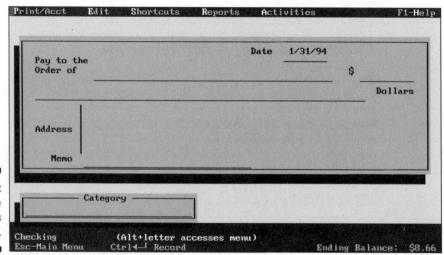

Figure 5-1:
The Write
Checks
screen.

Here's a little address-entry trick. You can copy the payee name to the first line of the address block of fields by typing a quotation mark (") or an apostrophe (') in the first field of the address block.

6. (Optional) Enter a description of the check.

Move the cursor to the Memo field and type the description you want to use, such as the account number or the invoice number that a check pays.

7. Enter the category.

Move the cursor to the Category field and type the name of the category name that summarizes the expense. If you don't remember the category name, press Ctrl-C (or choose the **C**ategorize Transfer command from the **S**hortcuts menu) to display a list of categories. Then use the arrow keys to select a category and press Enter. Figure 5-2 shows a rent check payable to the venerable Marlborough Apartments in the fictional town of Pine Lake.

Want to split categories for a check? You can assign a check to more than one category by using the Split Transaction screen — just as you can in using the register. You might use this feature when writing a check to pay your mortgage, for example, when part of the check pays the actual mortgage and part of the check goes into an escrow account for property taxes.

To split a check into multiple spending categories, press Ctrl-S (or choose the **S**plit Transaction command from the **E**dit menu). When Quicken displays the Split Transaction screen, indicate which categories and categorized amounts make up the check total. If you have questions about how this split transaction business works, refer to Chapter 4.

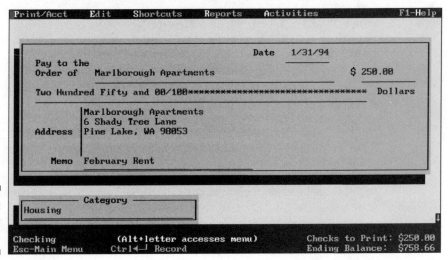

Figure 5-2:
A completed
rent check.

8. Record the check.

When all the information in the Write Checks screen is correct, move the cursor to the Category field and press Enter. Quicken displays a message box that asks whether you want to record the check.

9. Press Enter or 1 to answer yes.

Quicken updates the account balance, adds a Checks to Print total in the screen's lower right corner, and scrolls the completed check off the screen. Quicken displays a blank check screen, which you can use to write another check.

What if you make a mistake entering a check?

Don't worry; be happy. It's easy to fix mistakes if you haven't printed the check yet. Use the PgUp or PgDn keys to page through the checks you've entered using the Write Checks screen. You can display any check you've entered but not yet printed.

When you find an incorrect check, you can fix the mistake in two ways. If you incorrectly entered information, move the cursor to the field with the bad data and make the necessary changes. (If you have trouble, flip back to *Entering stuff into a screen* in Chapter 2.) You also can delete the entire check: press Ctrl-D or choose the **D**elete Transaction command from the **E**dit menu.

Don't delete a check you've already printed. Instead, void it: with the Register screen displayed, highlight the check you want to delete and then press Ctrl-V or choose the **V**oid Transaction command from the **E**dit menu. You should also write VOID in ink in large letters across the face of the check form. (This mark prevents some nefarious type — a cat burglar, your rebellious teenage son, or the neighbor lady — from cashing the check later.)

Printing a check you've entered

For some reason, my pulse quickens (no pun intended) when I get to this part of the discussion. I think there's just something terribly serious about actually writing a check for real money.

To lower my heart rate, let's print the darn check and get it over with. Here's how:

1. Place the checks in your printer.

Load checks the same way you load any other kind of paper. If you have questions, refer to the documentation that came with your printer. (Sorry I'm not more helpful. There are a million different printers out there.)

2. Choose the Print Checks command.

With the Write Checks screen displayed, press Ctrl-P or choose the **Print** Checks command from the **Print/Acct** menu. Quicken displays the Print Checks screen shown in Figure 5-3. At the top of the screen, Quicken indicates the number of checks it plans to print.

Remember that the **Print** Checks command only appears in the **Print/Acct** menu when the Write Checks screen is displayed. When the Register screen is visible, the **Print** Register command appears instead.

3. Tell Quicken to use the check printer description.

Move the cursor to the Print To field and press 3 if the field doesn't already show a 3. (*Chk* stands for Checks. But I bet you guessed as much.)

4. Indicate which checks Quicken should print.

Move the cursor to the Print All/Selected Checks field. Press A if you want Quicken to print all the checks you've entered by using the Write Checks screen. (This case is the most common.) Press S if you want to pick which checks to print.

5. Indicate which check form you're using.

Move the cursor to the Type of Checks to Print On field and then type the number that identifies the check form you purchased.

6. (For laser printers only) Indicate whether you want extra copies of the check form.

Enter the number of copies you want in the Number of Additional Copies (Laser Only) field.

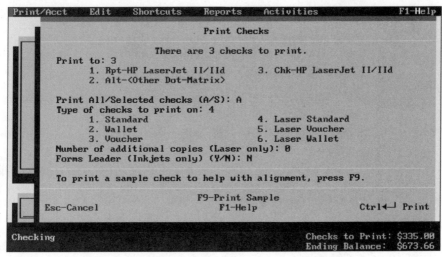

Figure 5-3:
The Print
Checks
screen.

If you use Quicken for business and you keep accounts payable files, it's not a bad idea to make a copy of a check and then attach the copy to the invoices that the check pays. If a vendor calls later and asks which check paid which invoices, you can check your accounts payable files and quickly find the answer.

7. (For ink jet printers only) Indicate whether you are using a forms leader.

Move the cursor to the Forms Leader (Ink Jet Only) field and press Y. I assume that if you've purchased a forms leader from Quicken, you'll know what one of these is. If you haven't, of course, you won't know. But it won't really matter, right? If you don't have a forms leader, you don't need to worry about this step.

8. (For nonlaser printers) Print a sample check.

If you're printing checks for the first time, you can print a test check to verify that you have the check forms lined up correctly in your printer. Just press F9 and Quicken prints a sample check. If this sample reveals problems, see step 12.

9. Let the games begin.

Press Ctrl-Enter to continue the printing process. Or, press Enter when the cursor is on the last field on the screen, the Forms Leader (Y/N) field.

10. (Optional) Select which checks to print.

If you tell Quicken that you want to pick which checks it prints, Quicken displays the Select Checks to Print screen (see Figure 5-4). Initially, Quicken marks all the checks dated on or before the current date with the word *Print*. (Refer to the far right column in Figure 5-4.) If you don't want to print a check, highlight the check and press the spacebar. The spacebar acts as an on-off switch, alternately telling Quicken to print or not print the selected check. When all the checks you want to print are marked Print, press Enter. Quicken displays the Enter Check Number screen (see Figure 5-5). In Figure 5-4, only the rent check is marked Print. (After all, you can avoid the Save the Whales people easier than the landlord.)

11. Indicate which check number to use for the first check.

Type the number that's already printed on the first check form in your printer. Don't press Enter yet.

12. (For nonlaser printers) Fix alignment problems revealed by the sample check.

If you're not using a laser printer and you printed a sample check to test the alignment, press F7 when the Enter Check Number screen appears. Quicken displays the Vertical Check Adjustment screen shown in Figure 5-6. If the check information printed too high on the form, indicate how many half lines the information should be moved down. Use the Full Page Adj

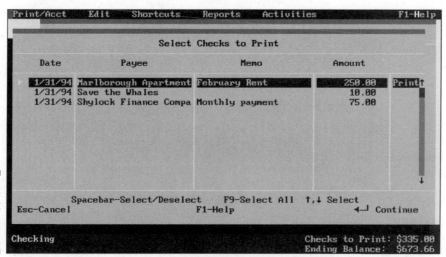

Figure 5-4:
The Select
Checks to
Print screen.

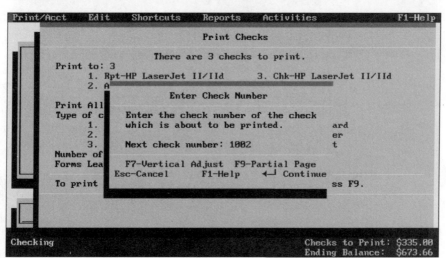

Figure 5-5:
The Enter
Check
Number
screen.

and Higher/Lower fields when you're printing forms on a full page, and use the Partial Page Adj and Higher/Lower fields when you're printing forms on a half page. Note that the adjustment you specify is in *half* lines. To move the check information a full line higher, enter the adjustment as 2 and the Higher/Lower setting as H. Press F10 or Enter when the cursor is on the screen's last field to return to the Enter Check Number screen.

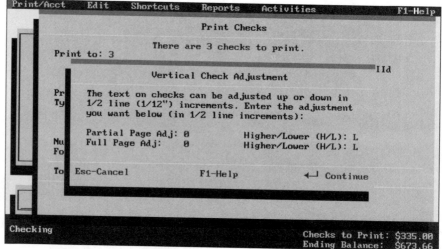

13. (Optional for laser printers) Tell Quicken that you're printing a partial page.

If you're printing a partial page of forms on a laser printer, press F9 when the Enter Check Number screen appears. Quicken displays the Start Printing on Partial Page screen shown in Figure 5-7. Indicate whether there are one or two check forms remaining on the partial page. Indicate whether the tear-off strip at the bottom of the partial page is still in place (press Y for yes or N for no). Press F10 or Enter when the cursor is on the screen's last field to return to the Enter Check Number screen.

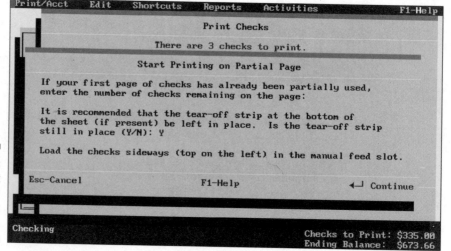

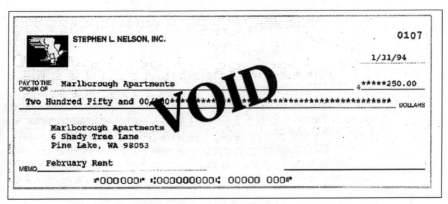

Figure 5-8:
A printed
check.

14. **When the Enter Check Number screen shows the correct check number (and any necessary alignment or partial page settings), press Enter.**

    Quicken prints the checks. If you're starting with a partial page of forms, your printer may prompt you to manually feed the first page of forms. When Quicken finishes, it asks whether it printed your checks correctly.

    Figure 5-8 shows a check made payable to Marlborough Apartments. At last, you get the landlord off your back.

15. **Review the printed check or checks.**

    If Quicken printed the checks correctly, press 1. Quicken then redisplays the Write Checks screen so that you can print more checks.

    If Quicken didn't print the checks correctly, press 2. You then need to repeat the steps for check printing. Note that you only need to reprint the bad checks. You don't have to print good checks again.

16. **Sign the printed checks. Don't forget to mail them.**

A few words about check printing

This check printing stuff is kind of complicated, isn't it?

For the record, I'm with you. I really wish it weren't so much work. I think you may find, though, that it gets easier after the first few times. Pretty soon, you can zip through the steps, skating around things like check form alignment problems.

What if you discover a mistake after you've printed a check?

This problem isn't as big as you might think.

If you've already mailed the check, there's not a whole lot you can do. You can try to get the check back if it hasn't been cashed yet; then replace the incorrect check with a correct one. (Good luck!) If the check has been cashed, there's no way to get the check back. If you overpaid (you wrote the check for more than you should have), get the person you overpaid to refund the difference. If you underpaid, write another check to make up the difference.

If you printed the check but haven't mailed it, void it. First, write VOID in large letters across the face of the check form. (Use a ballpoint pen for multipart forms so that the second and third parts are also voided.) Second, display the register, highlight the check, and then choose the Void Transaction command from the Edit menu. After you mark a check as voided, Quicken ignores it when figuring your account balance.

Printing a Check Register

You can print a check register (or, for that matter, a register for any kind of account). Choose the Use Register command from the Main Menu to display the Register screen; then press Ctrl-P or choose the Print Register command from the Print/Acct menu.

Quicken displays the Print Register screen shown in Figure 5-9. To print a register, just press Ctrl-Enter. Quicken prints a copy of the check register (see Figure 5-10).

Oh where, oh where, do unprinted checks go?

Quicken stores unprinted checks—those you've entered by using the Write Checks screen but haven't yet printed — in the register. To identify them as unprinted checks, Quicken changes their check numbers to ***** (five asterisks). So when you tell Quicken to print unprinted checks, Quicken prints all the checks with ***** check numbers.

This asterisk business raises two intriguing possibilities. To enter checks that you want to print directly into the register, just enter the check number as *****. (Note that you can't enter an address anywhere in the register, however, so this method isn't practical if you want addresses printed on your checks.) You also can reprint a check by changing its check number to *****. Of course, I can think of only one situation where you would want to reprint a check: if you accidentally print a check on plain paper and want to reprint it on a check form.

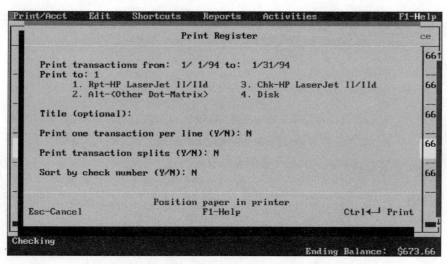

Figure 5-9:
The Print
Register
screen.

```
  Print/Acct    Edit    Shortcuts    Reports    Activities           F1-Help
 ┌─────────────────────────────────────────────────────────────────────┐
 │                         Print Register                            ce │
 │                                                                 ┌─┐ │
 │   Print transactions from:  1/ 1/94 to:  1/31/94               │66↑│ │
 │   Print to: 1                                                   ├─┤ │
 │          1. Rpt-HP LaserJet II/IId     3. Chk-HP LaserJet II/IId│66 │ │
 │          2. Alt-<Other Dot-Matrix>     4. Disk                  ├─┤ │
 │                                                                 │66 │ │
 │   Title (optional):                                             ├─┤ │
 │                                                                 │66 │ │
 │   Print one transaction per line (Y/N): N                       ├─┤ │
 │                                                                 │66 │ │
 │   Print transaction splits (Y/N): N                            ├─┤ │
 │                                                                 │66 │ │
 │   Sort by check number (Y/N): N                                └─┘ │
 │                                                                     │
 │                        Position paper in printer                    │
 │   Esc-Cancel                     F1-Help               Ctrl◄─┘ Print │
 │                                                                     │
 │ Checking                                                            │
 │                                        Ending Balance:   $673.66    │
 └─────────────────────────────────────────────────────────────────────┘
```

```
                            Check Register
Checking                                                    Page 1
4/ 2/94

Date  Num           Transaction         Payment  C  Deposit    Balance
----- -----  ------------------------------  ---------- -  ----------  ----------

1/01         Opening Balance                          X     4.16        4.16
1994 memo:
       cat: [Checking]

1/16 106     Movies Galore                   25.50                    -21.34
1994 memo: February
       cat: Utilities

1/16         Aunt Enid                                    100.00       78.66
1994 memo: Birthday gift
       cat: Gift Received

1/19         For Aunt Enid's next gift       50.00                     28.66
1994 memo: Def Leppard CD?
       cat: [Savings]

1/25 107     25th Street Market              20.00                      8.66
1994 SPLIT
       cat: Groceries

1/25         Salt Mine, Inc.                        1,000.00    1,008.66
1994 memo: January paycheck
       cat: Salary

1/31 107     Marlborough Apartments         250.00                   758.66
1994 memo: February Rent
       cat: Housing

1/31 *****   Save the Whales                 10.00                   748.66
1994 memo:
       cat: Charity

1/31 *****   Shylock Finance Company         75.00                   673.66
1994 memo: Monthly payment
       cat: Int Exp
```

Figure 5-10:
A real live
check
register.

If you want to change how Quicken prints a register, follow these magical steps:

1. **Limit the range of dates.**

   To print a register of something other than the current year's to-date transactions, use the Print Transactions From and To fields. Move the cursor to the From and To fields and enter the range of months the register should include (pretty obvious, eh?). Be sure that you enter the date in MM/YY format — in other words, enter May 1994 as **5/94.**

2. **(Optional) Choose the printer setting.**

   When you install Quicken, you tell it about your printer. With this information in hand, Quicken creates report print settings and a check print setting (*print settings* are basically just rules of the road). Quicken sticks a 1 in the Print To field to suggest that you use the first report print setting. If you want to experiment with print settings, go ahead and noodle around.

3. **(Optional) Enter a register title.**

   If you like to add your own special titles to things, move the cursor to the Title field and then enter a title or description. Quicken prints the title at the top of each register page.

4. **(Optional) Tell Quicken to use a single line per transaction.**

   To print each check and deposit transaction on a single line, move the cursor to the Print One Transaction Per Line field and press Y.

5. **(Optional) Tell Quicken to print split transaction information.**

   To print split transaction information — categories, memos, and amounts — move the cursor to the Print Transaction Splits field and press Y. I think that if you use split transactions, you should print the split transaction information.

6. **Tell Quicken to print transactions in check number order.**

   To print check and deposit transactions in check number order instead of transaction date order, move the cursor to the Sort By Check Number field and press Y. (If you do so, Quicken will usually list your deposits first — because most deposits don't have numbers.)

Go ahead and experiment with the different fields. You can't hurt anything — or anybody.

Printing Good Ol' Reports

You're on the home stretch. After you've printed a check and a register, printing anything else in Quicken seems easy.

Just the facts (of printing), ma'am

The information in a report comes from the transactions you enter in the Register screen and the checks you enter in the Write Checks screen.

You just need to tell Quicken which report you want to print.

To print a report, select the **C**reate Reports menu from the Main Menu or select the **R**eports menu from the menu bar on either the Register screen or Write Checks screen. Figure 5-11 shows the Reports menu.

To print a home, business, or investment report, simply select the report from the appropriate menu. For example, to print the Home Cash Flow report, select **H**ome Reports from the **R**eports menu and then choose the **C**ash Flow command from the Home Reports menu.

A Quicken timesaver: the numbered commands in the **R**eports menu list the last four reports printed. If you want to reprint one of these reports, you can just choose it from the menu.

After you choose which report you want to print, Quicken asks you to title the report and identify the range of dates that the report covers (see Figure 5-12). (By the way, Quicken provides a pop-up list of common report date ranges; press Ctrl-L to access this list. If you select the Include All Date entry from the pop-up list, you can then enter specific dates in the From and To fields.)

If you don't enter a report title, Quicken uses the command name, for example, Cash Flow Report (see Figure 5-13). If you don't enter a range of dates, Quicken assumes that you want transactions from the start of the current calendar year through the current month.

Print/Acct	Edit	Shortcuts	Reports	Activities		F1-Help
Date	Num	Payee	Memo	► Home Reports...		Balance
				Business Reports...		
1/25	107	25th Street Market		Investment Reports...		8 66↑
1994	SPLIT		Grocer	Other Reports...		
1/25		Salt Mine, Inc.		Memorized Reports		1,008 66
1994		January paychec→Salary		Redo Last Report Ctrl-Z		
				1: Monthly Budget Report		
1/31	107	Marlborough Apartments		2: Tax Summary Report		758 66
1994		February Rent Housin		3: Balance Sheet		
				4: Profit & Loss Statement		
1/31	*****	Save the Whales				748 66
1994	Memo:			Quick Report Alt-Z		
	Cat:	Charity				
1/31	*****	Shylock Finance Compan				673 66
1994		Monthly payment Int Exp				
1/25						
1994						
		END				

Create or customize standard reports for home use.

Figure 5-11:
The Reports menu.

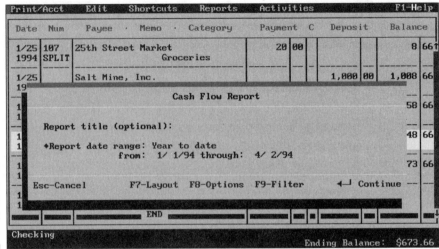

Figure 5-12:
The Cash
Flow Report
screen.

REMEMBER

A report that shows account balances — such as the Home Net Worth Report and the Business Balance Sheet — doesn't need a range of dates because it reports account balances as of a specific date. If you don't enter a date, Quicken assumes that you want account balances for the current date shown on your computer's internal clock.

When the Create Report screen looks right, press F10. Or press Enter when the cursor is on the last field. Quicken produces an on-screen version of the report.

You won't see all the on-screen version of a report unless your report is very small (or your screen is monstrously large). Use the PgUp and PgDn keys to scroll up and down; use Tab and Shift-Tab to move left and right.

Figure 5-13:
An on-
screen
version of
the Cash
Flow Report.

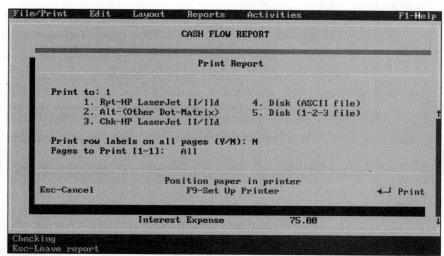

Figure 5-14:
The Print
Report
screen.

If a report doesn't fit on a single screen, Quicken provides vertical and horizontal *scroll bars,* which you can use to scroll up and down and move right and left. Just drag the square scroll bar marker in the direction you want to scroll. You also can click the arrows at either end of the scroll bars, or you can click the scroll bars themselves (the scroll bar marker moves toward the place where you clicked).

To print your report, press Ctrl-P or choose the **P**rint Report command from the **F**ile/Print menu. Quicken displays the Print Report screen, as shown in Figure 5-14.

Choose the correct printer option (you probably will use the first option). Press Enter to accept Quicken's suggested settings.

You'll never guess what happens next: Quicken prints the report and then redisplays the on-screen version of the report. To remove the on-screen version of the report, press Esc.

Reviewing the standard reports

Most of the time you want a report, you select one of the first three options in the **R**eports menu: Home Reports, Business Reports, or Investment Reports. After you make your selection, Quicken displays a list of possible reports.

Tables 5-1, 5-2, and 5-3 list and describe Quicken's personal, business, and investment reports. (Some of these babies may not make sense until you understand how to collect the information that goes into them.)

Table 5-1	Quicken's Home Reports
Report	**Description**
Cash Flow	Summarizes the money that flows into and out of an account by income and expense categories and by transfers. Cash is king, dude, so this report only includes transactions recorded in your bank, cash, and credit card accounts.
Monthly Budget	Summarizes income and expense categories and compares actual category totals to budgeted category amounts. This report only includes transactions recorded in your bank, cash, and credit card accounts. (For this report to make any sense, of course, you must set up a budget.)
Itemized Categories	Summarizes income and expense category accounts.
Tax Summary	Summarizes income and expense category totals for those categories marked tax-related. Like the itemized categories report, this report includes transactions from all accounts.
Net Worth	Lists all your accounts and their balances. Also identifies your net worth (the difference between the asset accounts and liabilities accounts).
Missing Check	Lists payment transactions in the current account in check number order. Gaps in the check number sequence may indicate a missing check.
Tax Schedule	Summarizes income and expense category totals for those categories marked tax-related and assigned to specific tax schedules. This report includes transactions from all accounts. (If you export Quicken information to a tax preparation package, such as TurboTax, this is the report that essentially gets passed to the tax preparation package.)

Table 5-2	Quicken's Investment Reports
Report	**Description**
Portfolio Value	Lists your investments and their actual or estimated values.
Investment Performance	A power user report. Calculates the internal rates of return delivered by each investment in your portfolio.
Capital Gains	Lists all realized gains on individual investments you've sold.
Investment Income	Summarizes income and expense categories for transactions recorded in your investment accounts.
Investment Transactions	Lists transactions recorded for all investment accounts.

Table 5-3	Quicken's Business Reports
Report	*Description*
P&L Statement	Summarizes income and expense category totals. This report, which includes transactions from all accounts, should help you answer the age-old question, "Am I being fairly compensated for the hassle and risk?"
Cash Flow	Summarizes the money that flows into and out of an account by income and expense categories and by transfers. This report only includes transactions recorded in your bank, cash, and credit card accounts.
A/P by Vendor	Summarizes unprinted checks by payee for all bank accounts. (A/P stands for accounts payable.)
A/R by Customer	Summarizes uncleared transactions for all other asset accounts. (A/R stands for accounts receivable.)
Job/Project	Summarizes income and expense category totals and displays each class's information in a separate column. For this report to make sense, you need to use an advanced Quicken feature called *classes* (refer to *Do You Need a Little Class?* in Chapter 2 for a definition of classes).
Payroll	Summarizes income and expense categories which begin with the word *Payroll.* Use this report to prepare quarterly and annual payroll tax reports (for more information, see Chapter 12).
Balance Sheet	Lists all your accounts and their balances. Also identifies your equity (the difference between the asset accounts and liabilities accounts). Identical to the Home Net Worth Report.
Missing Check	Lists payment transactions in the current account in check number order. Gaps in the check number sequence may indicate a missing check. Identical to the Home Missing Check Report.

The Other command in the Reports menu

When you want to know some financial tidbit, you almost certainly can get the information you want from one of the reports listed in the Home, Business, or Investment reports menus.

Quicken, though, is remarkably sophisticated in its reporting capabilities. In fact, when you select the **O**ther option from the **R**eports menu, Quicken lists several additional kinds of reports: Transaction, Summary, Budget, Account Balances, and Comparison. When you choose one of these reports, Quicken displays a special version of the Create Report screen; Quicken then lets you specify exactly what you want to appear in the report and how you want the report organized.

The Quicken Reports menu provides one other handy report command, QuickReport. QuickReport creates a quick-and-dirty report using information from the selected transaction and selected field. If a check to Armstrong Commons is the selected transaction and the cursor is on the Payee field, for example, QuickReport creates an on-screen report that lists all the checks to Armstrong Commons. If the cursor isn't in a transaction field, choosing QuickReport first causes Quicken to display the QuickReport screen which lets you pick which transaction field Quicken should use to create the report (see Figure 5-15).

Because the reports listed in the Home, Business, and Investment reports menus should serve all your needs, I'm not going to describe how the Create Report screen works — though undoubtedly there are some people out there who, late one night, will want to know how to filter, sort, and customize. Of course, there are also people out there who want to know how to replace the transmission on a 1971 Triumph Spitfire, and I'm not describing that here, either.

If you want to learn how these other reports work, just mess around with them. You can't hurt anything. To save any custom report specifications you create, press Ctrl-M or choose the **M**emorize Reports command from the **F**ile/Print

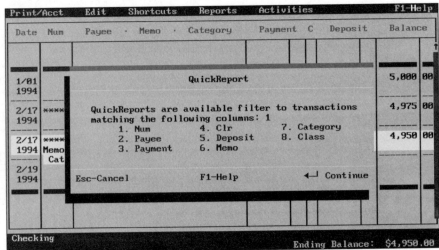

Figure 5-15:
The
QuickReport
screen.

menu that Quicken displays with an on-screen version of a report. Then name the report. From that point on, the program lists your custom report whenever you choose the **Memorized Reports** command from the **Reports** menu.

One other thing: if you want to create a custom report that looks just like the last one you printed, choose the **Redo Last Report** command.

The printing dog-and-pony show

You can do some neat things with the reports you create. Although I won't spend much time describing these things, I'll run down some of the most valuable tricks.

Got a question about a number? Just QuickZoom it

If you don't understand a number on a report, select the number (using either the arrow keys or the mouse) and then press Ctrl-Z or choose the QuickZoom command from the File/Print menu. Quicken lists all the transactions that make up the number. (I find QuickZoom extremely handy for understanding figures that appear on reports.)

Sharing report data with spreadsheets and word processors

From the Print Report screen, you can export a report as an ASCII file or as a 1-2-3 disk file (see Figure 5-14). Just indicate that you want to print a report as an ASCII file (press 4) or as a 1-2-3 disk file (press 5). Quicken prompts you for the filename and the path. (If you don't specify the path, Quicken puts the file in the Quicken directory — probably C:\QUICKEN.)

I'm going to go out a limb here: I bet your word processor can read an ASCII file. The mechanics depend on the program, of course, but every word processor I've come across imports ASCII files. If you don't know how to get your word processor to read an ASCII file, refer to the application's user manual.

I'm climbing out on another limb: I bet your spreadsheet can import a 1-2-3 disk file. Again, how you do so depends on the particular spreadsheet. But you should be able to use Quicken report data in any spreadsheet, because every spreadsheet since 1-2-3 imports 1-2-3 files. For help, refer to the spreadsheet's user manual.

Editing and rearranging reports

When Quicken displays an on-screen report, the menu bar lists five menus: File/Print, Edit, Layout, Reports, and Activities. I've not yet talked about the Edit and Layout menu commands.

You can use the **E**dit and **L**ayout menu commands to edit and rearrange a report. If you customize reports *after* you build them rather than *before,* you have fewer options available, but you can make some interesting changes.

I suggest that you experiment with the commands the next time you produce an on-screen version of a report. Don't worry, you can't hurt the data.

I could describe the commands, but I think that you will remember what you experience firsthand more readily. (OK, it's a cop-out, but it's also true.)

Charts Only Look Tricky

I love charts. That sounds goofy, I know. But *data graphics,* as the snobs and academics say, opens up wonderful opportunities for communicating.

Plus, Quicken's charts are really easy to use.

To produce a chart, select View **G**raphs from the Main Menu. Quicken displays the View Graphs menu, which lists four kinds of graphs: Income and Expense, Net Worth, Budget and Actual, and Investment.

When you select a graph option, Quicken lists the specific graphs that it can produce. If you choose Income and Expense graphs, for example, Quicken displays the list shown in Figure 5-16. To produce a graph, choose a graph command.

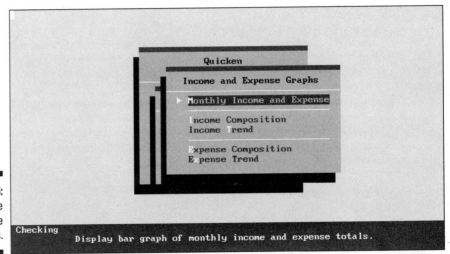

Figure 5-16:
The Income
and Expense
graphs.

By the way, Quicken tells you which commands produce which graphs. When you choose the first Income and Expense graph, for example, Quicken displays a message at the bottom of the screen:

```
Display bar graph of monthly income and expense totals.
```

After you choose a graph command, Quicken displays a Create Graph screen that asks which months of data you want to chart. Enter the months the same way you do for a report and then press Enter.

When you first choose a graph menu command, Quicken asks you for information.

  ✔ It asks you to select your computer's graphics adapter card from a list. (If you don't know, try the EGA & VGA Drivers option.)

  ✔ It asks whether you want to give the graphics portion or the text portion of the graph more space. (I suggest that you give the graphics more space.)

  ✔ If you have a color monitor, it asks whether you want the graphics in black and white or color. (Go with color.)

If you are confused by any of the graphics questions that Quicken asks, press Enter to accept Quicken's suggested settings. These settings are usually the best choices, anyway.

Figure 5-17 shows a bar graph of monthly income and expense totals. It's kind of cool, but you may have more fun looking at your own data in a picture.

If you want to print the graph, press Ctrl-P or click the Print button. To see a report summarizing the same data that the graph plots, choose the Report button. To remove the graph from the screen, press Esc or click the Esc-Cancel button.

Your computer works hard when printing a graph. Very hard, indeed. To let you know that it's not fooling around, Quicken displays a message box while it prints the graph. You may see this message box for several minutes. This wait is normal — even if it isn't all that fun.

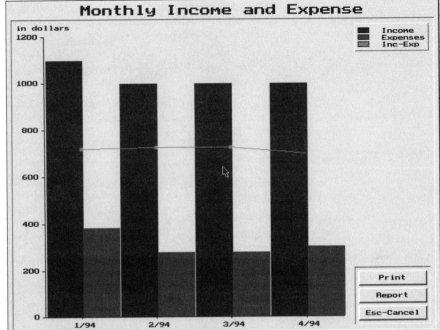

Figure 5-17:
A bar graph
of monthly
income and
expense
totals.

Chapter 6
Perfect Balance

● ●

In This Chapter

▶ Selecting the account you want to balance

▶ Telling Quicken that you want to balance an account

▶ Entering your bank statement balance

▶ Entering monthly service charges and interest income

▶ Marking account transactions as cleared and uncleared

▶ Verifying that the account difference is explained by uncleared transactions

▶ Ten things you should do if your account doesn't balance

● ●

*B*alancing a bank account in Quicken is very quick and very easy.

I'm not just trying to get you pumped up about an otherwise painfully boring topic. I don't think balancing a bank account is any more exciting than you do. (At the Nelson house, we never answer "What should we do tonight?" by saying, "Hey, let's balance an account!")

Although bank account balancing can be tedious, Quicken makes quick work of the drudgery.

Selecting the Account You Want to Balance

Choose the Select Account command from the Main Menu. Or if either the Register screen or the Write Checks screen is displayed, activate the Print/Acct menu by pressing Alt-P or F2 and then choose Select/Set Up Account. Quicken displays the Select Account to Use screen.

To select the account you want to balance, use the arrow keys to highlight the account and press Enter, or double-click the account.

Balancing a Bank Account

Balancing a bank account is remarkably easy. In fact, if you run into any problems, I bet they stem from, well, the sloppy record keeping that preceded your use of Quicken.

Enough of this blather, though. Time to get started.

Telling Quicken, "Hey, man, I want to balance an account"

To tell Quicken that you want to balance (or *reconcile*) your records of a bank account with the bank's records, choose the Reconcile command from the Activities menu. Quicken displays the Reconcile Register with Bank Statement screen, as shown in Figure 6-1.

It doesn't matter whether the Register screen or the Write Checks screen is displayed when you choose the Reconcile command. The Reconcile command appears in the Activities menu of both screens.

If you choose the Reconcile command when the Write Checks screen is displayed, though, Quicken replaces the Write Checks screen with the Register screen (you can see the screen underneath the Reconcile Register with Bank Statement screen). Another one of life's great mysteries, I guess.

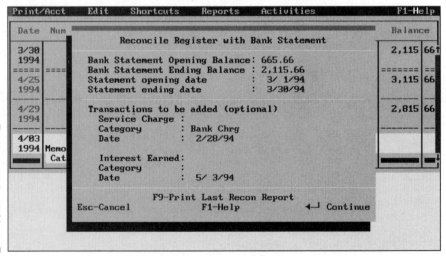

Figure 6-1: The Reconcile Register with Bank Statement screen.

Telling Quicken what the bank says

In a reconciliation, you compare your records of a bank account with the bank's records of same account. You should be able to explain any difference between the two accounts — usually by pointing to checks you've written but that haven't cleared the bank or deposits that the bank hasn't yet credited to your account.

Your first step, then, is to supply Quicken with the bank's account information (you get this information from your monthly bank statement):

1. **Verify the Bank Statement Opening Balance.**

   Quicken supplies a Bank Statement Opening Balance by guessing what the bank balance was at the start of the month. (If this is the first time you've reconciled, Quicken gets the opening balance figure from your starting account balance. If you've reconciled before, Quicken uses the Bank Statement Ending Balance that you specified the last time you reconciled.) Make sure that this figure is correct. If it isn't, replace it with the correct figure by moving the cursor to the field and then typing over the suggested figure.

2. **Enter the Bank Statement Ending Balance.**

   Move the cursor to the Bank Statement Ending Balance field and enter the ending (or *closing*) balance shown on your bank statement.

3. **Enter the Statement Opening Date.**

   Move the cursor to the Statement Opening Date field and enter the date in MM/DD/YY format. (For example, enter November 26, 1994, as **11/26/94.**) Get this information from your bank statement.

4. **Enter the Statement Ending Date.**

   Type the date in the Statement Ending Date field (also get this information from your bank statement). Then move your left foot in, move your left foot out, move your left foot in, and shake it all about.

5. **Enter the Service Charge.**

   If the bank statement shows a service charge and you haven't entered it in the register, move the cursor to the Service Charge field and enter the amount. Don't type the dollar sign. Do type the decimal point. (Enter $4.56 as **4.56**, for example.)

6. **Assign the service charge to a category.**

   Move the cursor to the first category field — the category field beneath the Service Charge field — and enter the expense category to which bank service charges should be assigned. If you're using the standard home categories list, you probably want to go with Bank Chrg. To select a category from the Category and Transfer list screen, press Ctrl-C, highlight the category, and press Enter.

7. Enter a Transaction Date for the service charge transaction.

Quicken supplies the current system date from your computer's internal clock, but you probably need to replace it with the correct date (just type over the suggested Service Charge Transaction Date). Remember, too, that you can adjust a date one day at a time by using the + and - keys.

8. Enter the account's interest income.

If the account earned any interest for the month and you haven't entered it in the register, enter the amount in the Interest Earned field. (For example, enter 17 cents as **.17**.)

9. Assign the interest to a category.

Move the cursor to the second category field and name the interest income category to which interest should be assigned. If you're using the standard home categories list, you probably want to go with Int Inc. To select a category from the Category and Transfer list screen, press Ctrl-C, highlight the category, and press Enter.

10. Enter a Transaction Date for the interest income charge transaction.

11. Tell Quicken that the reconciliation is complete.

Move the cursor to the Interest Earned Transaction Date field — the last field on-screen — and press Enter. Or press F10 with the cursor on any field.

Explaining the difference between your records and the bank's

Quicken now compares your register's account balance with the bank statement ending account balance. Quicken builds a list of checks and deposits that your register shows but that haven't yet been cleared or recorded by the bank. Quicken displays a screen that summarizes the reconciliation. You can view a screen that uses the regular, two-lines-per transaction approach employed by the Register screen (see Figure 6-2). Or, you can view an abbreviated, one-line-per-transaction view of the register transaction (see Figure 6-3). To toggle between these two views, press F9.

The reconciliation register shows both the register and some additional information at the bottom of the screen: the cleared balance (which is your account balance including only the transactions that you or Quicken has marked as cleared), the bank statement ending balance, the difference between these two figures, and the number of checks and deposits that you or Quicken has marked as cleared.

```
 Print/Acct     Edit    Shortcuts    Reports    Activities          F1-Help

  Date  Num   Payee  ·  Memo  ·  Category    Payment  C  Deposit    Balance

  2/25       Salt Mine, Inc.                              1,000 00   1,665 66↑
  1994 Memo: February paycheck
       Cat: Salary
  2/28 110   Marlborough Apartments       275 00                    1,390 66
  1994       March Rent        Housing

  3/25       Salt Mine, Inc.                              1,000 00   2,390 66
  1994       March paycheck   Salary

  3/30       Marlborough Apartments       275 00                    2,115 66
  1994       April Rent        Housing
 ===== =====================================  ======= == = ======= == ======= ==↓

                            RECONCILIATION SUMMARY
         Items You Have Marked Cleared (*)
        ─────────────────────────────────     Cleared (X,*) Balance      665.66
          0    Checks, Debits       0.00     Bank Statement Balance    2,115.66
          0    Deposits, Credits    0.00        Difference            -1,450.00

 Esc-Main Menu      F8-Mark Range       F9-View as List        Ctrl F10-Done
```

Figure 6-2:
The
reconciliation
version of
the register.

Press F9 to display an abbreviated version of the register, which lists just one line of information for each transaction (see Figure 6-3). You don't see the category and memo information for checks and deposits. But you probably don't need to see this stuff here, anyway.

Marking cleared checks and deposits

To tell Quicken which deposits and checks have cleared the bank (refer to the bank statement to find this information), follow these steps:

1. Identify the first cleared deposit.

Just leaf through the bank statement and find the first deposit listed.

2. Mark the first cleared deposit as cleared.

Scroll through the transactions listed on the reconciliation version of the register and find the deposit. Highlight the deposit and press the spacebar. Quicken puts an asterisk in the C column to mark this deposit as cleared and updates the cleared statement balance.

3. Record any missing but cleared deposits.

If you can't find a deposit, you haven't entered the transaction in the register yet. If you've been using the one-line, or list, version of the register, press F9 to view the unabridged register (see Figure 6-2). After you enter the deposit in the register, type an asterisk in the C column to tell Quicken that the deposit has already cleared the bank. To return to the one-line, or list, version of the Reconciliation Register screen, press F9 again.

4. Repeat steps 1, 2, and 3 for every deposit listed on the bank statement.

5. Identify the first cleared check.

No sweat, right? Just find the first check or withdrawal listed on the bank statement.

6. Mark the first cleared check as cleared.

Scroll through the transactions listed on the reconciliation version of the register and find the check or withdrawal. Highlight the check or withdrawal and press the spacebar. Quicken puts an asterisk in the C column to mark this transaction as cleared and updates the cleared statement balance.

7. Record any missing but cleared checks.

If you can't find a check or withdrawal, guess what? You haven't entered it in the register yet. After you enter the check or withdrawal in the register (remember that you can press F9 to view the unabridged register), type an asterisk in the C column to tell Quicken that the check or withdrawal has already cleared the bank.

8. Repeat steps 5, 6, and 7 for all checks and withdrawals listed on the bank statement.

The preceding steps shouldn't take you very long. It only takes me about two minutes to reconcile my account each month. I'm not joking or exaggerating. When I say two minutes, I really mean two minutes.

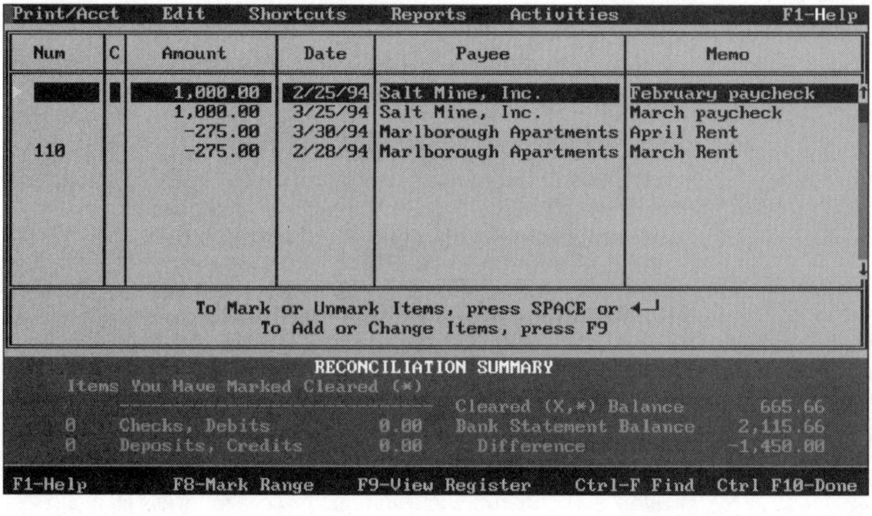

Figure 6-3:
The one-line, or list, version of the register.

Verifying that the uncleared transactions total explains things

After you mark all the cleared checks and deposits, the difference between the cleared balance and the bank statement's ending balance should equal zero. Notice that I say *should*. Figure 6-4 shows a Reconciliation register where everything is hunky-dory. Isn't life grand?

```
 Print/Acct    Edit    Shortcuts    Reports    Activities           F1-Help
┌───────┬─┬──────────┬─────────┬─────────────────────┬────────────────────────┐
│  Num  │C│  Amount  │  Date   │       Payee         │         Memo           │
├───────┼─┼──────────┼─────────┼─────────────────────┼────────────────────────┤
│       │*│ 1,000.00 │ 2/25/94 │Salt Mine, Inc.      │February paycheck      ↑│
│       │*│ 1,000.00 │ 3/25/94 │Salt Mine, Inc.      │March paycheck          │
│       │*│  -275.00 │ 3/30/94 │Marlborough Apartments│April Rent             │
│  110  │*│  -275.00 │ 2/28/94 │Marlborough Apartments│March Rent             │
│       │ │          │         │                     │                        │
│       │ │          │         │                     │                       ↓│
└───────┴─┴──────────┴─────────┴─────────────────────┴────────────────────────┘
            To Mark or Unmark Items, press SPACE or ↵
                To Add or Change Items, press F9

                      RECONCILIATION SUMMARY
      Items You Have Marked Cleared (*)
      ─────────────────────────────────      Cleared (X,*) Balance    2,115.66
        2   Checks, Debits      -550.00       Bank Statement Balance   2,115.66
        2   Deposits, Credits  2,000.00       Difference                   0.00

 F1-Help        F8-Mark Range    F9-View Register    Ctrl-F Find  Ctrl F10-Done
```

Figure 6-4:
A Reconciliation register.

If the difference equals zero, you're done. Press Ctrl-F10 to tell Quicken that you're finished. Quicken displays a congratulatory message, telling you how proud it is of you. Quicken also asks you whether you want to print a Reconciliation report.

If you want to print a Reconciliation report (no, you don't hafta), press Y and then Enter. Quicken displays a regular ol' Print Report screen asking where and how you want to print the report. Press Enter to print the report using the default print settings. (If you feel adventurous, go ahead and fool around with the fields and switches on the Print Report screen to change the way Quicken prints.)

Quicken changes all the asterisks to Xs to identify which transactions have been through the reconciliation process.

Can't decide whether to print a Reconciliation report? Unless you're a book-keeper for a business or an accountant who's reconciling a bank account for someone else — for example, your employer or a client — you don't need to print a Reconciliation report. A Reconciliation report simply proves that you reconciled the account. (Of course, if you are a bookkeeper or an accountant, the report is proof that you did your job.)

If the difference doesn't equal zero, you've got a problem. Press Ctrl-F10 and Quicken will try to explain why your account doesn't balance (see the message box shown in Figure 6-5, for example). Quicken also will tell you that you can force the two amounts to agree by simply pressing Enter. Tempting though it may sound, forcing the two amounts to agree is generally a bad idea. To do so, Quicken adds a cleared transaction equal to the difference. (I talk about this process later in the chapter.)

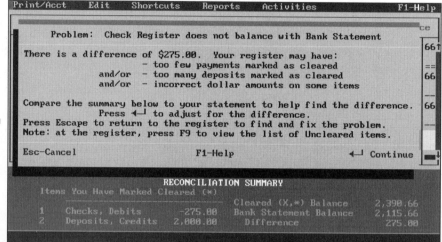

Figure 6-5:
The "Oops, there's a problem with your reconciliation" message.

If you press Esc when the Reconciliation register shows a difference, Quicken will tell you that the reconciliation isn't complete (see Figure 6-6). You can postpone reconciling the account by selecting the Leave Reconciliation (Your Work Will Be Saved) option.

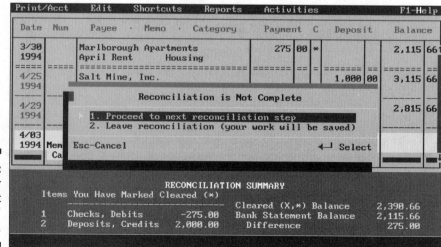

Figure 6-6:
The "Your work isn't done yet" message.

If you select the Leave Reconciliation (Your Work Will Be Saved) option, Quicken leaves your reconciliation work half done. The transactions that you've marked as cleared still have an asterisk in the C column. And, of course, you still have an unexplainable difference between the bank statement and your register.

Nevertheless, this approach is usually the safest. After postponing a reconciliation, you may be able to find the problems and fix them. Then you can restart the reconciliation and finish your work. (You restart a reconciliation the same way you start one.)

By the way, selecting the Proceed To Next Reconciliation Step option is the same thing as pressing Ctrl-F10. If the account balances, you see a congratulations message telling you what a wonderfully bright person you are.

If the account doesn't balance, Quicken tells you why this may be the case and displays a message that asks whether you want to force the two amounts to agree.

Ten Things You Should Do If Your Account Doesn't Balance

If you're sitting in front of your computer wringing your hands, the following tips might help you reconcile your account. Use these ideas as a sort of laundry list.

Verify that you're working with the right account

Sounds dumb, doesn't it? If you have a bunch of different bank accounts, however, it's darn easy to end up in the wrong account. So go ahead and verify that you're trying to reconcile your checking account at Mammoth International Bank by using the Mammoth International checking account statement, for example.

Look for transactions that you forgot to record

Go through your bank statement and make sure that you recorded every transaction that your bank recorded; cash machine withdrawals, special fees or charges (such as for checks or your safety deposit box), automatic withdrawals, and direct deposits are easy to overlook.

If the difference is positive — the bank thinks you have less money than you think — you may be missing a withdrawal transaction. If the difference is negative, you may be missing a deposit transaction.

Look for backward transactions

If you accidentally enter a deposit as a withdrawal or a withdrawal as a deposit, your account won't balance.

This sort of error can be very difficult to find. The Reconciliation register shows all the correct transactions, but the transaction amount appears in the wrong column. The amount of the check you wrote to pay Mrs. Travis for your son's piano lessons, for example, simply shows up as a deposit in the deposit column.

Look for a transaction that's equal to half the difference

If you entered only one transaction backwards, you may be able to find it by looking for a transaction that's equal to half the irreconcilable difference. For example, if the difference is $200, look for a $100 deposit you entered as a withdrawal or a $100 withdrawal you entered as a deposit.

By the way, if the difference is positive — the bank thinks you have less money than your register indicates — you probably entered a withdrawal as a deposit. If the difference is negative — the bank thinks you have more money than your register indicates — you're probably missing a deposit transaction.

Look for a transaction that's equal to the difference

If the difference between your records and the bank's records equals one of the transactions listed in your register, you probably either incorrectly marked the transaction as cleared or incorrectly left the transaction marked as uncleared.

Was that one too obvious? Sorry.

Check for transposed numbers

You transpose numbers when you flip-flop two digits — when you enter $45.89 as $48.59, for example.

These turkeys always cause accountants and bookkeepers headaches. When you compare a check for $45.89 in your register with a check for $48.59 on your bank statement, for example, both check amounts show the same digits: 4, 5, 8, and 9. They just show them in different orders, which can be difficult to detect with a quick glance.

Transposed numbers are tough to locate, but here's a trick you can try: divide the difference shown on the Reconciliation register by 9. If the result is an even number of dollars or cents, there's a good chance that you've transposed a number somewhere.

Get someone else to look over your statement and reconciliation

Even though this trick seems pretty obvious, I'm always amazed how often a second pair of eyes can find something you've been overlooking for 20 minutes.

If you're using Quicken at home, ask your spouse. If you're using Quicken at work, ask one of your coworkers — preferably that one person who always seems to have too much free time.

Look out for multiple errors

If you do find an error and there's still a difference, start checking from the top of this list again. After you find a transposed number, for example, you may remember that you entered another transaction backwards or that you incorrectly cleared or uncleared a transaction.

Try again next month (and maybe the month after)

If the difference isn't huge (in relation to your bank account), consider waiting until next month to try reconciling again.

Suppose that you reconcile your account in January and the difference is $24.02. Then you reconcile in February and the difference is again $24.02. And when you reconcile the account in March, surprise, surprise, the difference is still $24.02.

What's going on here? Well, your starting account balance was surely off by $24.02.

After the second or third month, I think it's OK to tell Quicken to enter an adjusting transaction for $24.02 so that your account balances. (As a general rule, though, this is the one time I think it's reasonable to tell Quicken to adjust your account so that it agrees with the bank.)

If you've successfully reconciled your account with Quicken before, don't have Quicken enter an adjusting transaction right away. The mistake could be (drum roll, please) the bank's! And in this case, there's something else you should do.

Get in your car, drive to the bank, and beg for help

Ask the bank to help you reconcile the account. Hint that you think the mistake is probably theirs. Smile a lot. And be sure that you ask about whatever product they're currently advertising in the lobby. Let them think that you want to buy that 180-month certificate of deposit.

In general, of course, the bank is usually pretty darn good at record keeping. In fact, I've never had a problem either as a business banking client or as an individual. (I've also been lucky enough to deal with well-run banks.)

However, it's possible that your bank has made a mistake. Be sure that you have a bank representative explain any transactions that you've learned about only by seeing them on your bank statement.

Chapter 7

Housekeeping

· ·

In This Chapter

▶ Backing up your data

▶ What to do if you lose your data and you did back up

▶ What to do if you lose your data and you didn't back up

▶ Working with more than one set of data

▶ Using automatic backup reminders

▶ Adjusting screen settings

▶ Setting up and changing file passwords

· ·

*I*f you live in a house or an apartment, you must do a little housekeeping from time to time — defrost the refrigerator, change the furnace filter, clean out the gutters.

Although you don't have to vacuum your computer, Quicken requires some occasional housekeeping. In this chapter, I describe the necessary chores so that you can do them right with minimal hassle.

Backing Up Is Hard to Do

First, and most important, on the spring cleaning list: back up your files. You should always back up the files that store your financial records. The following section explains how.

Backing up the quick-and-dirty way

You're busy. You don't have time to screw around. You just want to back up essential files quickly and efficiently. Here's what you do:

1. **Insert a blank formatted floppy disk into your floppy disk drive.**

2. **Verify that the file you want to back up is active.**

   Display the Register screen and make sure that it displays an account in the file you want to back up. (If you don't remember setting up more than one file, don't worry. Like most people who use Quicken, you probably only have one file.)

3. **Start the backup operation.**

   Choose the **B**ack Up File command from the **P**rint/Acct menu. Quicken displays the Select Backup Drive screen, as shown in Figure 7-1.

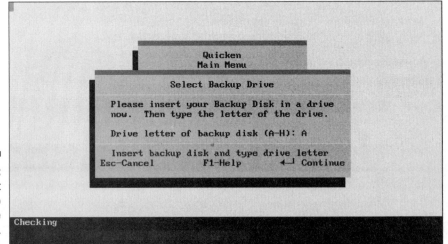

Figure 7-1:
The Select
Backup
Drive
screen.

You also can access the Back Up File command by choosing the **F**ile Activities command from the Main Menu (the File Activities menu also lists the Back Up File command).

4. **Identify the backup floppy drive.**

   Press A if you stuffed your floppy disk into the top floppy drive. The bottom floppy drive — if you have one — is usually named drive B.

5. **Press Enter.**

   Quicken flashes a message that says, "Aye, Cap'n, I'm working just as fast as I can" (or something like that, anyway). When Quicken finishes, it tells you that the backup is complete.

Formatting floppy disks

A floppy disk needs to be formatted before you can store information on it. You can buy either formatted or unformatted floppy disks. Just make sure that the disks you buy match your drive's size (5¼-inch or 3½-inch) and density (low or high).

Size is easy to determine. Get a ruler and measure one of the disks you use. It should be either 5¼- or 3½-inches wide. Simple, huh?

Density is somewhat trickier because you can use both high- and low-density disks in a high-density drive. If you don't know your drive's density, scrounge around for the paperwork that came with your computer. The documentation should tell you the drive's density code (HD for high-density and DS/DD for low-density) or the amount of storage space (for high-density: 1.2MB on a 5¼-inch floppy and 1.44MB on a 3½-inch floppy; for low-density: 360K on a 5¼-floppy or 720K on a 3½-inch floppy).

Of course, if you use high-density floppy disks (often marked HD), the drive is high-density. But remember, if you use low-density disks, the drive could be high- or low-density.

Anyway, to format a disk, exit Quicken to DOS. (You can do this by choosing the Use **D**os command from the **A**ctivites menu.) Stuff the floppy disk into the top floppy disk drive (drive A). Then type **format a:** at the C:\> prompt and press Enter. If you want to be different, stuff the floppy disk into the bottom floppy disk drive (drive B). Type **format b:** at the C:\> prompt and press Enter.

I should point out that computers sold nowadays often have one 5¼-inch disk drive and one 3½-inch disk drive. In this case, select the floppy drive based on the size of the floppy disk in your hand.

DOS asks you to insert a disk in the drive and then press Enter when you're ready. Because you already put your disk in the drive, go ahead and press Enter (don't worry about those grinding and gnashing sounds). When it's done, DOS asks you whether you want a *volume* for the disk. Just press Enter again. (There's no reason to get tricky here.)

After the computer tells you that the format is complete, it asks whether you want to format another disk. Press N to indicate "Heck, no," and then press Enter. Type **EXIT** at the C:\> prompt to return to Quicken.

There's more to this formatting business than I describe here. If you want more information and you're adventurous, check the DOS user's guide that came with your computer. If you're not that adventurous, you can buy preformatted floppy disks and save yourself all this trouble.

When and how often should you back up?

Sure, I could give you some tricky, technical spiel here and talk about fancy-schmancy backup strategies, off-site storage, and that kind of stuff. But I won't, OK?

Here's what *I* do: I back up every month after I reconcile. Then I stick the floppy disk in my briefcase. That way if something terrible happens at home, I don't lose both my files stored in my computer and the backup disk with the data.

I should admit, however, that my strategy has a couple of flaws. First, because I only back up monthly, I may have to reenter as much as a month's worth of data. If you have real heavy transaction volumes — in other words, you write a zillion checks a month — you may want to back up more frequently.

The second problem, a worst-case scenario, is only remotely possible but still worth mentioning: if something bad happens to the Quicken files stored on my computer's hard disk *and* to my backup floppy disk, I'm up the proverbial creek without a paddle. I would have to start over from scratch from the beginning of the year.

I should note, by the way, that a floppy disk is far more likely to fail than a hard drive. As a result, some people create backup backups to reduce the chance of widespread file loss.

If you lose your data and you did back up

First, I encourage you to feel smug. Get a cup of coffee, lean back in your chair, and gloat for, oh, a couple of minutes.

After you're done, carefully do the following:

1. **Get your backup floppy disk.**

   Find your backup disk and insert it in one of your disk drives. (If you can't find the backup disk, stop gloating and skip to the next section.)

2. **Start Quicken.**

   If Quicken is already running, exit it and then restart it.

3. **Select File Activities from the Main Menu.**

   Don't select anything other than the File Activities command from the Main Menu. This step is key. If you try to use a file by displaying one of its accounts in a register, Quicken won't let you restore that file.

4. **Choose the Restore File command from the File Activities menu.**

   Quicken displays the Select Drive to Restore From screen (see Figure 7-2).

5. **Identify the backup floppy drive.**

   Press **A** if the backup disk is in the top floppy drive or **B** if it's in the bottom floppy drive.

6. **Press Enter.**

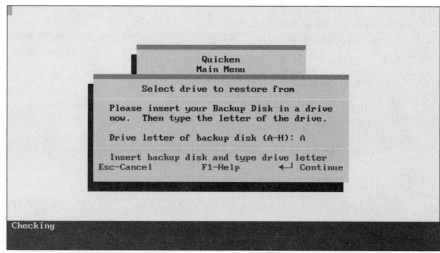

Figure 7-2:
The Select
Drive to
Restore
From
screen.

Quicken lists the files stored on the backup floppy disk (see Figure 7-3). If there's only one Quicken file on the disk — which is usually the case — Quicken lists only one file.

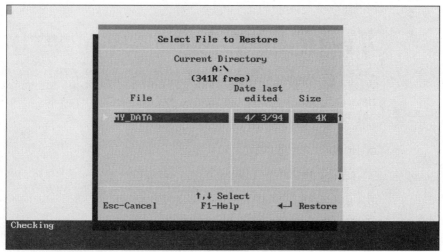

Figure 7-3:
The Select
File To
Restore
screen.

7. Select the file you want to restore.

Use the arrow keys or the mouse to highlight the file that you want to restore; then press Enter. If the file you select is the last one Quicken used, the program displays a message asking whether it's OK to *overwrite,* or replace, the open file with the file stored on the floppy disk.

When you restore a file, you replace the current, in-memory version of the file with the backup version stored on the floppy disk. Don't do so for fun. Don't do so for entertainment. Do so only if the current version is trashed and you want to start over by using the version stored on the backup floppy disk.

8. Press Enter.

Wait until Quicken tells you that it has restored the file. You're almost done.

9. Return to the Main Menu.

Press Enter to remove the on-screen message. Then press Esc twice to return to the Main Menu.

10. Update the accounts' registers as necessary.

Display the Register screen and then reenter each transaction you recorded since you created the backup. This step is important: your newly restored file doesn't contain transactions you entered since the last time you backed up.

Just to be on the safe side, back up the file after you completely update the accounts. They say lightning never strikes twice in the same place, but . . . if you have hard disk problems or something, whatever fouled up your file this time may rear its ugly head again soon.

If you lose your data and you didn't back up

Because there's a good chance that you don't back up your files — at least not regularly — you need to know what to do when you lose your data and you haven't backed up. (This situation may not be as big a hassle as you think, although it creates a lot of work.)

Here's what you do: reenter every transaction for the year.

Sure, this method isn't quick. It isn't all that pretty. But it works. And remember that you probably didn't spend any time backing up anyway. Not you. You were too busy for that.

If you have copies of the registers, use them as your information sources. If you don't have copies of the registers, use your bank statements and any other financial records you have.

Files, Files, and More Files

When you set up Quicken, you create what Quicken calls a *file*. All your accounts get stored in this file.

You can work with more than one Quicken file. For example, if you use Quicken at work and at home, you should probably create two Quicken files: one for your business accounts and one for your home accounts. When you use different files, you can better segregate your personal financial records from your business financial records.

There is a drawback to using more than one file: you can't record account transfer transactions between accounts in different files in one fell swoop. You have to record the transaction twice — once in the source account in one file and again in the destination account in the other file. If the two accounts involved in a transfer are in the same file, you just enter the account name in the Category field. Quicken then records the transfer in the other account for you.

Setting up an additional file

To set up a new file

1. **Select File Activities from the Main Menu.**

   Quicken displays the File Activities menu.

2. **Choose the Select/Set File command from the File Activities menu.**

   Quicken displays the Select/Set Up New File screen shown in Figure 7-4.

3. **Select the <Set Up New File> option.**

   Press Home and Enter. Or double-click the option. Quicken displays the Set Up New File screen (see Figure 7-5).

4. **Name the file.**

   Type some meaningful combination of up to eight letters and numbers in the Enter Name For File field. You can use the filename *business* if you're setting up a file for your business, for example.

It's a little tricky, but you can use the symbol characters on your keyboard when establishing a filename. Refer to either the user documentation or a good book on DOS for help.

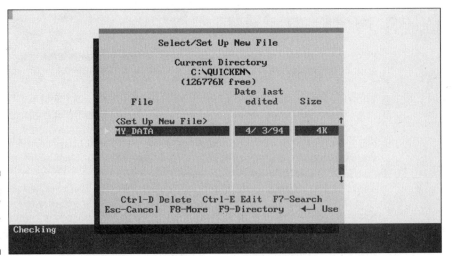

Figure 7-4:
The Select/
Set Up New
File screen.

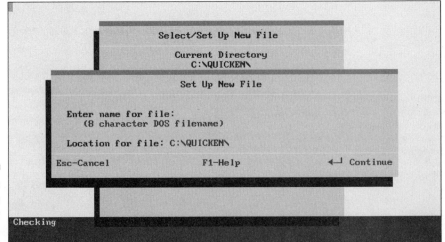

Figure 7-5:
The Set Up
New File
screen.

5. Use the default file location.

To accept Quicken's suggestion to store the file in the Quicken directory, move the cursor to the Set File Location field and press Enter. (There's no good reason to pick some other file location.) Quicken displays the Standard Categories screen and asks which preset category list you want to use. (Remember, you waltzed through this process when you first started the program.)

6. **Indicate which category list you want.**

   Press 1 if you use Quicken to track home finances. Press 2 if you use Quicken to track business finances. Press 3 if you use Quicken for both purposes. (Don't press 4. It makes for a bunch of work later.)

7. **Press Enter.**

   Quicken returns to the Select/Set Up New File screen (see Figure 7-4).

8. **Indicate which file you want to use.**

   Highlight the file and press Enter. (You can also use the Select/Set Up New File screen to flip-flop between files.)

When you use the new file for the first time, you must set up at least one account for the file. As a result, when you first select the new file, Quicken displays the Set Up New Account screen. Tell Quicken which type of account you want to set up, name the account, and provide starting account balance information. Chapter 2 talks about all this if you need help.

What Quicken refers to as a file is really a set of files with the same filename (such as HOME) but different file extensions (such as QDI, QDT, QIF, QMT, and QNX). For example, when Quicken refers to the HOME file, it really refers to the set of HOME files — HOME.QDI. HOME.QDT, HOME.QIF, HOME.QMT, and HOME.QNX.

Most of the time, you don't need to know this stuff. But if you use a third-party backup utility, then you need to know that you won't be backing up just one file but all the files with the same name.

Shrinking files

You can enter a large number of transactions in a Quicken file. In fact, you can record as many as 65,535 transactions in a file and as many as 30,000 transactions in a single account. Wowsers!

There are good reasons, though, to work with smaller files. The floppy disks you use for backing up have limited space, for example. You can fit about 2,500 transactions on a low-density 5¼-inch disk and about 5,000 on a low-density 3½-inch disk.

If your files have gotten too big for their own good, you can knock them down to size by creating a new file that contains only the current year's transactions. If you do so every year or every couple of years, your files should remain small enough to fit on one low-density floppy disk.

Call me a Nervous Nelson, but because shrinking a file involves wholesale change, please back up the file you want to shrink. There's no reason to get anxious, but if something does go wrong during the shrinking, I think that you'll want a backup copy of the file handy.

To shrink a Quicken file

1. Select File Activities from the Main Menu.

2. Choose the Year End command from the File Activities menu.

Quicken displays the Year End screen, as shown in Figure 7-6.

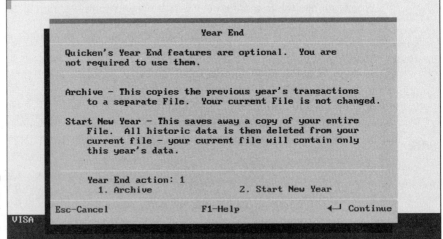

```
                           Year End

         Quicken's Year End features are optional.  You are
         not required to use them.


         Archive - This copies the previous year's transactions
               to a separate File.  Your current File is not changed.

         Start New Year - This saves away a copy of your entire
               File.  All historic data is then deleted from your
               current file - your current file will contain only
               this year's data.


            Year End action: 1
               1. Archive                  2. Start New Year

    Esc-Cancel                  F1-Help                ◄┘ Continue
```

Figure 7-6:
The Year End screen.

3. Enter the Year End Action as Start New Year.

With the cursor on the Year End Action field, press 2.

4. Press Enter.

Quicken displays the Start New Year screen (see Figure 7-7).

5. Enter a name in the Copy All Transactions to File field.

Type a name, using up to eight characters. By the way, at this point, the new file you're creating is an exact copy of the original file.

6. Specify a cutoff date.

Enter the date, or *cutoff point,* that determines whether a transaction goes in the new, shrunk file. I think you should use January 1.

7. Press Enter.

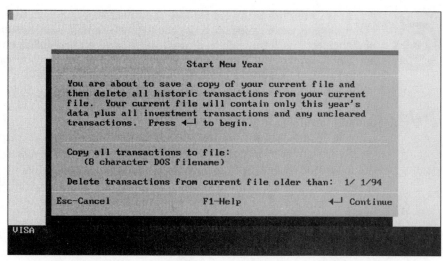

Figure 7-7:
The Start
New Year
screen.

Quicken creates the new file, which doesn't contain any transactions dated earlier than the cutoff point. After Quicken tells you that the file was copied successfully, it asks which file you now want to use: the original file or the new file. (Refer to Figure 7-8 to see the message box.)

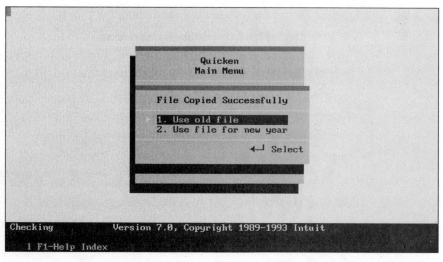

Figure 7-8:
The
message
that asks
whether you
want to use
the old file
or the new
file.

8. Select the file you want to use.

To use the new (or shrunk) file, press 2 to select the Use File for New Year file option.

If you ever want to see the old file, you can select it by using the **S**elect/Set Up File command, which appears in the File Activities menu. But don't enter any new transactions in the old file; if you do, you change the old file's ending account balance without changing the new file's beginning account balance.

Tweaking Quicken

Quicken provides a bunch of *tweaks,* or ways to customize your program. I don't cover them all here because most people want to make just three changes: automatic backup reminders, screen setting changes (specifically, color scheme changes), and passwords.

Automatic backup reminders

If you decide that this backing up business is just too important to be cavalier about, you can have Quicken take some of the responsibility. Specifically, you can tell the program to remind you to back up at regular intervals.

To have Quicken remind you to back up, do the following:

1. **Select File Activities from the Main Menu.**

2. **Choose the Set Backup Frequency command.**

   Quicken displays the Backup Reminder Frequency screen (see Figure 7-9), which asks how often you want Quicken to remind you to back up.

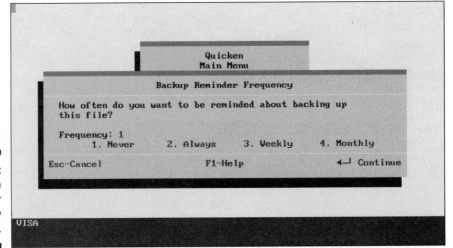

Figure 7-9:
The Backup Reminder Frequency screen.

3. **Pick a Backup Frequency.**

   Press 1 for Never, 2 for Always (which really means daily), 3 for Weekly, and 4 for Monthly.

4. **Save your settings change.**

   Press Enter to leave the Backup Reminder Frequency screen and save the new settings.

Quicken checks the backup reminder frequency whenever you want to exit the program. If it's time to back up, Quicken takes you through the backup process. Just follow the instructions.

Color you beautiful

If you don't like the color scheme that Quicken uses, you can change it. Here's how:

1. **Select Set Preferences from the Main Menu.**

2. **Select Screen Settings from the Set Preferences menu.**

   Quicken displays the Screen Settings menu, shown in Figure 7-10. (Refer to Table 7-1 for an explanation of the other screen settings commands shown in Figure 7-10.)

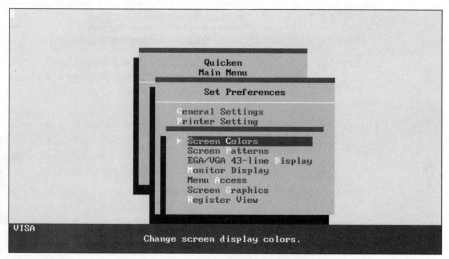

Figure 7-10:
The Screen
Settings
menu.

3. **Choose the Screen Colors command from the Screen Settings menu.**

   Quicken displays a list of color schemes (see Figure 7-11).

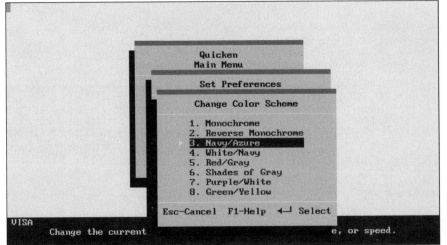

Figure 7-11:
The Change
Color
Schemes
menu.

```
                        Quicken
                       Main Menu

                     Set Preferences

                   Change Color Scheme

                   1. Monochrome
                   2. Reverse Monochrome
                   3. Navy/Azure
                   4. White/Navy
                   5. Red/Gray
                   6. Shades of Gray
                   7. Purple/White
                   8. Green/Yellow

            Esc-Cancel  F1-Help  ◄─┘ Select
  VISA
       Change the current                        e, or speed.
```

4. Get crazy and experiment.

Go wild. Pick a color scheme. If you don't like it, pick another.

Quicken's default color scheme is Navy/Azure. If you fool around a bit and then decide that the initial Quicken color scheme isn't so bad after all, just select the Navy/Azure option.

Table 7-1	Screen Settings Commands
Setting	*What it does and whether it matters*
Screen Patterns	Tells Quicken what pattern you want displayed in the screen area that surrounds the Main Menu. You can fool around with this option, but there's little reason to do so.
EGA/VGA 43-Line Display	Tells Quicken to pack more lines of stuff — 43 lines instead of the usual 25 lines — in a check register and in reports. If you're young, ambitious, and have good eyesight, go ahead and try changing the screen setting.
Monitor Display	Lets you choose between a fast monitor and slow monitor display. Ostensibly, this option trades screen quality for display speed. But you probably won't ever need to use this feature.

Setting	What it does and whether it matters
Menu Access	Over the years, Quicken has changed how you activate the menus on its menu bars. In the old days, you needed to use function keys. Nowadays, you use Alt-key combinations. The Menu Access command indulges your need to feel nostalgic and allows you to use function keys again.
Screen Graphics	Controls whether Quicken uses big or small characters on its graphs. If you're into Quicken's graphs, go ahead and experiment with this setting.
Register View	Tells Quicken whether it should display the one-line or list version (the compressed case) of the register or the three-line version (the normal case) of the register. In either view, all three lines of a transaction are displayed when the transaction is highlighted.

Using and abusing passwords

I have mixed feelings about passwords. Theoretically, they let you lock up your Quicken data so that your rebellious teenager (if you're using Quicken at home) or the night janitor (if you're using Quicken at work) can't look at your files, print checks, process automatic payments, and generally muck things up.

If someone tries to break into your files, Quicken says, "Oh, you want to see that file? Well, I need to see your password first." Sounds just like Jerry Seinfeld. I bet you didn't know that Quicken did impressions.

But let me remind you that a Quicken password really only prevents someone from accessing your data by using Quicken. Those nefarious types can still erase your files by using DOS. Or they can scramble your information by using a spreadsheet or word processor. Heck, it's even possible (though unlikely) that they can manipulate the data by using another checkbook or accounting program.

I think, then, that passwords are best left to computer systems that use them globally to control access to all programs and to computer systems that track all users by name.

Besides, there's another annoying little problem with passwords. You've got to *remember* them, darn it.

Setting up a new file password

After reading all this wishy-washy mumbo-jumbo, you still want to create a password? OK. With much trepidation, here's how to set up a password:

1. **Select the file.**

   If the file you want to password-protect isn't the active file, use the Select/ Set Up File command in the File Activities menu to select the file.

2. **Select Set Preferences from the Main Menu.**

3. **Choose the Password Settings command from the Set Preferences menu.**

   Quicken displays the Password Settings screen, which lists two options: File Password and Transaction Password.

4. **Choose the File Password option.**

   Quicken displays the Set Up Password screen shown in Figure 7-12.

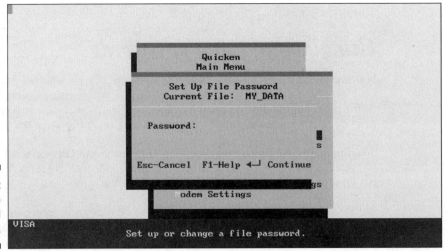

Figure 7-12: The Set Up Password screen.

5. **Type the password you want to use.**

   You can use up to 16 characters. Quicken doesn't differentiate between case, so Washington, wASHINGTON, and WASHINGTON mean the same.

6. **Press Enter.**

   Quicken displays the Confirm Password screen, which resembles the Set Up Password screen.

7. **Enter the password you want to use, again.**

   This step proves to Quicken that you know what you entered the first time.

8. Press Enter.

Quicken returns you to the Set Preferences screen. Press Esc to return to the Main Menu.

The next time you try to use this file (when you next start Quicken or when you next try to select the file by using the Select/Set Up File command), Quicken asks you for the file's password.

Changing a file password

After you set up a file password, you're not stuck with it forever. You can change it or even remove it. Just use the File Password command on the Password Settings screen.

If you've already set up a password, though, Quicken doesn't display the Set Up Password screen shown in Figure 7-12. Instead, Quicken displays a screen that asks for the current password and the new password. After you type both passwords, press Enter. From that point forward, use the new password to gain access to the file. If you leave the new password field blank, Quicken assumes that you don't want to use a password anymore.

What are transaction passwords?

When you choose the Passwords Settings screen from the Set Preferences menu, Quicken asks whether you want to create a file password or a *transaction password.*

A transaction password works like a file password, except that Quicken requires you to enter the transaction password only if you try to enter a transaction that's dated before a specified date. You specify the date, called a *cutoff date*, when you set up the transaction password.

I guess that you use a transaction password to keep some idiot from fouling up last year's or last month's transactions.

Transaction passwords don't make a lot of sense to me. I think that a couple other approaches are easier. First, you can create and safely store backup copies of a Quicken file for last year or last month. Second, just don't have idiots fooling around with your Quicken files in the first place. Jeepers, when somebody can't understand an instruction like, "Use the current date," do you really want that person mucking about in your books?

The 5th Wave — By Rich Tennant

"I THINK I'VE FOUND YOUR FILE, MARGARET! IT FEELS LIKE A SPREADSHEET! RIGHT?! RIGHT?!"

Chapter 8
Calculators, Schmalculators

In This Chapter

▶ How to use the Quicken calculator

▶ How to use the Investment Planning calculator

▶ How to use the Loan Calculator

▶ How to use the Refinance Calculator

▶ How to use the Retirement Planning calculator

▶ How to use the College Planning calculator

*T*he folks at Intuit have added several nifty little calculators to recent versions of Quicken. I strongly encourage you to use these tools. At the very least, the calculators should make your work easier. And if you invest some time, you should enhance your understanding of your financial affairs.

Using the Quicken Calculator

The Quicken calculator lets you perform simple arithmetic — like you do when you're entering transactions into a register or writing a check.

If you need to perform some basic arithmetic while the Register screen or the Write Checks screen is displayed, start the calculator by pressing Ctrl-O or by choosing the **Calculator** command from the **Activities** menu. Quicken displays the Calculator screen, as shown in Figure 8-1.

Getting started with the calculator

Use the calculator like you use any ten-key calculator. If you know how to work a calculator, skip the next discussion.

Adding

To add, type the first number and + (the plus symbol), the second number and +, the third number and +, and so on. Get the idea?

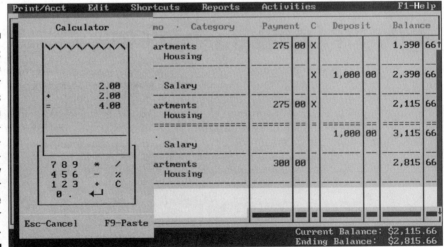

Figure 8-1:
The Quicken
calculator.

As you enter the numbers, Quicken displays them on the part of the Calculator screen that looks like the paper tape of a regular, sits-on-your-desk, ten-key calculator. To total the numbers (and print this total on the "tape"), press = (the equals sign) or press Enter (see Figure 8-2).

To clear the calculator, press C (the clear key).

Figure 8-2:
The
Calculator
screen looks
like a
typical, sits-
on-your-
desk, ten-
key
calculator
— replete
with paper
tape.

Subtracting, multiplying, and dividing

You can subtract, multiply, and divide with the calculator, too. To subtract, use – (the minus sign). To multiply, use * (the asterisk). To divide, use / (the slash). Sound simple? It is.

Table 8-1 provides some examples.

Table 8-1	Quicken Calculator Examples
Calculator Keys Pressed	*Final Calculator Display*
25 – 5 =	20
25 * 5 =	125
25 / 5 =	5

Working with percentages

The calculator's percent key (%) lets you add, subtract, multiply, and divide a number by some percentage of the number. For example, if you want to add 20 percent to 100, type **100+20%=.** The calculator displays the number 120 (100 plus 20 percent of 100 equals 120).

To subtract 20 percent from 100, type **100–20%=** (answer: 80). To find what number is 20 percent of 100, type **100*20%=** (answer: 20). To find what number 100 is 20 percent of, type **100/20%=** (answer: 500).

A cool calculator trick

You can use the numbers you calculate as inputs to fields.

To paste calculations that are displayed on the Calculator screen into the Register screen or Write Checks screen, do the following:

1. **Display the Register screen or Write Checks screen.**

2. **Move the cursor to the field you want to calculate.**

3. **Press Ctrl-O to display the Calculator screen.**

4. **Do the calculation and then press F9.**

Quicken pastes the calculation result into the field.

Putting the calculator away

To remove the calculator from your view, press Esc. To redisplay the calculator, press Ctrl-O or choose the **Calculator** command from the **Activities** menu.

For mouse users only

Got a mouse? You can select any of the calculator keys by clicking (pressing the mouse's left button). To add the numbers 4 and 8, for example, you could either type **4+8=** or you could

1. **Click the 4.**

2. **Click the +.**

3. **Click the 8.**

4. **Click the Enter key.**

Located under the plus symbol, the Enter key looks like a bent arrow.

Clicking the mouse's right button (as in right or left, not right or wrong) is like pressing Esc — Quicken removes the calculator from the screen.

Noodling Around with Your Investments

My favorite Quicken calculator is the Investment Planning calculator. I guess I just like to forecast portfolio future values and other similar stuff. (Note that you can't easily do this with a regular hand-held calculator.)

Using the Investment Planning calculator

To use the Investment Planning calculator, do the following:

1. **Display the Investment Planning calculator.**

   Select Financial Planning from the **Activities** menu; then choose the Investment Planning command from the Financial Planning menu. Quicken displays the Investment Planning calculator (see Figure 8-3).

2. **Enter the amount of your current investments.**

   Move the cursor to the Present Value field and input the amount of your current investments.

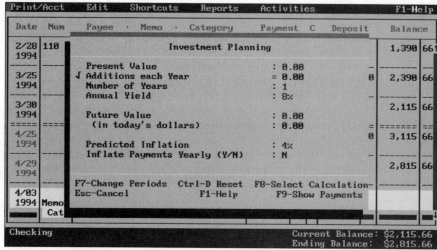

Figure 8-3:
The
Investment
Planning
calculator.

3. Tell Quicken how much you plan to add to your investments.

Move the cursor to the Additions Each Year field and input the amount you plan to add annually to your investment portfolio.

4. Indicate how long you plan to add to your investments.

Move the cursor to the Number of Years field and indicate how long you plan to add money to your investments. If you plan to add money for 25 years, for example, type **25**.

5. Enter the annual yield that you expect your investments to earn.

Move the cursor to the Annual Yield field and type the percent. If you plan to invest in the stock market and expect your savings to match the market's usual return of about 10 percent, for example, type 10 (don't type .10).

A timing assumption you should know: The Investment Planning calculator assumes that you will add to your portfolio at the end of the period — what financial planners call an *ordinary annuity*.

6. Enter the anticipated inflation rate.

Move the cursor to the Predicted Inflation field and enter the anticipated inflation rate percentage. By the way, from 1926 to 1992, the inflation rate has averaged just over 3 percent.

7. Indicate whether you plan to increase your annual contribution as a result of inflation.

Move the cursor to the Inflate Payments Yearly (Y/N) field. Press Y if you plan to annually increase — by the inflation rate — the amount you add to your investment portfolio. Press N if you want to contribute the same amount every year.

After you enter all the information, the Future Value field shows how much you'll accumulate in future day inflated dollars (the first line) and in current day uninflated dollars (the second line).

If you want to make another calculation, press Ctrl-D to erase the calculator's fields; then repeat the steps in the preceding list.

If you want to work with different contribution periods (quarterly, monthly, or weekly), press F7 to toggle your choices. *Toggle,* a computer buzzword, means to switch between modes. If you're not sure what I mean, display the calculator, press F7, and watch what happens. See how much fun it is to toggle. You may even want to throw toggle parties.

How to become a millionaire

To tell Quicken which investment planning field you want to calculate, press F8. Quicken toggles the check mark from financial variable to variable. Leave the check mark next to the variable that you want Quicken to compute.

For example, to calculate how much money you must invest each year to cause your portfolio to grow to $1 million, move the check mark to the Additions Each Year field and then enter all the other input variables. Be sure that you enter 1000000 in the Future Value field. The Investment Planning calculator computes how much you need to save to hit your $1 million target if you've give yourself 35 years to reach your financial goal and expect to earn 10 percent annually. (Over the last sixty or seventy years, the stock market has returned about 10 percent.)

Figure 8-4 shows the results of your calculations based on the Additions Each Year field.

Starting from scratch, it'll take 35 years of roughly $2,800-a-year payments to reach $1,000,000.00. (All those zeros look rather nice, don't they?) Note that this calculation assumes a 10 percent annual yield.

"Jeepers, creepers," you say. "This seems too darn good to be true, Steve."

Well, unfortunately, the calculation is a little misleading. With 3 percent inflation, your million bucks will only be worth $355,383 in current day dollars. Oh, well, I still think it's cool to be worth this much some day.

 Want a permanent copy of the calculations? No problem. Just press F9. Quicken produces on-screen a schedule of the amounts you plan to contribute, and the forecasted portfolio values you'll accumulate including both the contributions and the money you'll earn. To print the schedule, press Ctrl-P and Enter.

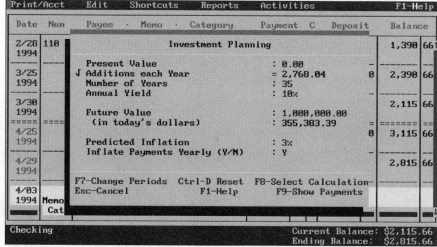

Print/Acct Edit Shortcuts Reports Activities F1-Help

Date	Num	Payee · Memo · Category	Payment	C	Deposit	Balance
2/28 1994	110	Investment Planning				1,390 66↑
3/25 1994		√ Present Value : 0.00				2,390 66
		Additions each Year = 2,768.04		0		
		Number of Years : 35				
		Annual Yield : 10%				
3/30 1994						2,115 66
		Future Value : 1,000,000.00				
		(in today's dollars) : 355,383.39		=		
4/25 1994				0		3,115 66
		Predicted Inflation : 3%				
		Inflate Payments Yearly (Y/N) : Y				
4/29 1994						2,815 66
		F7-Change Periods Ctrl-D Reset F8-Select Calculation				
4/03 1994	Memo	Esc-Cancel F1-Help F9-Show Payments				
	Cat					

Checking

Current Balance: $2,115.66
Ending Balance: $2,815.66

Figure 8-4:
The secret to your success: $2,800 a year for 35 years.

The Often Unbearable Burden of Debt

Quicken provides a couple of neat calculators to help you better manage your debts: the Loan Calculator, which helps you compute loan payments (and other loan figures), and the Refinance Calculator, which helps you decide whether to refinance the old mortgage.

Using the Loan Calculator to calculate payments

The Loan Calculator lets you calculate loan payments. So you may want to use this handy tool as a way to estimate what that new car might cost in the way of monthly payments. Or you maywant to use it to estimate what your brother-in-law's mortgage payment is. (You might do this, for example, if you're trying to figure out whether your brother-in-law can actually afford the mortgage he's signed up for. Any insights you gain, of course, can be shared with him at the next family gathering, right?)

To use the Loan calculator to calculate a loan payment, follow these steps:

1. **Display the Loan Calculator.**

   Select Financial Planning from the Activities menu and then the Loan Calculator command from the Financial Planning menu. Quicken displays the Loan Calculator — wouldn't you know it — which you can see in Figure 8-5.

```
Print/Acct    Edit   Shortcuts    Reports    Activities           F1-Help

 Date  Num    Payee  ·  Memo  ·  Category    Payment  C  Deposit    Balance

 2/28 110  Marlborough Apartments              275 00 X             1,390 66
 1994                        Loan Calculator                    __
 3/25                                                           00  2,390 66
 1994       Principal             : 0.00
            Annual interest rate  : 0%
 3/30       Total years           : 1.00                           2,115 66
 1994       Periods per year      : 12
=====  ===                                                      ==  ======= ==
 4/25     √ Regular payment        = 0.00                       00  3,115 66
 1994       US/Canadian loan (U/C)  : U
            Balloon at payment number: 12
 4/29                                                              2,815 66
 1994          F7-Set Up Loan   F8-Select Calculation        __
          Esc-Cancel   Ctrl-D Reset   F9-View Payment Schedule
 4/03
 1994 Memo:
      Cat:

Checking                                  Current Balance: $2,115.66
                                          Ending Balance:  $2,815.66
```

Figure 8-5:
The Loan
Calculator
screen.

2. **Enter the loan amount.**

   Move the cursor to the Principal field and input the loan amount.

3. **Enter the annual interest rate.**

   Move the cursor to the Annual Interest Rate field and input the interest rate percent. If a loan charges 8 percent interest, for example, press 8. (Don't enter the loan interest rate as a decimal value, such as .08. If you do, Quicken thinks the annual interest rate is 8/100 of a percent, not 8 percent.)

4. **Enter the number of years you want to take to repay the loan.**

   Move the cursor to the Total Years field and input the number of years you'll make payments.

5. **Indicate how many loan payments you plan to make a year.**

   Move the cursor to the Periods Per Year field and input the number of loan payments you'll make in a year. If you want to make monthly payments, for example, enter **12.**

6. **Indicate whether you're using US-style interest compounding or Canadian-style interest compounding.**

   Move the cursor to the US/Canadian Loan field; press U if you get the loan from a U.S. bank; press C if you get the loan from a Canadian bank.

7. **(Optional) Tell Quicken about any balloon payment.**

   If your loan includes a *balloon payment* — an amount you pay in addition to one of the regular payments so that you pay off the loan balance completely — indicate with which regular payment you plan to make the balloon payment. Suppose that you take a 30-year loan. After 10 years of monthly payments, you want to make a balloon payment to pay off the debt. Because you want to make a balloon payment with the 120th regular payment, type **120** into the Balloon At Payment Number field. (Quicken, by default, sets the Balloon At Payment Number field as the last regular payment, in case you still owe a few pennies on the loan and you need to pay these pennies off with a balloon payment.)

After you enter all the variables, Quicken calculates the loan payment, displaying the amount in the Regular Payment field.

Let's say that one Sunday afternoon, for example, you're wondering what the mortage payment is on one of those monster houses: tens of thousands of square feet, acres of ground, cottages for the domestic help, and so on. You get the picture — something that's a really vulgar display of wealth (that we all secretly covet).

To learn how the rich live, move the check mark to the Regular Payment field. Figure 8-6 shows the monthly mortgage payment on a 30-year, $9,999,999 mortgage if the money costs 7.5 percent. (By the way, $9,999,999.99 is the biggest loan amount the calculator can handle.)

How about $69,921.44 a month? A mere pittance.

Calculating other loan figures

To calculate some other loan figure — the principal amount, for example — press F8 to move the check mark and flag which loan figure you want to calculate. Then enter all the other variables.

Figure 8-6: The Loan Calculator with some sample data.

```
  Print/Acct    Edit    Shortcuts    Reports    Activities            F1-Help

  Date  Num     Payee  · Memo ·  Category    Payment  C   Deposit    Balance

  2/28  110   Marlborough Apartments          275 00 X             1,390 66↑
  1994                                                      ---     -------
                              Loan Calculator                 00    2,390 66
  3/25
  1994        Principal            : 9,999,999.00
             Annual interest rate  : 7.5%                      ---   -------
  3/30        Total years          : 30.00                           2,115 66
  1994        Periods per year     : 12
 =====       =====                                            ==   ======= ==
  4/25      √ Regular payment       = 69,921.44                00    3,115 66
  1994        US/Canadian loan (U/C) : U
             Balloon at payment number: 360                   ---   ------- --
  4/29
  1994           F7-Set Up Loan    F8-Select Calculation
             Esc-Cancel   Ctrl-D Reset   F9-View Payment Schedule --  ------- --
  4/03
  1994 Memo:
       Cat:

  Checking                                Current Balance: $2,115.66
                                          Ending  Balance: $2,815.66
```

Let's say, for example, that those $70,000-a-month payments seem more than a little outrageous. So let's calculate how much you can borrow if you make $1,000-a-month payments over 30 years and the annual interest rate is 7.5 percent.

Move the check mark to flag the Principal field. Enter the Annual Interest Rate as **7.5,** the Total Years as **30,** the Periods Per Year as **12,** and the Regular Payment as **1000.** The Loan Calculator computes a principal amount of 143,017.63. That's a heck of a lot more reasonable, don't you think?

Setting up a loan account

You can use the Loan Calculator information to set up a special account for tracking the loan. Just press F7 and Quicken displays a screen that asks you for some information. You fill in a few fields, and bang, you've set up a special loan account.

I think that this whole loan account business is pretty handy. If you want to see how it works, refer to Chapter 10.

Using the Refinance Calculator

Deciding whether to refinance is very perplexing. As you may know, you can't just compare your existing loan's interest rate to the rate that a local bank is advertising this week; the bank undoubtedly will charge you a fee and, possibly, points to refinance.

The Refinance Calculator calculates the difference in mortgage payments if you make lower payments; then it tells you how long it would take with these lower payments to pay back the refinancing costs you incur. If it costs $50 to refinance, for example, and you save $10 a month because of a lower payment, the calculator tells you that it would take five months to recoup your $50.

To use the Refinance Calculator to calculate how long it takes for the savings from a new, smaller loan payment to pay back your refinancing costs, do the following:

1. **Display the Refinance Calculator.**

   Select Financial Planning from the **Activities** menu and then choose the Refinance Calculator command from the **Financial Planning** menu. Quicken displays the Refinance Calculator, as shown in Figure 8-7.

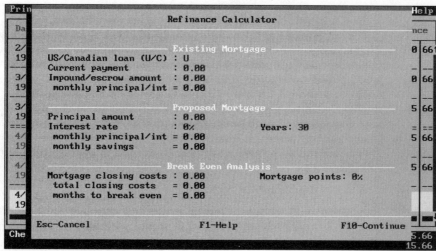

Figure 8-7:
The
Refinance
Calculator.

2. Indicate whether the loan uses U.S.-style or Canadian-style interest calculations.

Move the cursor to the US/Canadian Loan field; press U if the loan is from a U.S. bank; press C if the loan is from a Canadian bank.

3. Enter the current loan payment.

Move the cursor to the Current Payment field and input the total payment amount.

4. Enter the nonprincipal and noninterest portion of the current payment.

Move the cursor to the Impound/Escrow Amount field and input the portion of each payment that represents property taxes, private mortgage insurance, and anything else that's neither principal nor interest. After you enter this figure, Quicken calculates the principal and interest portion of the payment.

5. Enter the principal amount you plan to refinance.

Move the cursor to the Principal field and input the loan amount you plan to borrow for your new loan.

A word to the wise: The principal amount should be the same as the current loan's existing loan balance if you see refinancing as a way for you to swap high-interest-rate debt for low-interest-rate debt. If you see refinancing as a way to borrow more money or as a tax-deductible way to borrow money, this whole exercise is really kind of moot (which rhymes with snoot).

6. Enter the interest rate.

Move the cursor to the Interest field and input the interest rate percent. If a loan charges 8 percent interest, for example, type **8.** (Don't enter the interest rate as a decimal value, such as .08. If you do, Quicken thinks the annual interest rate is $\frac{8}{100}$ of a percent, not 8 percent.)

7. Enter the number of years you plan to take to repay the loan.

Move the cursor to the Years field and input the number of years you'll make payments. After you enter this amount, Quicken calculates the new loan's monthly payment and the payment difference between the old and new loans.

8. Enter the refinancing costs.

Move the cursor to the Mortgage Closing Costs field and input any fees the bank's going to charge you for refinancing the loan.

9. Enter the points (if needed).

Move the cursor to the Mortgage Points field and input the points you must pay. If you must pay 2 points, for example, type **2.** Be careful not to double count here. For example, if a lender plans to charge you two points, or $2,000, on a $100,000 loan, don't enter 2000 in the Mortgage Closing Costs field and 2 in the Mortgage Points field. If you do, Quicken will count the $2000, two-point fee twice.

After you enter all the variables, Quicken calculates how long it will take to repay the refinancing costs. Like I said earlier, there's nothing tricky here.

Do you really want to save money?

Unfortunately, the Refinance Calculator won't tell you whether it truly makes financial sense to refinance. Quicken simply tells you how long it takes to pay back refinancing costs with lower payments.

Here's a tip: you should refinance debts when you can lower your true overall interest rate. For example, if you can trade your 8 percent debt for a 6 percent debt, it's a good deal, all other things being equal.

Of course, all the other things are never equal.

Nonetheless, you still can save money as long as you borrow the *same amount* of money and you make the *same number* of payments. Then, if the annual percentage rate (or APR) on the new loan is less than the interest rate on the old loan, you'll save money by refinancing. By the way, the new lender may (and really should) be willing to calculate the APR. And you can get the old loan's interest rate from your loan contract.

Here's why this kind of refinancing works: the APR is the implicit interest rate on the new loan, including closing costs and any points. So if this implicit interest rate is lower than the rate you're paying on your current mortgage, you'll save money.

Let me make a couple observations about these refinancing decisions. First, it's this "time value of money" angle that usually makes these decisions so darn complicated — which, of course, is why people pass around vague and largely inaccurate rules of thumb, such as "Well, Dolores, you should refinance any time the rates drop 2 percent."

Also, be careful that you don't get caught on the refinancing merry-go-round. For example, a friend of mine has refinanced her house about four or five times over the last 15 years. I think it made sense to refinance the first time. According to the pundits, though, refinancing made sense each time because mortgage interest rates had dropped a bit. Here's what my friend now finds a little hard to swallow, though: if she had used the refinancing money to pay down her mortgage, by now she would have paid off her mortgage. Instead, she has 30 years of payments left. Kind of depressing, isn't it?

I'm not writing to criticize my friend (I assume she's still my friend). I just want to suggest that you use my friend's mistake to your benefit. If you do refinance, make sure that you still have your mortgage paid off in the not-too-distant future. If your first mortgage should be paid off when you're 59, for example, don't sign up for a new mortgage that won't be paid off until you're 83.

Using the Retirement Planning Calculator

I think this is the book's most important section. No joke. Your financial future is much too consequential to go for easy laughs or cheap shots.

The dilemma in a nutshell

By the time the 30-something and 40-something crowd reaches retirement, social security coverage probably will be scaled back. As you may know, the current recipients are getting everything they paid in as well as most of what we pay in.

If you currently receive social security, please don't feel defensive or betrayed. I think your generation overcame challenges far more important (World War I, the Great Depression, World War II, the Cold War, the end of segregation, and so on) than the problem of inadequate social security funding we young'uns face.

I know this sentiment sounds corny, but I think you've left the world a better place. I hope my generation does the same.

But the problem isn't just social security. More and more often, employer-provided pension plans are defined contribution plans, which add specific amounts to your pension (like 2 percent of your salary), rather than defined benefit plans, which promise specific pension amounts (like $1,000 a month). As a result, although you know that someone will throw a few grand into your account every so often, you don't know how much you'll have when you retire.

I urge you, I *implore* you, to think ahead about your financial requirements. Fortunately, the Retirement Planning calculator can help you.

I'll get off my soapbox now. Thank you.

Making retirement planning calculations

You don't need to be a rocket scientist to figure this stuff out. To use the Retirement Planning calculator, just follow these steps:

1. **Display the Retirement Planning calculator.**

   Select Financial Planning from the Activities menu. Then choose the Retirement Planning command from the Financial Planning menu. Quicken displays the Retirement Planning calculator shown in Figure 8-8.

2. **Enter what you've already saved as your Present Savings.**

   Move the cursor to the Present Savings field and input your current retirement savings; use it, for example, if you have some individual retirement account money or you've accumulated a balance in an employer-sponsored 401(k) account. Don't worry if you don't have anything saved — most people don't.

3. **Indicate whether you plan to save retirement money in a tax sheltered investment.**

   Move the cursor to the Tax Sheltered (Y/N) field. Press Y if your retirement savings earns untaxed money. Press N if it is taxed. Tax sheltered investments are things like individual retirement accounts, annuities, and

```
                          Retirement Planning

      Present Savings      : 0.00        Tax Sheltered (Y/N)   : Y
      Annual Yield         : 8%
      Yearly Payments      : 0.00        Inflate payments (Y/N) : N
      Current Tax Rate     : 28%         Retirement Tax Rate   : 15%

      Current Age          : 30
      Age At Retirement    : 65
      Withdraw Until Age   : 79

      Predicted Inflation  : 4%

      Retirement Income
        Other Income (SSI,etc.): 0.00
    J After-tax Income       = 0.00
        (in Future dollars)  : 0.00

    F8-Select Calculation                          F9-Show Payments
    Esc-Cancel                    F1-Help          F10-Continue
                                                                    8
```

Figure 8-8:
The Retirement Planning calculator.

employer-sponsored 401(k)s and 403(b)s. A 403(b) is kind of a profit-sharing plan for a nonprofit agency. As a practical matter, tax sheltered investments are the only way to ride. By deferring income taxes on your earnings, you earn interest on the money you otherwise would have paid as income taxes.

4. Enter the annual yield that you expect your retirement savings to earn.

Move the cursor to the Annual Yield field and input the percent. If you plan to invest in the stock market and expect your savings to match the market's usual return of about 10 percent, for example, type **10** (don't type .10).

5. Enter the annual amount added to your retirement savings.

Move the cursor to the Yearly Payments field and input the amount that you or your employer will add to your retirement savings at the end of each year.

A timing assumption you should know: The Retirement Planning calculator assumes that you or your employer will add to your retirement savings at the end of the year — what financial planners call an *ordinary annuity*. If you or your employer will add to your retirement savings at the beginning of the year, you actually will earn an extra year of interest. Accordingly, your after-tax income will be more than Quicken shows.

6. Indicate whether the annual additions will inflate.

Move the cursor to the Inflate Payments field and press Y if the annual additions will increase by the inflation rate. Press N if they won't.

7. Enter your current marginal tax rate.

Move the cursor to the Current Tax Rate field. Then input the combined federal and state income tax rate that you pay on your last dollars of income. (As I'm writing this, Congress is talking about changing the federal income tax rates. Even so, most people still will be taxed 15 or 28 percent. Remember, if your state taxes income, you need to add the state income tax rate to the federal income tax rate.)

8. Enter your anticipated retirement tax rate.

Yeah, right. This is a complete shot in the dark. Who knows what the rates will be next year, let alone when you're retired. I think you should enter **0,** but remember that the Annual Income After Taxes is really your pretax income (just like your current salary is really your pretax income).

9. Enter your current age.

Move the cursor to the Current Age field and enter a number. You're on your own here, but let me suggest that this is a time to be honest.

10. **Enter the age at which you plan to retire.**

    Move the cursor to the Age At Retirement field and enter a number. Again, purely a personal matter. (Figure 8-8 shows this age as 65, but you should retire when you want.)

11. **Enter the age to which you want to continue withdrawals.**

    Move the cursor to the Withdrawal Until Age field and enter a number. Let's not beat around the bush here. This number is how old you'll think you'll be when you die. I don't like the idea any better than you do. Let me say, though, that ideally you want to run out of steam — there, that's a safe metaphor — before you run out of money. So go ahead and make this age something terribly old — like 95 (sorry, Grandma).

12. **Enter the anticipated inflation rate.**

    Move the cursor to the Predicted Inflation Rate field and input the anticipated inflation rate percentage. By the way, from 1926 to 1992, the inflation rate has averaged just over 3 percent.

13. **Enter any other income you'll receive — such as social security.**

    Again, just move the cursor and then input a value.

After you enter all the information, take a peek at the After-Tax Income fields, which show how much you'll be able to withdraw annually from your retirement savings in current day dollars (the first line) and in future day dollars (the second line).

If you're now bummed out about retirement

First, don't feel depressed. At least you know *now* if your golden years seem a little tarnished. After all, you acquired Quicken to help you sort out your finances. Now you can use Quicken and your newly gained knowledge to help improve your financial lot.

Basically, retirement planning depends on just three things:

✔ The number of years that the retirement savings will earn interest

✔ The real yield (that is, adjusted for inflation) you earn — in other words, the annual yield, or interest rate, minus the predicted inflation

✔ The yearly payments

Anything you do to increase one of these variables will increase your retirement income.

If you invest, for example, in something that delivers higher real yields, such as the stock market, you should see a big difference (of course, you usually bear more risk). Or if you wait an extra year or two to retire, you wind up making more annual payments and earning more interest. Finally, if you boost the yearly payments (for example, by participating in an employer-sponsored 401(k) or 403(b) plan, where your employer matches a portion of your contribution), you'll see a huge change.

Noodle around with the variables. See what happens. You may be surprised.

Playing retirement roulette

To determine a retirement income variable, press F8 to toggle the check mark next to the financial variable that you want Quicken to compute.

To calculate the yearly payment required to produce a specific level of retirement income, for example, move the check mark so that it flags the Yearly Payments field. Then enter all the other variables — including the desired after-tax income. The Retirement Planning calculator calculates how much you need to save to hit your target retirement income.

Planning for the Cost of College

Ouch. I have a couple of daughters, so I know how you feel. Man, oh man, do I know how you feel.

Using the College Planning calculator

The College Planning calculator works like the Retirement Planning calculator:

   1. **Display the College Planning calculator.**

Looking at the nitty-gritty

If you want to see your retirement planning calculations on a year-to-year basis, press F9. Quicken produces a schedule of contributions, withdrawals, and year-end retirement savings (or balances).

If you want to print the schedule, press Ctrl-P and then Enter. (If you want to know more about printing, refer to Chapter 5.)

Select Financial Planning from the Activities menu. Then choose the College Planning command from the Financial Planning menu. Quicken displays the College Planning calculator shown in Figure 8-9.

2. Enter the annual college tuition.

Move the cursor to the Current Tuition (annual) field. Input the current annual tuition at a school Junior may attend.

3. Enter the number of years until enrollment.

Move the cursor to the Years Until Enrollment field and enter a number. For example, if Junior will start college in 16 years, enter **16**.

4. Enter the number of years enrolled.

Move the cursor to the Number Of Years Enrolled field and enter a number. Assuming Junior doesn't fool around, enter **4** or **5**.

5. Enter how much you or the student (yeah, right) has already saved.

Move the cursor to the Present Savings field and enter an amount.

6. Enter the annual yield that you expect the college savings to earn.

Move the cursor to the Annual Yield field and type the percent. If you plan to invest in the stock market and expect your savings to match the market's usual return of about 10 percent, for example, type **10**.

7. Enter the inflation rate anticipated in college tuition.

Move the cursor to the Predicted Inflation field and enter the inflation rate percent. Unfortunately, college costs have increased at a rate much greater than the general inflation rate.

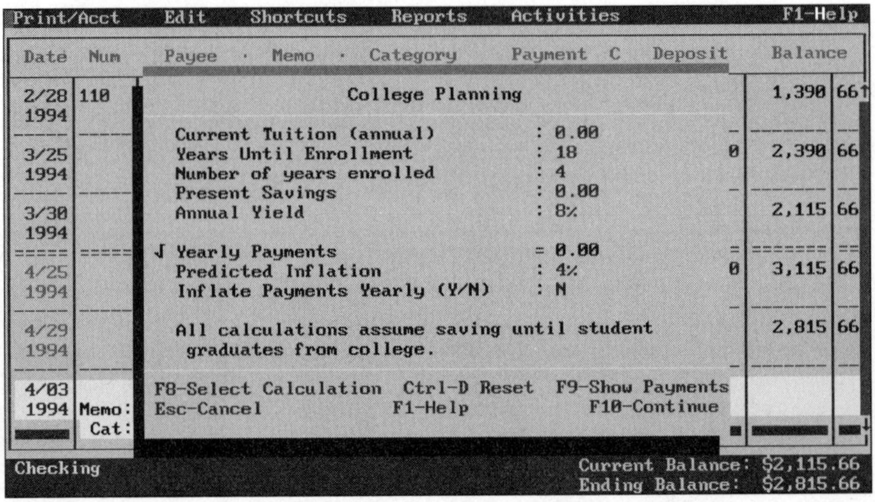

Figure 8-9:
The College Planning calculator.

8. Indicate whether you plan to increase your annual contribution as a result of inflation.

Move the cursor to the Inflate Payments Yearly (Y/N) field and press Y if you plan to annually increase — by the annual inflation rate — the amount you save. Press N if you don't plan to increase your contribution.

After you enter all the information, the Yearly Payments field shows how much you need to save each year until the child graduates from college.

Figure 8-10 shows how much you need to save for someone who won't attend college for another 16 years and who will attend four years at a college that currently costs $9,500 a year. Because you expect to earn 9 percent annually and anticipate 3 percent annual inflation, you must ante up $1,548.60 every year.

If you're now bummed out about college costs

Look at the positive side: you now understand the size of the problem and the solution.

College planning depends on four things:

- College costs
- The number of years that the savings will earn interest

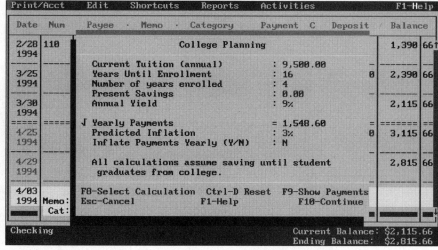

Figure 8-10: The College Planning calculator with some sample data.

- ✔ The real yield (that is, adjusted for inflation) you earn — in other words, the annual yield minus the predicted inflation
- ✔ The yearly payments

I don't mean to sound like a simpleton, but there are three basic ways to successfully save for a college education:

- ✔ Reduce the costs (find a less expensive school)
- ✔ Invest in things that deliver higher real yields
- ✔ Boost the yearly payments

I'm truly sorry there's not some easy answer here. Lottery tickets. A multilevel marketing scheme. Some tricky tax tactic. I encourage you to experiment with the input variables and see what happens.

Remember, too, that you can ask Quicken to determine a particular variable. Just press F8 to toggle the check mark next to the college planning variable that you want Quicken to compute. Then enter all the other variables. The College Planning calculator computes the flagged variable.

And one other thing: you can press F9 to see the college planning calculations on a year-to-year basis. To print the schedule, press Ctrl-P and Enter. (If you want to know more about printing, refer to Chapter 5.)

This chapter wraps up the Quicken for DOS basics. If you plan to use Quicken mostly at home, Part III talks about Quicken's record-keeping tools for loans and investments. If you use Quicken at your business, skip ahead to Part IV.

Part III
Home Finances

The 5th Wave   By Rich Tennant

"ALL RIGHT, NOW, WE NEED SOMEONE TO PLAY THE PART OF THE GEEK."

In this part...

Are you going to be using Quicken for personal financial stuff? If so, you should know that there's more to the program than just the checkbook-on-a-computer business described in the previous part. Quicken can help you manage and monitor things like credit cards, home mortgages, and investments. If this sounds interesting, then keep reading.

Chapter 9
Credit Cards (and Debit Cards, Too)

In This Chapter

▶ Tracking credit cards

▶ Setting up a credit card account

▶ Selecting a credit card account so that you can use it

▶ Recording a credit card charge

▶ Changing charges you've already entered

▶ Paying credit card bills

▶ Reconciling a credit card balance

▶ Handling debit cards

▶ Deciding whether to use IntelliCharge

*Y*ou can use Quicken to track your credit cards in much the same way you use Quicken to keep a checkbook. However, there are a few wrinkles.

Should You Even Bother?

I use a credit card for many purchases, but I don't need Quicken to track my balance because I always pay off my bill in full every month. (It's like a natural law that CPAs have to do this.)

If you're in the same boat — you use a credit card but don't carry an unpaid balance — you don't need to use anything special to track your credit card purchases and, of course, you don't need Quicken to tell your account balance because it's always zeroed out at the end of the month.

If you do carry a credit card balance (and most people do, it turns out), you can set up a credit card account to track your purchases.

What's more, if you need to keep track of how much you've charged during the month (even though you're going to pay the balance off in full), you also may need to set up a credit card account in Quicken.

Of course, when I pay my credit card bill, I easily use the Split Transaction screen (see Chapter 4) to describe my spending categories: $3.53 on food for lunch, $52.64 for car repairs, $217.54 for books (my personal weakness).

A credit card account, however, will help you track not just what you charged (using spending categories), but also where you charged it (using the Payee field).

My father-in-law, for example, uses a credit card account. Although he doesn't carry a balance (or so he says), he likes to know what he spends at International House of Pancakes, at Kmart, and at Buck's truck stop. Sure, he could use the Split Transaction screen to record his spending on breakfast, clothing, and gasoline when he pays the credit card bill at the end of the month. But he can't use the Split Transaction screen to record where he said, "Charge it."

Setting Up a Credit Card Account

If you want to track credit card spending and balances with Quicken, you need to set up a credit card account. (In comparison, you use bank accounts to track things like the money that flows into and out of a checking account.)

Adding a credit card account

To set up a credit card account, you follow roughly the same steps as you do when establishing a bank account. Starting from the Quicken Main Menu, here's what you do:

1. **Choose the Select Account command from the Quicken Main Menu.**

   Quicken displays the Select Account to Use screen, as shown in Figure 9-1.

2. **Select the <New Account> option from the list of accounts.**

   You can do this by pressing Home because <New Account> is the first item listed. Or, you can use the up- and down-arrow keys to highlight the <New Account> line and then press Enter. Quicken displays the Set Up New Account screen (see Figure 9-2).

3. **Indicate that you want to set up a credit card account.**

   With the cursor on the Account Type field, press 2.

4. **Name the account.**

   Move the cursor to the Name For This Account field and type a name.

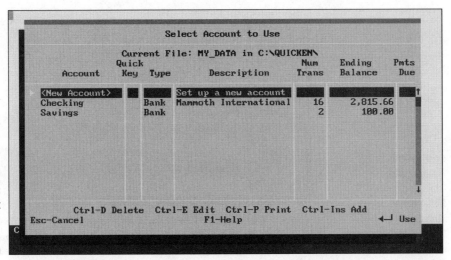

Figure 9-1:
The Select
Account to
Use screen.

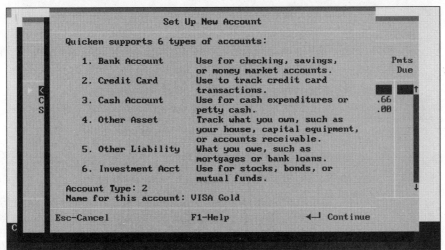

Figure 9-2:
The Set Up
New
Account
screen.

5. Press Enter.

Quicken displays the Starting Balance and Description screen, as shown in
Figure 9-3.

**6. Enter the balance you owed at the end of the last credit card billing
period after making your payment.**

Move the cursor to the Balance field and input the balance value using the
number keys.

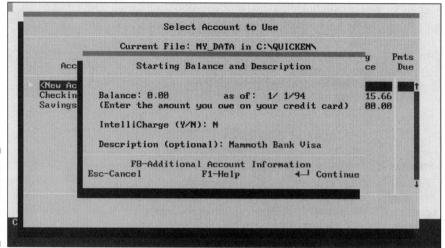

Select Account to Use

Current File: MY_DATA in C:\QUICKEN\

Starting Balance and Description

Balance: 0.00   as of: 1/ 1/94
(Enter the amount you owe on your credit card)

IntelliCharge (Y/N): N

Description (optional): Mammoth Bank Visa

F8-Additional Account Information
Esc-Cancel   F1-Help   ↵ Continue

Figure 9-3:
The Starting
Balance and
Description
screen.

7. Enter the date on which you started keeping records for the credit card account.

This date should probably be the date you made your payment. Move the cursor to the As Of field and type the date.

8. Indicate whether you plan to use IntelliCharge.

If you want to use Quicken's IntelliCharge feature, which allows you to get a list of your credit card charges on disk or though a modem, move the cursor to the IntelliCharge field and press Y. (I'll ramble about IntelliCharge later in this chapter.)

9. (Optional) Enter a description for the account.

Move the cursor to the Description field and type a description of the account or some other important piece of account information, such as the credit card account number.

10. (Optional) Record additional credit card information.

Quicken lets you enter additional information about the credit card account. Sure, you don't have to do this. If you want to, press F8. Quicken displays a screen that you can use to store a bunch of extra info: bank name and address, account number, and interest rate. Press Ctrl-Enter when you want to return to the Starting Balance and Description screen. Or press Enter when the cursor is on the last field of the Additional Account Information screen.

11. Press Enter.

Quicken displays the Specific Credit Limit screen. If you want, enter your credit limit. I don't show this simple, one-field screen as a figure, so don't waste any time looking for it.

12. Press Enter.

Quicken redisplays the Select Account to Use screen, as shown in Figure 9-1. Mysteriously, the screen will list an additional account: the credit card account you've just created.

Selecting a credit card account so that you can use it

In Quicken, you work with one account at a time: one bank account, one cash account, one credit card account, and so on. To tell Quicken which account you want to work with, use the Select Account to Use screen — the same one shown in Figure 9-1.

If the Select Account to Use screen isn't already displayed, choose the Select Account command from the Quicken Main Menu. Or if either the Register screen or Write Checks screen is displayed, choose the Select/Set Up Account command from the **P**rint/Acct menu.

After you've reached the Select Account to Use screen, highlight the account you want (using the arrow keys) and press Enter. Quicken displays the Register screen, and you can begin recording transactions.

Entering Credit Card Transactions

After you've selected credit card accounts, Quicken displays a special version of the Register screen (see Figure 9-4).

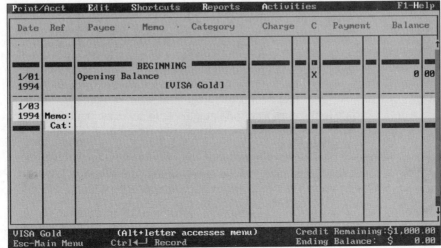

Figure 9-4:
The credit card version of the Register screen.

```
 Print/Acct     Edit     Shortcuts     Reports     Activities          F1-Help

  Date  Ref    Payee  ·  Memo  ·  Category    Charge   C  Payment    Balance

                           BEGINNING
  1/01        Opening Balance                          X                 0 00
  1994                     [VISA Gold]
 -----------
  1/03  Memo:
  1994  Cat:




 VISA Gold            (Alt+letter accesses menu)    Credit Remaining:$1,000.00
 Esc-Main Menu       Ctrl◄┘ Record                  Ending Balance:  $    0.00
```

A whirlwind tour of the credit card register

The credit card register works like the regular ol' Register screen you use for a bank account: you enter transactions into the rows of the register. When you record a charge or payment, Quicken updates the credit card balance. You also can use the commands that appear on the **P**rint/Acct, **E**dit, **S**hortcuts, **R**eports, and **A**ctivities menus the same way you do for a bank account.

Recording a credit card charge

Recording a credit card charge works basically like recording a check or a bank account withdrawal.

Suppose that you've charged $30.47 for lunch at your favorite Mexican restaurant, Mommasita's Cantina. Here's how you record this charge:

1. **Enter the charge date.**

   Move the cursor to the Date field (if it isn't already there) and type the date, using the MM/DD format. Enter July 4, 1994, for example, as **7/4.** You usually won't have to enter the year because Quicken retrieves the current year from the little clock inside your computer.

2. **Record where you used the credit card.**

   Move the cursor to the Payee field and type the name of the person or business you're paying. For example, type **Mommasita's Cantina.**

3. **Enter the charge amount.**

   Move the cursor to the Charge field and enter the total charge amount. Don't type a dollar sign. Do type a period to indicate the decimal place. For example, type **30.47.**

4. **Enter a description of the charge.**

   Move the cursor to the Memo field and enter a description of the charge. For example, you might note that the lunch was a special date with your spouse or an important business meeting.

5. **Enter the category.**

   Move the cursor to the Category field and type the category that summarizes this charge. You might classify a restaurant charge as "Entertain," for example.

If you don't remember the category names you've set up, press Ctrl-C to see the Category and Transfer List screen. Use either the arrow keys or the mouse to highlight the correct category; then press Enter.

6. Record the charge.

With the cursor on the Category field, press Enter. Quicken displays a message box that asks you whether it's OK to record the transaction. Press Enter or press 1 to indicate that it's OK to record the charge. Quicken beeps reluctantly, calculates the new balance, and moves the cursor to the next row in the register.

What if you make a mistake? If you don't want to record the charge because you made an error, press 2 when Quicken asks whether it's OK to record the transaction. Fix the incorrect field or fields. Then press F10 and Enter, or press Ctrl-Enter.

If you've already recorded the transaction, skip to the next section.

Figure 9-5 shows the charge at Mommasita's Cantina — one of your finer dining establishments. Good food at reasonable prices. You can't ask for much more.

By the way, I'm not making fun of Mexican restaurants or Mexican food. I love both.

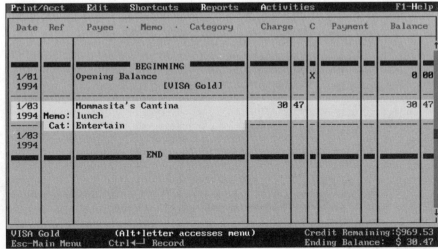

Figure 9-5:
The charge at Mommasita's Cantina.

Changing charges you've already entered

Here's how to change charges you've already entered: use the arrow keys to highlight the charge you want to change. Use Tab or Shift-Tab to move the cursor to the field you want to change. (You can also click the field with the mouse.) Make your fix. Then record the transaction by pressing F10 and Enter, by pressing Ctrl-Enter, or by choosing the **R**ecord Transaction command from the **E**dit menu.

Paying credit card bills

Quicken offers you two ways to pay a credit card bill if you're tracking the credit card account balance with a credit card account. Of course, if you're not using a credit card account, you record a check paying a credit card bill the same way you record any other check that pays a bill.

A most bodacious way to pay a credit card bill

This method is pretty simple, so don't blink. You may miss the action.

Look at your credit card statement. Decide how much you want to pay. Select the bank account on which you'll write the check. Write the check and record it in the register as a transfer to the credit card account (see "Recording Account Transfers" in Chapter 4).

You're done.

If you have questions, take a peek at the highlighted check transaction shown in Figure 9-6. The check pays $100 of the credit card balance; the money has been transferred to the credit card account.

If you look at the credit card account register, you should see that this check reduces the credit card balance by $100.

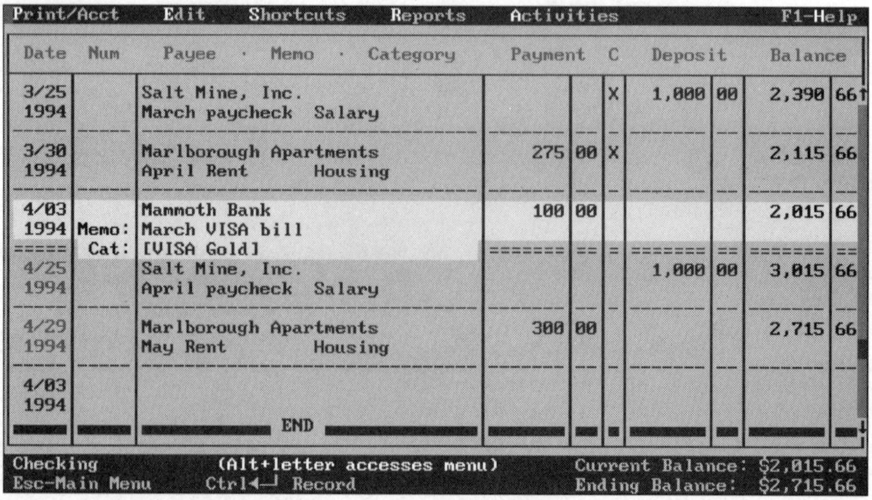

Figure 9-6:
The highlighted check transaction shows a check paying a portion of a credit card balance.

Print/Acct	Edit	Shortcuts	Reports	Activities			F1-Help

Date	Num	Payee · Memo · Category	Payment	C	Deposit	Balance
3/25 1994		Salt Mine, Inc. / March paycheck Salary		X	1,000 00	2,390 66↑
3/30 1994		Marlborough Apartments / April Rent Housing	275 00	X		2,115 66
4/03 1994	Memo: Cat:	Mammoth Bank / March VISA bill / [VISA Gold]	100 00			2,015 66
4/25 1994		Salt Mine, Inc. / April paycheck Salary			1,000 00	3,015 66
4/29 1994		Marlborough Apartments / May Rent Housing	300 00			2,715 66
4/03 1994						

END

Checking	(Alt+letter accesses menu)	Current Balance: $2,015.66
Esc-Main Menu	Ctrl◄┘ Record	Ending Balance: $2,715.66

A less bodacious way to pay a credit card bill

You also can tell Quicken that you want to pay some portion of the credit card bill as part of reconciling the credit card's account balance. I think that this method is slightly more difficult, but you may find it more convenient — especially if you're going to reconcile your credit card balance. I call this method "that crazy reconciliation trick."

That crazy reconciliation trick

You know that trick where you compare your record of, say, your checking account with the bank's record of the same checking account? Where the difference between your account balance and the bank's understanding of your balance is supposed to equal the total of the transactions floating around in the system? You can do this same trick using a credit card account.

To reconcile a credit card account, first grab your credit card statement. Then display Quicken's credit card account register.

What the nasty credit card company says

To tell Quicken what that nasty credit card company says, try these dance steps (put on some music if you can't seem to get the rhythm right):

1. **Choose the Reconcile/Pay Credit Card Bill command from the Activities menu.**

   Press Alt to activate the menu bar, **A** to select the Activities menu, and then **e** to select the Reconcile/Pay Credit Card Bill command. Quicken displays the Credit Card Statement Information screen (see Figure 9-7).

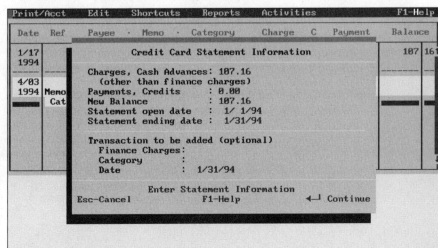

Figure 9-7:
The Credit
Card
Statement
Information
screen.

2. **Enter the charges and cash advances your statement shows.**

   Move the cursor to the Charges, Cash Advances field and then input the amount.

3. **Enter the payments and credits your statement shows.**

   You know the drill: move the cursor and input the amount. Do-si-do and swing your partner.

4. **Enter the ending balance per the credit card statement.**

   Even if you can't believe you charged that much.

5. **Enter the statement's opening date in the Statement Open Date field.**

   Now this was a surprise, I'll bet.

6. **Enter the statement's ending date in the Statement Ending Date field.**

   This is getting kind of boring, isn't it? Move and type, move and type; that's all I ever seem to say.

7. **Enter the monthly interest charged on the unpaid balance in the Finance Charges field.**

   Let us pause for a moment of silence here if this is a sad, sad topic for you.

8. **Assign the monthly interest to an appropriate spending category, such as Int Exp.**

   Move the cursor to the Category field and type the category name. (Remember that you can press your keystroke combination friend, Ctrl-C, to see the Category and Transfer List screen.)

9. **Press Enter.**

   Quicken displays a special version of the Credit Card Register screen, as shown in Figure 9-8. Then again, maybe the screen isn't so special after all. It just allows you to inform Quicken of the credit card charges and payments that appear on your statement.

Ouch! Did I really spend that much?

After you've given Quicken an overview of your credit card situation, you're ready to note which charges have and which charges haven't cleared.

If you're comfortable whipping through a bank reconciliation, you probably can do this with your eyes closed. If you need some help, keep your eyes open — so you can read the steps that follow:

1. **Find the first charge listed on the credit card statement.**

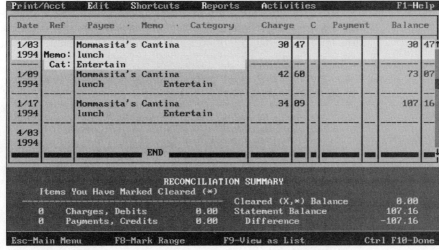

Print/Acct	Edit	Shortcuts	Reports	Activities		F1-Help

Date	Ref	Payee · Memo · Category	Charge	C	Payment	Balance
1/03 1994	Memo: Cat:	Mommasita's Cantina lunch Entertain	30 47			30 47↑
1/09 1994		Mommasita's Cantina lunch Entertain	42 60			73 07
1/17 1994		Mommasita's Cantina lunch Entertain	34 09			107 16
4/03 1994						
		=========== END ===========				

```
                         RECONCILIATION SUMMARY
       Items You Have Marked Cleared (*)
                                         Cleared (X,*) Balance       0.00
        0     Charges, Debits         0.00  Statement Balance       107.16
        0     Payments, Credits       0.00  Difference             -107.16
```

Esc-Main Menu	F8-Mark Range	F9-View as List	Ctrl F10-Done

Figure 9-8: The reconciliation version of the credit card register.

2. Mark the charge as cleared.

Scroll through the transactions listed on the reconciliation register until you find the charge. Highlight the charge, using the arrow keys or the mouse; then press the spacebar. Quicken adds an asterisk to the C column, marking this charge as cleared. Then Quicken updates the cleared statement balance.

TIP

You can fit more charges and payments onto the screen by using the one-line, or list, version of the register. But if you want to see more information, you can display a two-line, register-like view. To toggle between these two views, press F9.

3. Enter any missing charges.

If you can't find a charge, you haven't entered it into the register yet. Enter the charge in the usual way — except add an asterisk to the C column. (The asterisk tells Quicken that the charge has already cleared.)

4. Repeat steps 1, 2, and 3 for each charge listed on the credit card statement.

Or until you're blue in the face.

5. Find the first payment or credit listed on the credit card statement.

6. Mark the payment or credit as cleared.

Scroll through the transactions listed on the reconciliation register until you find the first payment or credit. Highlight the payment or credit; then press the spacebar. Quicken adds an asterisk to the C column, marking this payment or credit as cleared. Then Quicken updates the cleared balance.

7. Enter any missing payments or credits.

If you can't find a payment or credit (and you probably know this), you haven't entered it into the register yet. Enter the darn thing. And be sure that you add an asterisk to the C column to say, "Hey, this baby's cleared."

8. Repeat steps 5, 6, and 7 for each payment or credit listed on the credit card statement.

Oh. . . . that explains things

After you've marked all the cleared charges and payments, the difference between the credit card's cleared balance and the statement's ending balance should equal zero.

Figure 9-9 illustrates this phenomenon: the statement shows your balance as 107.16. The sum of your cleared transactions is, magically, also 107.16. The difference is zero. For once, you and your credit card company agree.

By the way, it's darn easy to reconcile with fictitious data.

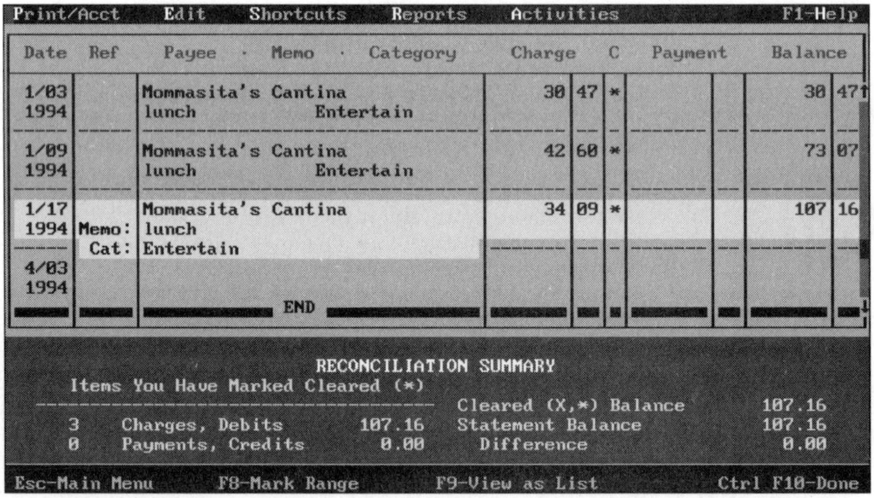

Figure 9-9:
After the smoke clears — you're done reconciling an account when the total cleared transactions equals the statement balance.

Finishing up the reconciliation

If the difference equals zero, you're cool. You're golden. Stick a fork in it; you're done. (This sort of makes you sound like a sausage, doesn't it? Sorry, I won't use this phrase again.)

Press Ctrl-F10 to tell Quicken that you're done. Quicken displays a congratulatory message telling you how proud it is of you; then it asks whether you want to print a reconciliation report.

If you want to save a tree, skip the report. If you like paperwork or know someone who works in the timber industry, print the report.

As part of "finishing up," Quicken changes all the asterisks to Xs, identifying those transactions that have already been reconciled.

If the difference doesn't equal zero, you've got a problem. Press Ctrl-F10 and Quicken will explain cursorily why your account doesn't balance.

Quicken also will tell you that you can force the two amounts to agree by pressing Enter. But forcing the two amounts to agree isn't a very good idea. In fact, it's actually a pretty crummy idea. If you choose to do this, Quicken adds a cleared transaction equal to the difference.

I know it's tempting to let Quicken make the problem disappear, but you should try to find why the difference isn't zero. In Chapter 6, I provide some hints to help you figure out why a bank account won't balance. You can apply the same list of tips to credit card reconciliations if you're in a bad way.

Postponing the inevitable

If you press Esc when the reconciliation register shows a difference other than zero, Quicken tells you (via a message box like the one shown in Figure 9-10) that the reconciliation isn't complete.

You can postpone reconciling the account by selecting the Leave Reconciliation option (your work will be saved). Quicken basically leaves your reconciliation work half done. Transactions you've marked as cleared still show the asterisk in the C column. And you still have an inexplicable difference between the statement's balance and your credit card's cleared balance.

Figure 9-10:
The
Reconciliation
is Not
Complete
message
box
basically
says,
"Leaving so
soon?
You've only
just begun."

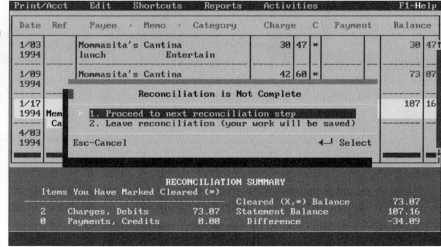

Postponing a reconciliation is usually better than forcing the two balances to agree. By postponing, you give yourself time to find (and fix) the problem (or, gulp, problems). Then you can restart the reconciliation and finish your work. (You restart the same way you originally started.)

By the way, selecting the Proceed To Next Reconciliation Step option is the same thing as pressing Ctrl-F10. If the account balances, you see a congratulatory message telling you what a wonderfully bright person you are. If the account doesn't balance, Quicken tells you why this might be the case, and Quicken asks whether you want to force the two amounts to agree.

Paying the bill as part of the reconciliation

After you finish or postpone the reconciliation, Quicken politely asks whether you want to pay the bill. If you do, Quicken displays the Make Credit Card Payment screen and collects the necessary data (see Figure 9-11).

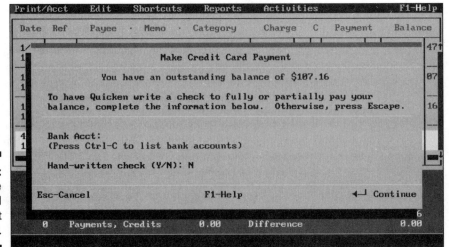

Figure 9-11:
The Make Credit Card Payment screen.

You probably can figure out how to use this baby yourself, but, hey, I'm on a roll. . . . So, here are the steps: roll 'em:

1. Enter the bank account on which you'll write the check.

Move the cursor to the Bank Acct field and enter the name. Notice that you can press Ctrl-C to see the accounts. Nice touch.

2. Indicate whether you'll write the check by hand.

Press Y to tell Quicken "yes." Press N to tell Quicken "no."

3. Press Enter.

If you tell Quicken that you want to write the check by hand, Quicken displays the Register screen (see Chapter 4 for more information); Quicken assumes that you want to pay the entire credit card balance. If you tell Quicken that you don't want to write the check by hand, Quicken displays the Write Checks screen; then you can tell Quicken to print a check (see Chapter 5 for information on how to do this task).

4. Enter the check into the Register screen or the Write Checks screen.

Describe the check that you plan to write by hand or that you want Quicken to print.

As I said earlier, this process isn't the easiest way to pay a credit card bill. But you're an adult. You make your own choices.

So What About Debit Cards?

Debit cards, when you get down to details, aren't really credit cards at all. They're more like bank accounts. To withdraw money, however, you don't write a check, you use a debit charge.

Although a debit card looks (at least to your friends and the local merchants) like a credit card, you should treat it like a bank account.

In a nutshell, here's what you need to do:

- ✔ Set up a bank account with the starting balance equal to the deposit you make with the debit card company.

- ✔ When you use your debit card to charge something, record the transaction just as you would record a regular check.

- ✔ When you replenish the debit balance by sending more money to the debit card company, record the transaction just as you would record a regular deposit.

If all this sounds simple, that's because it is. In fact, I'd go so far as to say that if you've been rambling along, doing just fine with a bank account, you'll find keeping track of a debit card is as easy as eating an entire bag of potato chips.

The IntelliCharge Hoopla

IntelliCharge refers to a special credit card account — specifically provided for people who have the Quicken Visa credit card.

The big hoopla concerning this account is that with IntelliCharge you don't have to enter the credit card transactions into a register. Instead, you retrieve them from a floppy disk (which the Quicken credit card people send you) or by using a modem.

Is IntelliCharge something you should look into? Does it really save you time? Is it a good deal? Inquiring minds want to know.

Let me tell you what I think (and this is just my humble opinion). Although there isn't an annual fee and the interest rate seems pretty competitive, IntelliCharge (at least at the time I'm writing this) still isn't all that cheap. The floppy disk monthly delivery fee is $4.50 and the monthly modem charge is $3. So you're looking at $40 to $50 a year. You do save some data entry time, of course, so maybe it's worth it. (If you're a heavy hitter who runs up 20 or 30 grand a month in credit card charges, your time savings should be pretty substantial.)

One thing that sort of bothers me about the whole deal, however, is that you're really just receiving an electronic version of your statement. So that reconciling your bank statement against, well, your bank statement isn't going to make a whole heck of a lot of sense. (Golly, gee, Batman. The charge to Mulva's Pet School appears on both statements, too!)

Another thing is that you have to do some extra fiddling. Now there's nothing particularly complicated about grabbing credit card charges off a floppy disk. And you don't need to know any special tricks to use a modem. (Your computer and the Quicken credit card computer have a secret handshake, but you'll learn about this after you join the club.) Nevertheless, the fiddling takes time.

I guess it all boils down to this: IntelliCharge is kind of a cool idea, but it has some drawbacks. IntelliCharge won't eliminate the need to keep records and, hey, it's not free.

If you've read all this stuff about IntelliCharge and are muttering things like "That bozo . . .," you're probably hot to trot on this IntelliCharge thing. If this is the case, you should know that IntelliCharge has an additional hardware requirement if you want to use a modem to retrieve your credit card transactions. You need at least 640K of memory. (Normally, in comparison, you only need 512K of memory).

If you're into debt management, turn to the next chapter. I describe how you use Quicken to track things like mortgages and car loans.

If you're not into the debt management thing, go ahead and flip ahead. Chapter 11 describes how to wrestle your way through Quicken's investment record-keeping feature — and how to make sure that you win.

Chapter 10
Other People's Money

In This Chapter

▶ Tracking loans, mortgages, and other debts

▶ Setting up liability accounts

▶ Calculating the payment principal and interest portions of a payment

▶ Recording loan payments

▶ Handling mortgage escrow accounts

▶ Adjusting principal-interest breakdowns

A popular financial self-help writer says that one of the secrets to financial success is using other people's money: the bank's, the mortgage company's, the credit card company's, your brother-in-law's. . . . You get the idea.

But I'm not so sure that using other people's money is the key to financial success. I do know that borrowing other people's money can turn into a nightmare.

Quicken can help you out here, though. No, the folks at Intuit won't make your loan payments. But they provide you with a tool to help monitor the money you owe and the costs of your debts.

Should You Bother to Track Your Debts?

I think it's a good idea to track your debts (such as car loans, mortgages, student loans, and so on) if the lenders fail to tell you how much you're paying in annual interest or how much you owe after each payment.

If the lenders do keep you well informed, why use Quicken to track their money? Heck, let them do the work.

If your lenders have half a clue, they send you a 1098 tax form at the end of every year. The amount shown on that form equals your tax deduction if the interest stems from a mortgage, business, or investment loan.

Personal interest expenses aren't deductible anymore, so there's little reason to track them unless you crave unnecessary work.

What Should I Do First?

To track other people's money with Quicken, you need to set up a *liability account*. Liability is a big word — which accountants love — for debts.

Thank goodness it's easy to set up a liability account because you need a separate baby for every loan or debt. To establish a liability account

1. **Choose Select Account from the Main Menu.**

   Accustomed to your sure-footed direction, Quicken displays the Select Account to Use screen.

2. **Select the <New Account> option.**

   Press Home and then Enter. Quicken displays the Set Up New Account screen.

3. **Press 5 to indicate that this account is a liability account.**

4. **Name the liability account.**

   Type something clever in the Name for This Account field.

5. **Press Enter.**

   Quicken alerts you that you're diving into something complicated. Pay no attention. You're in good hands.

6. **Press Enter again.**

   Quicken displays the Starting Balance and Description screen, as shown in Figure 10-1. (Do you feel a sense of déjà vu? You see this screen every time you set up an account.)

7. **Enter the amount you currently owe on the loan.**

   If you don't have this figure — and who does — call your lender. Then move the cursor to the Balance field and input the amount.

8. **Enter the date of your last payment.**

   Move the cursor to the As Of Date field and enter the date on which you owe the starting balance (which you entered in step 7). Type the date in MM/DD/YY fashion. (For example, enter May 31, 1994, as **5/31/94.**)

9. **(Optional) Describe the account.**

   If the account name isn't descriptive enough, you can provide the account number or the lender's name, for example.

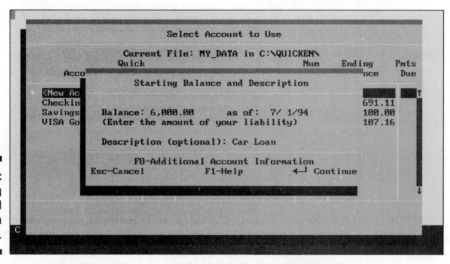

Select Account to Use

Current File: MY_DATA in C:\QUICKEN\

Starting Balance and Description

Balance: 6,000.00   as of: 7/ 1/94
(Enter the amount of your liability)

Description (optional): Car Loan

F8-Additional Account Information
Esc-Cancel   F1-Help   ↵ Continue

Figure 10-1:
The Starting
Balance and
Description
screen.

If you want to store more information about the liability, press F8. Quicken displays a screen that lets you record a bunch of additional data — such as the lender's name, the lender's address, whether they give away toasters, and the loan interest rate.

10. Press Enter.

Quicken adds the liability account and then redisplays the Select Account to Use screen, which now contains the newly added liability account.

When you want to use the liability account, select it from the Select Account to Use screen. Quicken displays the liability version of the register, which looks just like your old friend, the regular register. Notice, though, that the Payment and Deposit columns have different names — Increase and Decrease.

Delivering a Pound of Flesh (a.k.a. Making a Payment)

After you set up a liability account, you can give the lender a pound of flesh. That's Shakespeare, folks, for "make the darn payment."

Describing the payment principal and interest

OK, you can do this part the hard way or the easy way. Your choice.

The easy way to break down principal and interest

Get this: the easy way to break down principal and interest is (drum roll, please) *not* to do it. That's right. Don't do it yourself. Just ask the bank.

In fact, the bank may already do it for you — check your monthly loan statement. If so, you're home free.

Of course, there's a tiny catch: the current month's statement almost surely shows the *preceding* month's breakdown. But this small discrepancy need not be a major hassle. Just give an estimate of the interest expense and principal reduction figures when you record a check. When you receive your next statement, replace the estimate with the real McCoy.

The hard way to break down principal and interest

Of course, you can use Quicken to calculate how payments break down into principal reduction and interest expense. To get Quicken to describe the loan and explain how interest calculations work, do the following:

1. **Display the Memorized Transaction List screen.**

   From either the Register screen or the Write Checks screen (see Figure 10-2), choose **R**ecall Transaction from the **S**hortcuts menu.

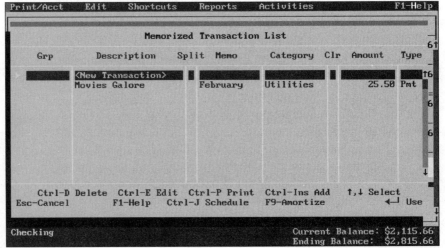

Figure 10-2:
The
Memorized
Transaction
List screen.

2. Press F9.

This action tells Quicken that you want to set up a memorized loan payment transaction, and it tells Quicken to break down the loan payment into its principal and interest components. The Set Amortization Information screen appears, as shown in Figure 10-3.

There's a secret back door to the Set Amortization Information screen. When the Loan Calculator is visible, press F7 and Quicken displays the Set Amortization Information screen. (Refer to Chapter 8 for more information about the Loan Calculator.)

3. Enter the loan payment amount.

Move the cursor to the Regular Payment field and then input the loan payment amount (which includes only interest and principal) and not some larger amount that includes extra money for things like insurance and escrow accounts.

4. Indicate how many payments you make each year.

Move the cursor to the Periods Per Year field and enter the number of payments you make in a year. If you make monthly payments, for example, type **12.**

5. Record the annual interest rate.

Move the cursor to the Annual Interest Rate field and enter the annual interest rate. Sounds easy, right? But this step can get tricky. Be sure that you enter the interest rate — not the Annual Percentage Rate (APR). The APR lets you sort of compare the overall costs of two loans; you don't use it to calculate loan interest.

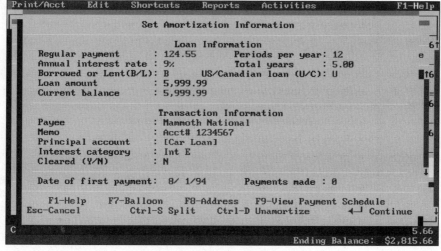

Figure 10-3:
The Set
Amortization
Information
screen.

6. Indicate how long (in years) you plan to take to pay off the loan.

Type the number in the Total Years field. If you plan to make payments during the next 99 years, for example, type **99**. (Quicken will calculate loan payments only for loans that are paid back in 100 years. Besides, it's probably best not to borrow money that your great-, great-, great-grand-children would have to pay back.)

7. Indicate whether you're acting as the borrower or the lender.

Move the cursor to the Borrowed or Lent field. To indicate that you're the borrower, press B. To indicate that you're the lender, press L. (Through-out this gripping discussion, I assume that you're the borrower, not the lender. If you do serve as the bank, however, things work basically as I describe here — except that you set up an asset account rather than a liability account to track the loan. Stay tuned for more on this asset vs. liability business.)

8. Indicate whether you're using US-style interest compounding or Cana-dian-style interest compounding.

Move the cursor to the US/Canadian Loan (U/C) field; press U to indicate US; press C to indicate Canadian. I think it's safe to assume that the interest-compounding type is determined by where you live, but you might want to double-check if you live in one country and are borrowing from someone who lives in the other country.

9. Enter the loan amount in the Current Balance field.

Enter the current loan principal figure in the Current Balance field. You know the drill: move the cursor and type an amount.

Quicken calculates the loan amount — based on the information that you enter — and sticks this estimate in the Loan Amount field. Don't worry if the estimate is off a few pennies.

10. Designate the payee.

11. (Optional) Enter a memo description.

12. Name the loan account.

Enter the name of the loan account in the Principal Account field. If you're the borrower, the account should be a liability account. If you're the lender, the account should be an asset account.

13. Enter the interest category.

Move the cursor to the Interest Category field and then enter the category you use to describe loan interest. If you're the borrower, the category should be an expense category, such as Int Exp. If you're the lender, the category should be an income category, such as Int Inc. (You can press Ctrl-C to see the Category & Transfer List.)

14. Indicate whether the loan payment transaction should be marked as cleared when it's recorded in a register.

Why would you mark a loan payment transaction as cleared when you record it? If the bank automatically deducts the loan payment from your account, the payment clears your account at the very same time you record it in your register.

15. Tell Quicken when you made (or plan to make) the first payment.

Type the date in the Date of First Payment field.

16. Tell Quicken how many payments you've already made.

You may need to do some figuring — feel free to use your fingers. Type the number in the Payments Made field.

17. Tell Quicken about any balloon payment.

Press F7 if your loan includes a *balloon payment* — an amount you pay in addition to one of the regular payments so that you pay off the loan balance completely. Quicken displays the Set Balloon Payment screen, which allows you to tell Quicken with which regular payment you plan to make the balloon payment. Simple enough, huh?

18. (Optional) If you want to print a check with Quicken, enter an address.

Press F8. When Quicken displays the Memorized Transaction Address screen, enter the check address the same way you enter an address in the Write Checks screen.

19. (Optional) Display and print an amortization schedule.

You can display an on-screen amortization schedule by pressing F9. Try it — it's pretty cool. If you want to print the schedule, press Ctrl-P. Quicken displays a Print Report screen.

20. Enter any additional payment categories.

If you pay other expenses or receive income as part of the loan payment, press Ctrl-S to display the Split Transaction dialog box. Then enter these additional payment categories, using the third and subsequent split transaction lines. Quicken uses the first and second lines to show the interest and principal portions of the payments. After you describe these additional payments, press Ctrl-Enter to close the Split Transaction dialog box.

When you pay $50 for insurance in addition to the regular loan payment of $124.55, for example, the Split Transaction dialog box should look something like Figure 10-4. Notice that Quicken categorizes the entire loan payment as a transfer to the loan account. Don't worry: Quicken doesn't perform the actual loan interest calculations until you record the loan payment.

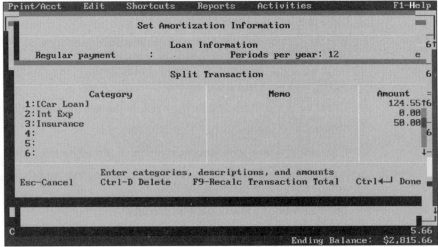

Figure 10-4:
The Split
Transaction
screen with
sample loan
payment
data.

21. Press Enter.

Quicken displays the Select Amortized Payment Type screen (see Figure 10-5). Press 1, 2, or 3 to indicate how you plan to make the loan payment. Then press Enter again. At long last, you're done.

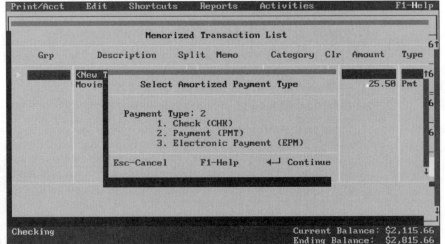

Figure 10-5:
The Select
Amortized
Payment
Type
screen.

Recording a loan payment

When you want to record a loan payment, display the Bank Account register and then follow these steps:

1. Display the Memorized Transaction List screen.

Press Ctrl-T or choose the **R**ecall Transaction command from the Short-cuts menu.

2. Highlight the memorized transaction and press Enter.

Quicken displays the Use Amortize Transaction screen (see Figure 10-6).

3. Confirm the current loan balance, current interest rate, and regular payment amounts.

Quicken gets these figures from the memorized transaction that you set up for the loan amortization transaction. If one of the figures is incorrect — if the interest on a variable rate loan has changed, for example — you can tell Quicken the updated amount by using the fields on the Use Amortize Transaction screen.

4. (Optional) Record any additional principal payment.

If you pay an extra amount to pay off the loan in less time, enter the extra amount in the Additional Prepayment field.

5. Record the loan payment transaction in the register.

After you verify that the information on the Use Amortize Transaction screen is correct, you're ready to rock. If the cursor is on the screen's last field, press Enter. If the cursor is on some other field, press F10. Quicken records the transaction in the register, automatically calculating the

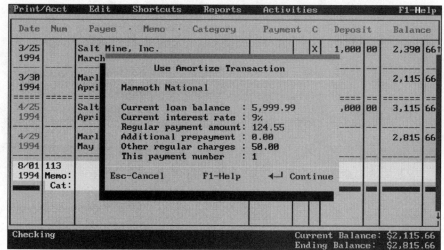

Figure 10-6:
The Use
Amortize
Transaction
screen.

interest and principal portions of the loan payment. Life doesn't get much better, does it? Figure 10-7 shows a loan payment that's been split between principal and interest with an extra $50 thrown in for insurance.

You jump through a few extra hoops, and in the end, Quicken calculates

✔ What part of your payment pays off what part of the interest

✔ What part of your payment pays off what part of the principal

Those who think that they have better things to do and therefore skip the step sequence for setting up the memorized transaction just get these numbers from the lender.

You take the loan payment and you split it and one part of the split is the interest expense. The other part is the account transfer to the liability account. Whew. This process is as close as you'll get to rocket science in your financial record keeping.

Handling mortgage escrow accounts

I should talk about one minor mortgage record-keeping annoyance — mortgage escrow accounts.

If you have a mortgage, you should know the basic procedure. While your mortgage payment may be $795 a month, for example, your friends at the mortgage company (who insist that they trust you completely) make you pay

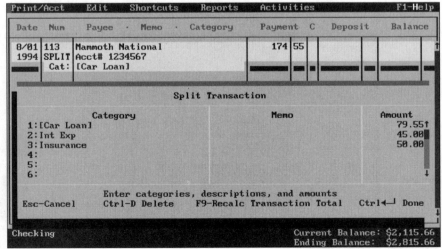

Figure 10-7:
A loan
payment
transaction.

an extra $150 a month for things like property taxes. In other words, though you're only paying $795 a month in principal and interest, you pay the mortgage company $945 a month.

Your friends at the mortgage company save this money for you in an escrow account or a set of escrow accounts. A couple times a year, they pay your property taxes and your homeowner's insurance. If you have private mortgage insurance, they may pay it every month. And so it goes.

You can treat this stuff in two ways. As with most things, there's an easy way, which is rough, dirty, and unshaven. And there's a hard way, which is precise, sophisticated, but cumbersome.

Choose the method you prefer. It's your life.

The rough, dirty, and unshaven method

Suppose that you pay an extra $150 a month. You can treat this $150 as another expense category, such as Other Housing, Property Expenses, or Escrow Fund. (I'm making these categories up as I go along.) Nice. Easy. No muss. No fuss. Figure 10-8 shows an example of a Split Transaction screen filled out this way.

Let me make a confession, though. The rough, dirty, and unshaven method doesn't tell you how much moola you've got stashed away in your escrow accounts. This method also doesn't tell you how much you really spend for homeowner's insurance, what you're entitled to claim as a property tax deduction, or how much the bank is bleeding you for private mortgage insurance.

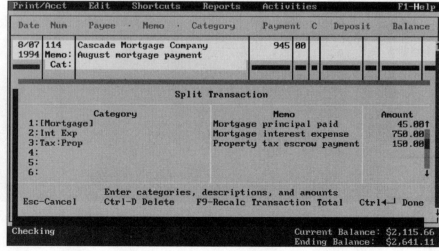

Figure 10-8:
You can treat the escrow account component of a mortgage payment as an expense category.

To find these figures, peruse the monthly and annual mortgage account statements. Or call the mortgage lender and demand the information.

The precise, sophisticated, but cumbersome method

So if you can't live with the uncertainty or the stress, then set up *other asset* accounts for each escrow account for which the mortgage company collects money.

You set up other asset accounts the same way you set up other liability accounts. First, set up an asset account with its starting balance equal to the current escrow account balance. To do so, display the Select Account to Use screen. Indicate that you want to create a new account. Identify the account as another asset account and give it a name. Then tell Quicken how much money is already in the account as of a certain date.

If you've set up an account or two in your day, this process should take you about 40 seconds.

After you set up your other asset account and record its current balance, you're ready to cruise. Record payments in the escrow as account transfers whenever you record the actual loan payment. Figure 10-9 shows an example of how the Split Transaction screen looks when you do so, assuming that there's only one escrow account.

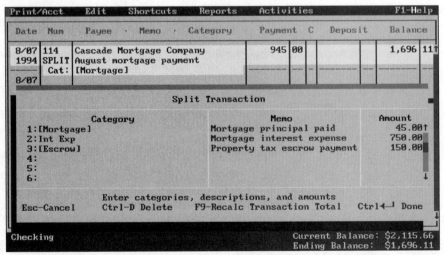

Figure 10-9:
You can record the escrow component of a mortgage payment as an account transfer.

When you set up an escrow account, you need to complete some additional record-keeping tasks. You must record the payments that the bank makes from your escrow account to the county assessor for property taxes. And you must record the payments that the bank makes from your escrow account to the insurance company for things like homeowner's and private mortgage insurance. (I know that all this work seems bogus. But I don't make the rules.)

You don't know when these payments are really made, so watch your monthly mortgage account statements carefully.

When the mortgage company disburses money from the escrow account to pay your first property tax assessment, for example, you need to record a decrease in the escrow account equal to the payment and then categorize the decrease as property taxes. This step isn't that tricky (see Figure 10-9). The account increases every loan payment (see the first transaction); the account decreases when there's a disbursement (see the second transaction).

Figure 10-10 depicts the other Asset Account version of the register, which looks just like your old friend, the regular register. Notice, though, that the Payment and Deposit columns have different names — Decrease and Increase.

Figure 10-10: The Asset Account version of the register — all dolled up for an escrow account.

Print/Acct	Edit	Shortcuts	Reports	Activities				F1-Help
Date	Ref	Payee · Memo · Category		Decrease	C	Increase	Balance	
		BEGINNING						
8/01 1994		Opening Balance [Escrow]					0	00
8/07 1994		Cascade Mortgage Company August mortgage→[Checking]				150 00	150	00
8/30 1994	Memo: Cat:	County Tax Assessor property tax payment Tax:Prop		150 00			0	00
8/30 1994		**END**						

Escrow
Esc-Main Menu   (Alt+letter accesses menu)   Current Balance: $0.00
                       Ctrl◄┘ Record   Ending Balance: $0.00

Fixing Your Principal-Interest Breakdown

I don't want to bum you out, but your principal-interest breakdown won't be right unless you use the bank's statement. You may calculate interest expense as $712.48, for example, while your bank may calculate your interest expense as $712.47. A few pennies here, a few pennies there, and pretty soon your account balance and interest expense tally are, well, a few pennies off.

Go ahead and call the bank, explain to them what bozos they are, and then tell them the correct balance. (If this trick works for you, let me know.)

Mending your evil ways

A more practical solution: adjust your records to agree with the bank's. Here's how:

1. **Display the register for the liability.**

2. **Choose the Update Account Balance command from the Activities menu.**

   Quicken displays the Update Account Balance screen shown in Figure 10-11.

3. **Input the correct (at least according to the bank's records) account balance.**

   Move the cursor to the Update This Account's Balance To field and enter the correct amount. (You probably should get this figure from the year-end or month-end loan statement.)

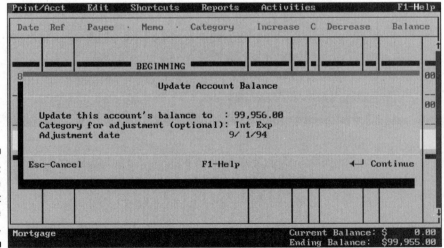

Figure 10-11:
The Update
Account
Balance
screen.

4. **Enter the interest expense category that you want to use.**

   Type the correct category name in the Category for Adjustment field. To see a list of categories, press Ctrl-C.

5. **Enter the last day of the month or year for which you're making the adjustment.**

   Move the cursor to the Adjustment Date field and type a transaction date. (The trick is to use a transaction date that sticks the correcting transaction into the right month or year.)

6. **Record the adjustment.**

   When the Adjust Account Balance screen correctly describes the needed adjustment, record the adjustment. To do so, move the cursor to the screen's last field and press Enter. Or press F10. Or Ctrl-Enter.

7. **If you use a memorized transaction, update it.**

   If you use a memorized transaction for principal-interest breakdowns, Quicken asks whether you want to update the memorized transaction for the balance adjustment when you record the balance adjustment transaction. Press Enter to answer yes.

You think this adjustment business is kooky?

Does the whole adjustment transaction business make sense to you? I know it can seem kind of backwards at times.

Remember, though, as you record loan payments, you split the loan payment between the interest expense category and a principal account transfer that reduces the liability.

But suppose that the liability isn't getting reduced enough or that it's getting reduced too much. Then you need to fix the liability balance as well as the principal-interest split.

For example, if (despite your best efforts) you record $.17 too little interest expense — and therefore record $.17 too much principal reduction during a year — you need to increase both the liability account balance and the interest expense figure by $.17. Quicken raises both amounts when you enter the interest expense category in the Category For Adjustment field. Pretty cool, huh?

The 5th Wave — By Rich Tennant

"IT SAYS HERE IF I SUBSCRIBE TO THIS MAGAZINE, THEY'LL SEND ME A FREE DESK-TOP CALCULATOR. DESKTOP CALCULATOR?!! WHOOAA – WHERE HAVE I BEEN?!!"

Chapter 11
Investments in a Nutshell

. . . .

In This Chapter

▶ Knowing when to use Quicken's investment record keeping

▶ Tracking mutual fund investments

▶ Tracking stocks and bonds in a brokerage account

▶ Recording dividends, capital gains, and other investment income

▶ Recording margin interest, miscellaneous income and expenses, and return of capital

▶ Updating share prices and balances

. . . .

I don't mean to scare you, but I think investment record keeping is Quicken's most complicated feature.

It's time to get down to business. Time to stop pussyfooting around. Time to earn my pay.

Should You Bother?

Quicken's investment record-keeping feature lets you do three important things:

✔ Track your interest and dividend income

✔ Track real and potential capital gains and losses

✔ Measure an investment's performance by calculating an internal rate of return

If you're a serious investor, these things probably sound worthwhile. But before you invest any time learning how Quicken's investment record keeping works, be sure that you need all this power.

Are your investments tax-deferred?

If your investments are tax-deferred (if, for example, you're using Individual Retirement Accounts (IRAs), 401(k)s, or Keoghs), you don't really need to track investment income and capital gains and losses. Tax-deferred investments have no effect on your personal income taxes. You get a tax deduction for the money you stick into IRAs, for example, and anything you take out is taxable. But, because you can track these amounts in your bank account (when you write the check or withdraw from the IRA), you don't have to set up a special investment account.

With tax-deferred investments, you record all that you should need to know through your checking account. Checks earmarked for investment are categorized as "IRA Deductions," for example, while investment account withdrawals deposited into your checking account are categorized as "Income."

Are you a mutual fund fanatic?

If you're a fan of mutual funds, you won't need Quicken to measure the fund's annual returns. The fund manager provides these figures for you in quarterly and annual reports.

Some investors don't need Quicken

Let me give you an example of someone who doesn't need to use Quicken's investments feature — me. Once upon a time I bought and sold common stocks, fooled around with half a dozen mutual funds, and learned firsthand why junk bonds are called junk bonds. Over the last few years, though, I've simplified my financial affairs considerably.

I don't invest directly in stocks, bonds, or mutual funds these days; instead, I stick money in an IRA. My investments don't produce taxable dividends or interest income, nor taxable or tax-saving capital gains or losses. Money I put into the IRA is tax-deductible. And money I ultimately take out of the IRA will be taxable.

I'm also sticking with a handful of mutual funds, but I don't need to calculate the annual return — that's what mutual fund managers do. So I don't need to separately figure, for example, what my shares of Vanguard Index Trust delivered as an annual return when I include both the 3 percent dividend and the 10 percent price drop.

Because I don't need to track investment income, nor track capital gains and losses, nor calculate the progress of my investment portfolio, I don't need to use Quicken's investment record keeping.

Many investors do need Quicken

Of course, many people do benefit from Quicken's investment record keeping. If you routinely buy stocks and bonds, you probably want to calculate your annual returns. What's more, if you try to monitor your capital gains and losses intelligently — and you should — you want to know which securities have gone up and which have gone done.

The size of your investment portfolio isn't an issue. For example, I have two daughters who are saving money for college. (Actually, in a cruel twist of fate, I am saving; they're simply accumulating.) Although Beth and Britt haven't saved much money, and although they use mutual funds to keep things simple, they do three things that cause nightmarishly complex record keeping for their poor, overworked, and grossly underpaid accountant (can you say "Daddy"): they reinvest their quarterly dividend income, pay annual maintenance fees, and coerce their parents into adding more money to their investment portfolios.

What's the big deal? All three things adjust the *basis* in the fund. And when Beth and Britt sell their mutual fund shares, their gain (or loss) will be determined by subtracting the basis from the sales proceeds.

The bottom line: even though Beth and Britt don't have much money, I need to use Quicken to track their investments.

Tracking a Mutual Fund

If you still think that you need to track a mutual fund investment, you need to know how to set up a mutual fund account and then record your investment activities.

Even if you don't invest in mutual funds, you shouldn't skip this section.

Setting up a mutual fund investment account

Setting up an investment account works the same way as setting up any other account:

1. **Choose Select Account from the Main Menu.**

   Quicken, ever the faithful companion, displays the Select Account to Use screen.

2. **Select the <New Account> option.**

   Press Home and then Enter. Quicken dutifully displays the Set Up New Account screen.

3. **Press 6 to indicate that this is an investment account.**

4. **Name the investment.**

   Move the cursor to the Name for This Account field; then enter the name of the mutual fund.

5. **Press Enter.**

   Quicken displays the Investment Account Type and Description screen, as shown in Figure 11-1.

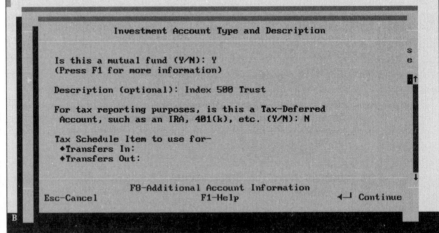

Figure 11-1: The Investment Account Type and Description screen.

```
            Investment Account Type and Description

    Is this a mutual fund (Y/N): Y
    (Press F1 for more information)

    Description (optional): Index 500 Trust

    For tax reporting purposes, is this a Tax-Deferred
    Account, such as an IRA, 401(k), etc. (Y/N): N

    Tax Schedule Item to use for-
    ◆Transfers In:
    ◆Transfers Out:


                 F8-Additional Account Information
    Esc-Cancel              F1-Help              ◄─┘ Continue
```

6. **Press Y.**

   This action tells Quicken, "Yeah, this account is a mutual fund investment account."

7. **(Optional) Enter a description for the account.**

   Move the cursor to the Description field and type something.

You can skip any step marked optional. If you decide later that you want to do something that's linked to an optional step, you can backtrack. Just thought you'd like to know.

8. **Indicate whether this account is a tax-deferred account.**

   Move the cursor to the For Tax Reporting Purposes, Is This A Tax-Deferred Account, Such As An IRA, 401(k), Etc. field (that's easy for you to say). Press N or Y. N means "Nope." Y means "Yeah." As I mention earlier, I can't think of a good reason for tracking a tax-deferred mutual fund. But, hey, I just work here.

9. **(Optional) Describe the tax effect of transfers to a tax-deferred investment.**

   If the investment is tax-deferred and you want to export data from Quicken to a tax preparation package (like TurboTax), move the cursor to the Transfers In field and enter the tax schedule and line on which Quicken should record transfers into the account. Then move the cursor to the Transfers Out field and enter the tax schedule and line on which Quicken should record transfers out of the account.

   I'm not a big fan of exporting directly to a tax preparation package, so I encourage you to skip this step if you're perplexed or bored.

10. **(Optional) Describe the investment account in more detail.**

    Press F8 to display the Additional Account Information screen, which lets you describe things like the mutual fund management company's address and phone number, as well as other heart-stopping information.

11. **Press Enter.**

    Quicken displays the Set Up Mutual Fund Security screen, as shown in Figure 11-2. The Name field shows the name that you entered in step 4.

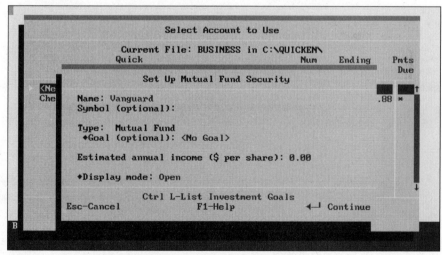

Figure 11-2:
The Set Up
Mutual Fund
Security
screen.

12. **(Optional) Enter the mutual fund symbol.**

    If you're going to turn wild and crazy and try downloading share price information through a modem, move the cursor to the Symbol field and enter the mutual fund's stock symbol.

13. (Optional) Indicate why you're investing.

Move the cursor to the Goal field. Press Ctrl-L to see Quicken's list of investment goals (college fund, growth, high risk, income, or low risk). You can select one of these preset goals, <Set Up New Goal> (which lets you define a different kind of goal), or <No Goal>. I think this investment stereotyping is sort of goofy, though. Are there really people who want high-risk investments?

14. (Optional) Enter the estimated annual income.

Move the cursor to the Estimated Annual Income ($ Per Share) field and enter a value.

15. (Optional) Indicate whether you want Quicken to display the mutual fund security on its investment list.

Move the cursor to the Display Mode field. After you press Ctrl-L, Quicken lists three display choices: Always, Open, and Never. Select Always if you want Quicken to always show the investment in its investment list — even if you're in another investment account. Select Open if the investment should show only when you're in this account. Select Never if (I bet you can guess this one) the investment should never appear in Quicken's list of investments.

16. Press Enter.

Quicken redisplays the Select Account to Use screen — except now it lists the new investment account. Hubba-hubba.

Recording your initial investment

After you set up your mutual fund account, you can record an initial purchase of fund shares.

Of course, you need to know the original price of those first shares. So dig through that kitchen drawer where you stuff bank statements, financial records, and those kooky birthday cards from Aunt Enid.

When you find the proper paperwork that shows the number of shares you purchased and the price per share, here's what you do:

1. Select the investment account.

Display the Select Account to Use screen, highlight the investment account with the arrow keys, and press Enter. Quicken displays the screen shown in Figure 11-3, which asks for your starting account balance.

Don't — I repeat, don't — record your initial purchase with the Create Opening Share Balance screen.

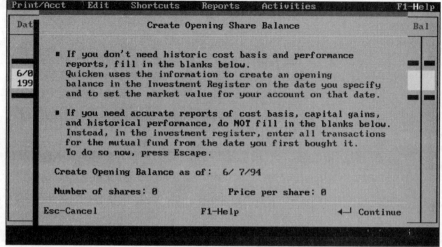

| Print/Acct | Edit | Shortcuts | Reports | Activities | F1-Help |

Dat | Create Opening Share Balance | Bal

■ If you don't need historic cost basis and performance
  reports, fill in the blanks below.
  Quicken uses the information to create an opening
  balance in the Investment Register on the date you specify
  and to set the market value for your account on that date.

6/0
199

■ If you need accurate reports of cost basis, capital gains,
  and historical performance, do NOT fill in the blanks below.
  Instead, in the investment register, enter all transactions
  for the mutual fund from the date you first bought it.
  To do so now, press Escape.

Create Opening Balance as of: 6/ 7/94

Number of shares: 0   Price per share: 0

Esc-Cancel   F1-Help   ◄┘ Continue

Figure 11-3:
The Create
Opening
Share
Balance
screen.

2. Press Enter four times. Don't enter anything in the Create Opening Share Balance screen.

After you press Enter after the third time, Quicken displays a message, No adjustment required, but don't worry. After you press Enter the fourth time, Quicken (tired of you beating on it) asks, "Hey, buddy, what gives?" Well, not really. After you press Enter the fourth time, Quicken displays the Portfolio Details screen (see Figure 11-4).

At this point, my friend, we come to a fork in the road. You can keep investment records with Quicken in two ways:

✔ You can use a special version of the familiar Quicken register. I describe this method in this chapter.

✔ You can use what Quicken calls the Portfolio approach.

I think that the register-based method is easier because the investment register works like a bank account register. If you're interested in the other method, however, take a look at this chapter's last section, "The Path Not Taken" — but only after you're comfortable with the register method.

4. Choose the View Register command from the View menu.

Quicken displays the investment version of the register (see Figure 11-5). You're in the big leagues now.

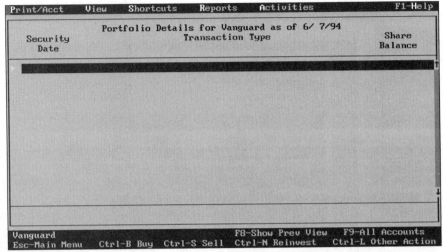

Figure 11-4:
The
Portfolio
Details
screen.

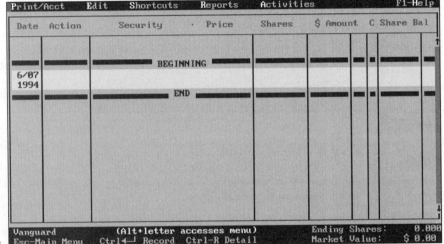

Figure 11-5:
The
Investment
Register
screen.

5. Enter the date you first purchased fund shares into the first row's Date field.

Move the cursor to the Date field and enter the date, using the MM/DD/YY format. Enter May 23, 1987, for example, as **5/23/87**.

6. Indicate that you're recording the prior purchase of shares.

Move the cursor to the Action field. Press Ctrl-L to display a list of investment actions, shown in Figure 11-6. Select Add/Remove Shares.

Quicken lists two possible Add/Remove Shares actions: ShrsIn (for Shares Into the account) and ShrsOut (for Shares Out of the account) (see Figure 11-7).

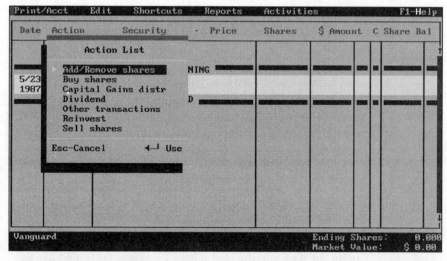

Figure 11-6:
The list of investment actions.

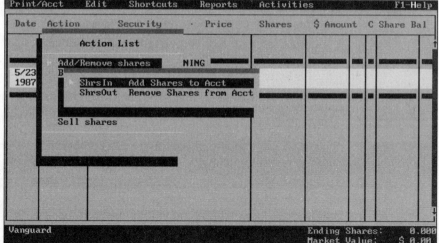

Figure 11-7:
The list of Add/ Remove Shares actions.

7. Select ShrsIn.

This action tells Quicken, "I bought some shares of this mutual fund, but don't go deducting money from my checking account because I made the purchase a long time ago and I recorded it then."

8. Accept the suggested security name.

The security name is the mutual fund account's name. Move the cursor to the Security field and press Enter.

9. Indicate what you paid per share.

With the cursor on the Price field, enter the share price. You can enter a fractional price — such as 10¼ — but your mutual fund shares probably cost something in dollars and cents — such as 10.25.

10. Indicate the size of your purchase.

Tell Quicken the size of your initial investment — either total number of shares or total price. To enter the total number of shares, move the cursor to the Shares field (fractional shares are OK). To enter the total price, move the cursor to the $ Amount field.

Quicken calculates the piece of data that you didn't enter. Let's say, for example, you spent $500 to purchase 48.7805 shares of a mutual fund that cost $10.25 per share. If you enter the share price as $10.25 and the number of shares as 48.7805, Quicken calculates the total price. If you enter the share price as $10.25 and the total purchase as $500, Quicken calculates the number of shares purchased.

Life doesn't get much better than this, huh?

11. (Optional) Enter a memo description.

If you want to tie the purchase to a confirmation order number, for example, enter the data into the Memo field. I suppose you could use this field to record anything: Kilroy was here. Save the Whales. Don't tread on me.

12. Record the initial purchase of mutual fund shares.

You can do so several ways. Press Ctrl-Enter. Choose the **R**ecord Transaction command from the Edit menu. Press F10. Or if the cursor is on the last field, press Enter. (I think the folks at Intuit should add a few more ways to record transactions, don't you?)

Quicken beeps in agony and then records the transaction into the register. Figure 11-8, for example, shows a register that records a $500 purchase of shares in the Vanguard Index mutual fund.

Figure 11-8:
How to record an initial purchase of mutual fund shares if you made the purchase a long time ago.

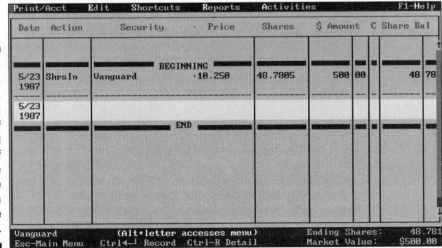

Buying near

As you purchase shares — by sending a check to the mutual fund management company or by reinvesting dividends and capital gain distributions — you should record these transactions in the investment register.

By writing a check

To buy shares by writing a check, first display your friend, the investment register. Then do the following:

1. **Enter the purchase date into the first empty row's Date field.**

2. **Tell Quicken that you're purchasing new shares by check.**

   Move the cursor to the Action field and press Ctrl-L to display a list of investment actions. Select Buy Shares. Quickens enters the Buy Shares action abbreviation, BuyX, into the Action field. (After you learn the Action abbreviations, you can type them directly into the field.)

3. **Accept the suggested security name.**

4. **Indicate what you paid per share.**

5. **Indicate the size of your purchase.**

   Tell Quicken the size of your investment — either total number of shares or total price.

6. **(Optional) Enter a memo description.**

7. **Enter the commission or fee that you paid**

   Move the cursor to the Comm/Fee field and enter the commission or fee that you paid to purchase the shares. (Quicken includes this amount in the figure shown in the $ Amount field.)

8. **Enter the bank account on which you'll write the check that pays for the shares.**

   Move the cursor to the Account field and enter the account name. (If you don't know the name by heart, press Ctrl-C or choose Categorize/Transfer from the Shortcuts menu.)

9. **Enter the account transfer amount.**

   Move the cursor to the XFer field and press Enter. Quicken beeps with enthusiasm and then records the purchase of new shares. You are now, by definition, a capitalist. Congratulations!

Figure 11-9 shows a new shares purchase transaction (a $100 addition to the mutual fund) recorded in the investment register.

```
Print/Acct     Edit     Shortcuts     Reports     Activities              F1-Help

  Date   Action       Security      · Price     Shares    $ Amount   C Share Bal

════════════════════════ BEGINNING ════════════════════════
  5/23  ShrsIn   Vanguard          ·10.250    48.7805      500 00          48 78
  1987
 ═════ ════════ ═══════════════════════════ ═════════ ═════════ ══ ═ ═════════ ══
  6/30  BuyX     Vanguard          ·13.450    7.4349       100 00          56 21
  1994    Memo:                               Comm/Fee:
 ─────  Account: [Checking]                   Xfer Amt:   100 00  -       ──   ──
  6/30
  1994  ════════════════════════   END   ════════════════════════

Vanguard           (Alt+letter accesses menu)        Ending Shares:    56.215
Esc-Main Menu    Ctrl◄─┘ Record  Ctrl-R Detail        Market Value:    $756.10
```

Figure 11-9: How to record a purchase of additional mutual fund shares.

By reinvesting dividends or capital gains

To buy shares by reinvesting dividends or capital gains, display the investment register and do the following:

1. Enter the purchase date into the first empty row's Date field.

2. Tell Quicken that you're purchasing new shares by reinvesting.

Move the cursor to the Action field and press Ctrl-L to display a list of investment actions. Select Reinvest. Quicken lists four reinvestment transactions: reinvest dividend income, reinvest interest income, reinvest long-term capital gain, and reinvest short-term capital gain. Using the arrow keys or the mouse, select how you want to reinvest; then press Enter.

Quicken enters the appropriate reinvestment action abbreviation into the Action field:

- ReinvDiv (reinvest dividends)
- ReinvInt (reinvest interest)
- ReinvLg (reinvest long-term capital gains)
- ReinvSg (reinvest short-term capital gains)

After you learn the Action abbreviations, you can type them directly into the field.

To choose the right reinvestment action, you don't need to determine whether the amounts you reinvest are dividends, interest, long-term capital gains, or short-term capital gains. The mutual fund statement tells you this stuff. If you reinvest more than one type of gain, though, you need to record more than one transaction. For example, if you reinvest $50, but part of the money is long-term capital gain and part is dividend income, you need to record two transactions: one for the long-term capital gain reinvestment and one for the dividend income reinvestment.

3. Accept the suggested security name.

4. Indicate what you paid per share.

5. Indicate the size of your purchase.

Tell Quicken the size of your investment — either total number of shares or total price.

6. (Optional) Enter a description into the Memo field.

7. Enter the commission or fee that you paid.

Move the cursor to the Comm/Fee field and enter the commission or fee that you paid to reinvest. (Quicken includes this amount in the figure shown in the $ Amount field.)

8. Press Ctrl-Enter to record the reinvestment transaction.

Quicken asks you to confirm your reinvestment transaction. After you do, Quicken records the reinvestment.

Figure 11-10 shows how Quicken records a reinvestment of $56.78 in dividends — through the purchase of mutual fund shares (at $13.65 per share). Other reinvestments work basically the same way, except that you use a different reinvestment action.

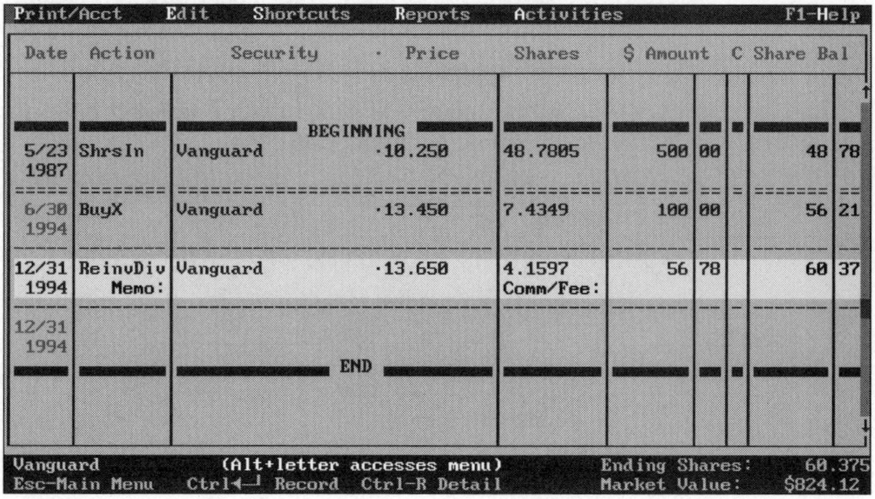

Figure 11-10: How to record dividends reinvestment.

```
Print/Acct      Edit      Shortcuts      Reports      Activities              F1-Help

  Date  Action          Security    ·  Price        Shares      $ Amount   C Share Bal

                                 BEGINNING
  5/23  ShrsIn    Vanguard           ·10.250     48.7805          500 00           48 78
  1987

  6/30  BuyX      Vanguard           ·13.450      7.4349          100 00           56 21
  1994

 12/31  ReinvDiv  Vanguard           ·13.650      4.1597           56 78           60 37
  1994    Memo:                                   Comm/Fee:

 12/31
  1994                               END

Vanguard                  (Alt+letter accesses menu)           Ending Shares:      60.375
Esc-Main Menu    Ctrl◄─┘ Record   Ctrl-R Detail                Market Value:      $824.12
```

Recording your profits

You may receive distributions directly from the mutual fund company. Retirees, for example, often tell mutual fund managers to send dividend checks and capital gains directly to the investor rather than reinvesting these amounts.

To record these kinds of distributions, you follow a process similar to those described earlier:

1. **Enter the distribution date into the first empty row's Date field.**

2. **Tell Quicken that you're receiving a distribution from the mutual fund.**

   Move the cursor to the Action field and press Ctrl-L to display a list of investment actions. Select either Dividend (DivX) or Capital Gains dDistr. If you select the Capital Gains dDistr action, Quicken lists two possible capital gains distribution actions: Llong-term capital Ggains & Transfer distribution (CGLongX) and Sshort-term capital Ggains Ddistr & Transfer distribution (CGShortX). Again, after you learn the Action abbreviations — DivX, CGLongX, and CGShortX — you can type them directly into the field.

   To choose the right distribution action, you don't need to determine whether a distribution is a dividend, long-term capital gain, or short-term capital gain. The mutual fund statement tells you this stuff.

3. **Enter the dividend or capital gains distribution amount in the $ Amount field.**

   When you tab past the Security field, you implicitly accept Quicken's suggested security name for the mutual fund. Don't worry, dude. This is correct.

4. **(Optional) Enter something into the Memo field.**

   Enter your wedding anniversary, the name of your dog, or even some data related to the dividend or distribution.

5. **Tell Quicken which bank account you want to deposit the dividend or distribution in.**

   Move the cursor to the Account field and type the account name.

6. **Press Ctrl-Enter to record the dividend or distribution transaction.**

   Quicken politely asks you to confirm whether you want to record the transaction. Press Enter and Quicken records the reinvestment. Bip. Bap. Boom.

Figure 11-11 shows $50 of long-term capital gains distribution being deposited into a checking account cleverly named *Checking*.

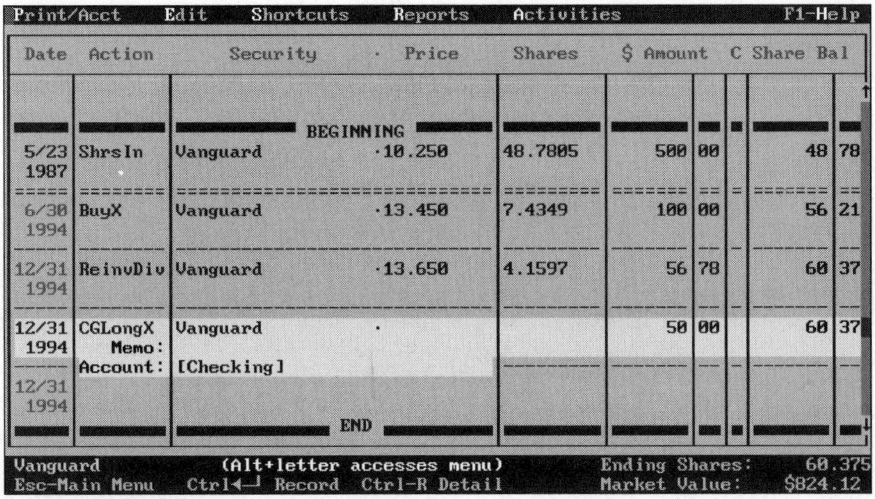

Print/Acct	Edit	Shortcuts	Reports	Activities		F1-Help

Date	Action	Security	· Price	Shares	$ Amount	C Share Bal
		BEGINNING				
5/23 1987	ShrsIn	Vanguard	·10.250	48.7805	500 00	48 78
6/30 1994	BuyX	Vanguard	·13.450	7.4349	100 00	56 21
12/31 1994	ReinvDiv	Vanguard	·13.650	4.1597	56 78	60 37
12/31 1994	CGLongX	Vanguard	·		50 00	60 37
	Memo:					
	Account:	[Checking]				
12/31 1994		END				

Vanguard   (Alt+letter accesses menu)   Ending Shares: 60.375
Esc-Main Menu   Ctrl◄┘ Record   Ctrl-R Detail   Market Value: $824.12

Figure 11-11: How to record a long-term capital gains distribution.

Selling dear

Selling mutual fund shares works like buying mutual fund shares. If you want to record the sale and what you do with the sale proceeds (such as transfer them into your checking account), do the following steps:

1. **Enter the sales date into the next empty row's Date field.**

2. **Tell Quicken you're selling shares.**

   Move the cursor to the Action field and press Ctrl-L to display a list of investment actions. Select Sell Shares. Quicken enters the Sell Shares action abbreviation, SellX, into the Action field. Of course, you also can type **SellX** directly into the field.

3. **Accept the suggested security name.**

4. **Indicate the price per share that you received.**

   With a little luck, this price is more than you paid.

5. **Indicate the size of your sale.**

   Tell Quicken the size of your sale — either total number of shares or total price. Quicken calculates whatever you don't enter.

6. **(Optional) Enter something into the Memo field.**

7. **Enter the commission or fee that you paid.**

   Move the cursor to the Comm/Fee field and enter the commission or fee that you paid to sell the shares. No wonder Bernie, your broker, does so well. He makes money whether you do or not.

8. **Enter the bank account into which you are planning to deposit the sale proceeds.**

   Move the cursor to the Account field and enter the account name. (If you don't know the name by heart, press Ctrl-C or choose **C**ategorize/Transfer from the **E**dit menu.)

9. **Enter the account transfer amount.**

   Move the cursor to the XFer field and press Enter. Quicken beeps cheerfully and then records the sale of new shares.

Figure 11-12 shows shares being sold to pay for Beth's first-semester college tuition. Wait a minute. This is too sudden. Just a few pages ago, Beth was a little girl. And now she's leaving home. They grow up fast, don't they?

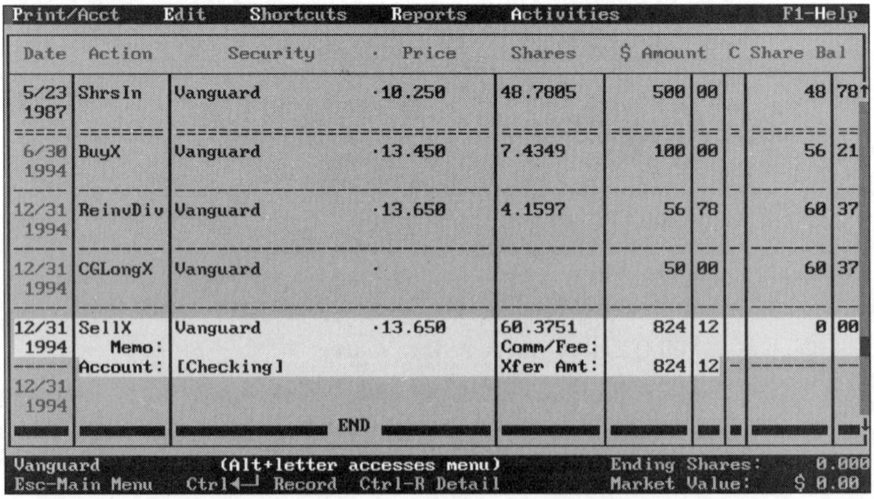

Print/Acct	Edit	Shortcuts	Reports	Activities			F1-Help

Date	Action	Security	· Price	Shares	$ Amount	C	Share Bal
5/23 1987	ShrsIn	Vanguard	·10.250	48.7805	500|00		48|78↑
6/30 1994	BuyX	Vanguard	·13.450	7.4349	100|00		56|21
12/31 1994	ReinvDiv	Vanguard	·13.650	4.1597	56|78		60|37
12/31 1994	CGLongX	Vanguard	·		50|00		60|37
12/31 1994	SellX Memo: Account:	Vanguard [Checking]	·13.650	60.3751 Comm/Fee: Xfer Amt:	824|12 824|12		0|00
12/31 1994				END			

Vanguard   (Alt+letter accesses menu)   Ending Shares: 0.000
Esc-Main Menu   Ctrl◄┘ Record   Ctrl-R Detail   Market Value: $ 0.00

Figure 11-12: How to record a sale of mutual fund shares.

Slightly tricky mutual fund transactions

I didn't describe every single possible mutual fund transaction — although I did describe every one I've encountered in the last dozen years. You should know, however, that Quicken enables you to record three additional, almost magical, kinds of transactions: shares out, stock split, and reminder.

Removing shares from an account

You can tell Quicken to remove shares from an account without moving the money represented by the shares to some other account.

To remove shares, press Ctrl-L to display a list of investment actions. Select Add/Remove Shares and then choose ShrsOut Shares Out. (Or type **ShrsOut** directly into the Action field.)You only need to use this action if

✔ You erroneously added shares to the account using the ShrsIn action, and you now need to remove them.

✔ You are using an investment account to record old investment activity — such as from last year. In this case, you don't want to transfer the proceeds of a mutual fund sale to a checking account because you already recorded the proceeds as a deposit.

The stock split and then doubled

Stock splits don't occur very often with mutual funds. When they do, the mutual fund manager, in effect, gives you new shares for each old share you own.

To record a stock split, move the cursor to the Action field and press Ctrl-L to display a list of investment actions. Select Other Transactions and then choose StkSplit.

Indicate the ratio of new to old shares. For example, with a two-for-one split, you tell Quicken that you receive two new "split" shares for each old "unsplit" share. This stuff is really pretty easy, but I wouldn't worry much about it. You probably won't ever need to know.

Quicken, will you remind me of something?

A *reminder transaction* is the electronic equivalent of a yellow sticky note. If you put a reminder transaction in the investment register, Quicken's Billminder utility will tell you that there's a reminder message on the reminder date.

You can't goof up anything by trying out reminders. If you're curious, enter a reminder transaction for tomorrow and see what happens. This crazy thing may give you the extra incentive that you need to jump out of bed tomorrow morning.

Tracking a Brokerage Account

Believe it or not, now that you understand how Quicken handles mutual fund investments, you should have no problems working with a brokerage account — what Quicken calls a *cash investment account*.

Setting up a brokerage account

You set up a brokerage account basically the same way you set up a regular mutual fund account, except for two minor, predictable differences. When Quicken asks you whether the account is a mutual fund account, you press N for "No." Meanwhile, you don't ever see the Set Up Mutual Fund Security screen (see Figure 11-2).

Setting up security lists

With a brokerage account, you don't have just one kind of security (unlike a mutual fund account, which has only mutual fund shares). You might have shares of Boeing, General Motors, Chase Manhattan. Shoot, you name it and someone owns it.

As a result, you must create a list of the securities — stocks, bonds, or whatever — that you plan to hold in the account. To do so, follow these steps — after you set up the brokerage account:

1. **Choose the Security List command from the Shortcut menu.**

   Quicken displays the Security List screen, as shown in Figure 11-13. If you've set up any mutual funds, they appear on the list as securities.

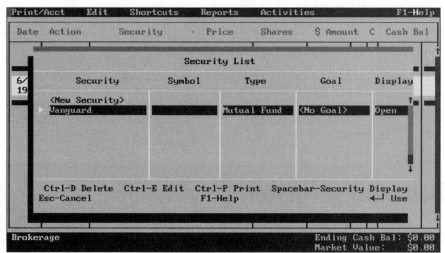

Figure 11-13:
The Security
List screen.

2. **Choose the <New Security> item.**

   Press Home and then Enter. Quicken displays the Set Up Security screen, as shown in Figure 11-14.

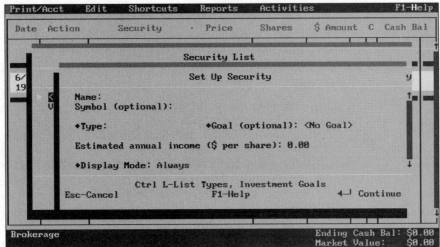

```
 Print/Acct    Edit    Shortcuts    Reports    Activities         F1-Help

 Date  Action        Security    · Price    Shares    $ Amount  C  Cash Bal

                              Security List
 6/
 19                          Set Up Security                          y

          Name:
          Symbol (optional):

          ◆Type:                    ◆Goal (optional): <No Goal>

          Estimated annual income ($ per share): 0.00

          ◆Display Mode: Always

                    Ctrl L-List Types, Investment Goals
          Esc-Cancel              F1-Help              ↵ Continue


 Brokerage                                  Ending Cash Bal: $0.00
                                            Market Value:    $0.00
```

3. Enter a name for the security.

4. (Optional) Enter the mutual fund symbol.

If you want to try downloading share price information through a modem, move the cursor to the Symbol field and enter the security's stock symbol.

5. (Optional) Indicate the type of security you're setting up.

Move the cursor to the Type field and press Ctrl-L to see Quicken's list of investment types: bond, CD, mutual fund, or stock. You can select one of these preset types or you can even select <Set Up New Type>, which lets you set up a new type. (I find this stereotyping thing a bit quirky, so don't get too hung up on it.)

6. (Optional) Indicate why you're investing.

Do you have a special purpose?

Move the cursor to the Goal field. Press Ctrl-L to see Quicken's list of investment goals . You can select one of these preset goals, <Set Up New Goal> (which lets you define a different kind of goal), or <No Goal>.

Move the cursor to the Goal field and press Ctrl-L to see Quicken's list of investment goals (college fund, growth, high risk, income, or low risk). Or select <Set Up New Goal> to create a new investment goal, such as "Sure-fire," "Easy money," or "Unconscionable profits." If you don't have goals, select <No Goal>.

7. (Optional) Plug your guestimate of how much you'll make off the security into the Estimated annual income (dollars per share) field.

8. **Use the Display field to indicate when Quicken should show the security on the screens.**

   Always means interestingly enough, always. Never means, well, never. And Open means only if you're actually holding shares.

9. **Press Enter.**

   Quicken redisplays the Set Up Security screen — except now it lists the new investment account.

10. **Practice, practice, practice.**

    As necessary, repeat steps 1 through 9 until either you're sick of the routine or you've described each security in your brokerage account.

Working with cash

Unlike a mutual fund account, a brokerage account has a cash management, or *money market*, account attached.

When you first set up the brokerage account, your check goes into the money market account. (This is the meeting where the broker buys you a doughnut and coffee, remember?) When you purchase your first shares, the cash from this account funds your purchase. And when you sell shares, your proceeds go into this account.

Transferring cash in and out of an account

Because you work with cash in a brokerage account, you need to know how to record the cash that you put into and take out of the account.

To record a cash transfer into a brokerage account (such as when you open an account)

1. **Tell Quicken that you're recording a cash transfer into the account.**

   Move the cursor to the Action field and press Ctrl-L to display a list of actions. Select Transfer Cash and then the Cash In (XIn) option. Of course, you also can type **XIn** directly into the field.

2. **Enter the amount in the $ Amount field.**

Figure 11-15 shows the record of a cash transfer into a brokerage account — which usually occurs. Notice that there's a cash balance figure in the lower right corner of the screen.

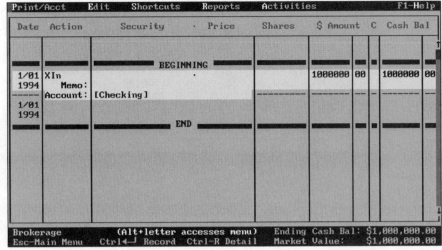

Print/Acct	Edit	Shortcuts	Reports	Activities			F1-Help

Date	Action	Security	· Price	Shares	$ Amount	C	Cash Bal
1/01 1994	XIn Memo: Account: [Checking]		·		1000000 00		1000000 00
1/01 1994							

BEGINNING

END

Brokerage   (Alt+letter accesses menu)   Ending Cash Bal: $1,000,000.00
Esc-Main Menu   Ctrl◄┘ Record Ctrl-R Detail   Market Value: $1,000,000.00

Figure 11-15:
How to record cash going into your brokerage account.

To record a cash transfer out of a brokerage account (such as when you write a draft on the money market)

1. Tell Quicken that you're recording a cash transfer out of the account.

Move the cursor to the Action field and press Ctrl-L to display a list of actions. Select Transfer Cash and then the Cash Out (XOut) option. Of course, you also can type **XOut** directly into the field.

2. Enter the amount in the $ Amount field.

Sure, cash transfers aren't all that complicated. But they will impress your friends.

Adding shares to a brokerage account

You add shares to a brokerage account the same way that you add shares to a mutual fund account — by using the ShrsIn action. (I describe this earlier in the chapter.)

As with mutual funds, you add shares to your account when you need to stick the shares somewhere, but you don't want to affect either your brokerage account cash or your checking account. You probably only need to use the ShrsIn action when you're first establishing a brokerage account.

Figure 11-16 shows a register with a ShrsIn transaction. I want to assure my friends that I'm not suffering delusions of grandeur. Alas, nor did I win the lottery. These transactions are fake.

```
 Print/Acct    Edit    Shortcuts      Reports     Activities              F1-Help

  Date  Action          Security    ·   Price      Shares    $ Amount   C  Cash Bal

  ━━━━━ ━━━━━━━━━━━━━━━ BEGINNING ━━━━━━━━━━    ━━━━━━━━ ━━ ━ ━━━━━━━━ ━━
  1/01 XIn                          ·                         1000000 00   1000000 00
  1994

  1/04 ShrsIn  Gnarlywear, Inc.   ·7 3/8     100,000       737,500 00   1000000 00
  1994  Memo:

  1/04
  1994
  ━━━━━ ━━━━━━━━━━━━━━━━ END ━━━━━━━━━━━━━    ━━━━━━━━ ━━ ━ ━━━━━━━━ ━━

 Brokerage           (Alt+letter accesses menu)   Ending Cash Bal: $1,000,000.00
 Esc-Main Menu   Ctrl←┘ Record  Ctrl-R Detail     Market Value:    $1,737,500.00
```

Figure 11-16:
A ShrsIn
transaction.

Removing shares from a brokerage account

You also can take shares out of an account — for example, because you've sold shares but don't want to adjust your brokerage account cash or your checking account. (Presumably, you've already recorded the cash proceeds as a ShrsOut, or Remove Shares, transaction.)

Load versus no-load mutual funds

Treat the mutual fund shares you hold in a brokerage account the same way you treat other stocks and bonds. Confused? While many mutual funds are sold by brokers to clients, many are sold directly to the public by the mutual fund manager.

I really don't want to delve into the subject of "load" versus "no-load" mutual funds. But if you're interested, flip open the *Wall Street Journal* and look for advertisements from no-load fund managers, such as Vanguard, Scudder, and T. Rowe Price. Ask one to tell you why they think it's a good idea for you to bypass the middleman

— a.k.a. your broker. Then ask your broker why you shouldn't bypass the middleman.

What's that? You want my opinion? Well, with much trepidation, here it is: I always use no-load mutual funds, so I like the do-it-yourself approach. I also think, however, that a *good* broker is well worth the "load" if you are saved from making an expensive mistake or two — especially if you're not paying an 8 percent load on a huge investment (like a $100,000 rollover from a pension fund). That's all I'm saying; I think I'm in enough hot water at this point.

Buying near and selling dear

Buying and selling securities works like buying and selling mutual fund shares, except for a couple minor differences.

First, when you buy or sell a share in a brokerage account, Quicken wants to know, "Hey, dude, like where did you get or stash the cash?"

For mutual funds, you use the BuyX action to tell Quicken that you just bought mutual fund shares with cash from some other account (usually a checking account). Similarly, you use the SellX action to indicate that you sold mutual fund shares and put the cash proceeds into some other account (again, probably checking, especially since the under-the-mattress method has become passé).

In a brokerage account, you also use BuyX if you buy with cash from another account and SellX if you deposit cash proceeds into another account. But when the cash stays in the brokerage account's cash account, you use two new actions: *Buy* tells Quicken that the cash for buying a security comes from the brokerage account's cash; *Sell* indicates that the cash proceeds from selling a security goes into the brokerage account's cash account.

Second, tell Quicken which security you're buying or selling or whatever.

Take a peek at Figure 11-17, which shows four brokerage account transactions. The first shows shares of Boeing being purchased using cash in the brokerage account. The second shows shares of Boeing being purchased using money from a checking account. The third shows shares of Boeing being sold with the sales proceeds going into the brokerage account as cash. The fourth shows the shares of Boeing being sold with the sales proceeds going into the checking account. A broker's dream come true.

Figure 11-17: Some examples of buy and sell transactions — a broker's dream come true.

Print/Acct	Edit	Shortcuts	Reports	Activities				F1-Help
Date	Action	Security	· Price	Shares	$ Amount	C	Cash Bal	
1/04 1994	Buy	Boeing	·35 5/8	3,000	107,325 00		892,675 00↑	
1/09 1994	BuyX	Boeing	·37 1/2	3,000	112,950 00		892,675 00	
1/09 1994	Sell	Boeing	·37 7/8	3,000	113,175 00		1005850 00	
1/12 1994	SellX Memo: Account:	Boeing [Checking]	·37 3/8	3,000 Comm/Fee: Xfer Amt:	111,625 00 500 00 111,625 00		1005850 00	
1/12 1994								

END

Brokerage   (Alt+letter accesses menu)   Ending Cash Bal: $1,005,850.00
Esc-Main Menu   Ctrl◄┘ Record   Ctrl-R Detail   Market Value: $1,743,350.00

Dividends, capital gains, and other goodies

This whole brokerage account cash business also comes into play when dealing with dividends and capital gains.

Whenever an investment action affects cash, Quicken needs to know whether the cash goes into (or, for that matter, comes out of) the brokerage account's cash or some other account, such as your checking account.

Actions indicating that cash goes into (or comes out of) some account other than the brokerage account cash end in *X*. Quicken, of course, also has equivalent actions indicating that the cash goes into or comes out of the brokerage account cash.

When you record dividends received on stock held in a brokerage account, you must specify where the dividend money ends up — in the brokerage account or some other account. To tell Quicken that your dividend money goes back into the brokerage account as cash, use the Div action. To indicate that your dividend money goes into some other account, use the DivX action; then specify the account.

The DivX action works for brokerage accounts like it works for mutual fund accounts. Remember, though, to specify the security on which you received the dividend check.

Capital gains distributions work the same way as dividends. Again, when you record these transactions, you need to tell Quicken where the money ends up. To indicate that your capital gains distribution money goes back into the brokerage account as cash, use either the CGLong (for long-term capital gains) or CGShort (for short-term capital gains) action. To indicate that your capital gains distribution goes someplace else, use either the CGLongX or CGShortX action; then tell Quicken into which account you put the money.

"I still don't get it — where's the cash?"

This brokerage account cash business usually boils down to a single burning question: Where does the cash go to or come from?

Don't panic, even if this stuff seems terribly confusing. Just put the book down and think about this question for a few minutes over the next day or so. I bet things will click for you, and suddenly the answers will seem crystal clear.

Some other not-so-tricky transactions

Surprise, surprise, Quicken lets you record other kinds of transactions in a brokerage account — but not just Reminder and Stock Split actions, like I described for mutual fund accounts. You can do a whole bunch of other things, too.

I briefly describe these other transactions here, illustrating them in Figure 11-18. The first transaction shown in Figure 11-18 is the purchase of some fictitious bonds.

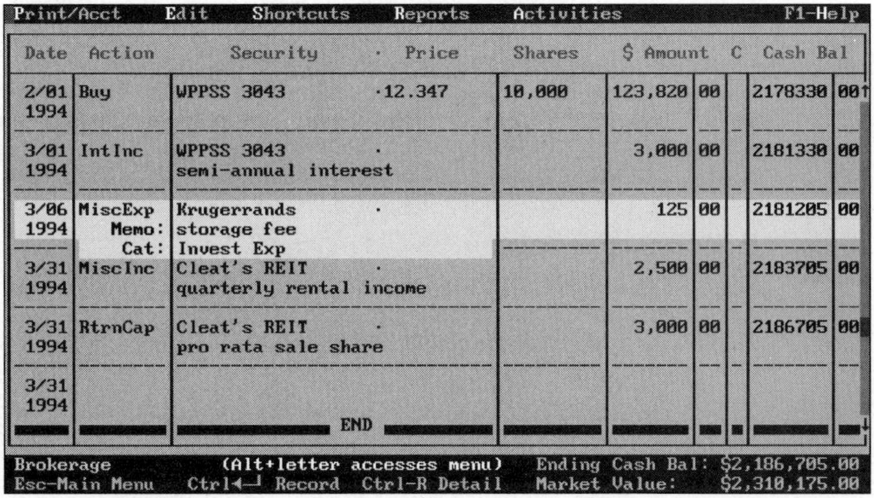
Print/Acct Edit Shortcuts Reports Activities F1-Help
Date Action Security Price Shares $ Amount C Cash Bal
2/01 1994 Buy WPPSS 3043 12.347 10,000 123,820 00 2178330 00
3/01 1994 IntInc WPPSS 3043 semi-annual interest 3,000 00 2181330 00
3/06 1994 MiscExp Krugerrands Memo: storage fee Cat: Invest Exp 125 00 2181205 00
3/31 1994 MiscInc Cleat's REIT quarterly rental income 2,500 00 2183705 00
3/31 1994 RtrnCap Cleat's REIT pro rata sale share 3,000 00 2186705 00
3/31 1994
END
Brokerage (Alt+letter accesses menu) Ending Cash Bal: $2,186,705.00
Esc-Main Menu Ctrl↵ Record Ctrl-R Detail Market Value: $2,310,175.00

Figure 11-18: The record of several transactions in a brokerage account. The first is . . . my word, it's a bond!

Recording interest income

To record interest income, use the Int Inc (Interest Income) action — which you should find after you select Interest from the main investment action list. This transaction is listed second in Figure 11-18.

By the way, you also use the Interest Income action for recording interest income on things like certificates of deposit (or other debt securities).

Are you on the margin?

The MargInt (Margin Interest) action records margin interest expense. You should find this action after you select Interest from the main investment action list.

I assume that if you're using margin, you're a smart cookie. You can figure out how to tell Quicken what it needs to know.

Oh, that's just a miscellaneous expense

Sometime, you may need to pay an expense. Although I've never seen this occur for a stock or bond, I must admit that my investing has been pretty conventional.

Expenses may crop up with mutual fund shares (which can be stored in a brokerage account), real estate partnership interests (which can be treated like common stock shares), or precious metal investments (which also can be treated like common stock shares).

If you need to pay some fee for account handling, for example, use the MiscExp (Miscellaneous Expense) action. If you do use this action, you need to categorize the expense using an expense category from your regular category list.

To use the MiscExp action, select the MiscExp option after you select Other Transactions from the main investment action list.

The third transaction listed in Figure 11-18 — the highlighted transaction — shows a miscellaneous expense associated with a fictitious Krugerrand investment. (Krugerrands are one-ounce South African gold coins.) Note the category, "Investment Expense."

Or how about some miscellaneous income?

No big surprise here. Quicken also provides a MiscInc (Miscellaneous Income) action, which works the same as the MiscExp action, except that you use it to record investment income that can't be recorded using one of the other investment income actions (dividends, interest income, or capital gains distributions).

I've seen this used most often relating to investments in things other than stocks or bonds. For example, if you invest in a real estate limited partnership, the quarterly distributions made by the general partner are neither interest nor dividends: they're rental income. When you use the MiscInc action, Quicken enables you to specify an income category for the transaction; so you can use an income category that you've set up to track rental income.

To use the MiscInc action, select the MiscInc option after you select Other Transactions from the main investment action list.

The fourth transaction in Figure 11-18 is a miscellaneous income transaction showing money that you might have received for your share of a real estate investment trust's quarterly net rental income.

A return of capital

I should touch on the old "return of capital" trick. Sometimes the money that you receive because you own a security isn't really income. Rather, it's a partial refund of the purchase price.

In my experience, you see this "return of capital" most often when you buy a mortgage-backed security — like a Ginnie Mae bond — where the mortgagee (the person who borrowed the mortgage money) pays not only periodic interest, but also a portion of the mortgage principal. Obviously, you shouldn't record the principal portion of any payment you receive as income. You should record this money instead as a mortgage principal reduction — a return of capital.

You also might see a return of capital transaction when the thing that you invested in starts liquidating and, as a result, returns money.

To record a return of capital action, select RtrnCap after you select Other
Transactions from the main investment action list. The fifth transaction shown
in Figure 11-18 shows a return of capital transaction.

Updating Securities Prices

Whether you're working with a mutual fund account or a brokerage account,
you can collect current market prices and then store this information with the
Quicken account information.

To do so, display the investment account with the mutual fund shares or the
securities that you want to update. Then, choose the **Update Prices** command
from the **Activities** menu. Quicken displays the Update Security Prices screen,
as shown in Figure 11-19.

```
 Print/Acct    View      Shortcuts     Reports    Activities              F1-Help
        Portfolio Update Prices for Brokerage as of 6/ 7/94
          Security      Type   Market   Shares     Market      Last      Chg
            Name               Price               Value       Price   Mkt Val
   ┌──────────────────┬───┬────────┬──────────┬────────────┬────────┬──────────┐
   │ UPPSS 3043       │Bon│12.347 *│ 10000.00 │ 123,470.00 │12.347  │          │
   │ Krugerrands      │Met│350    *│   100.00 │  35,000.00 │350     │          │
   │ Cleat's REIT     │Rea│1,000  *│   100.00 │ 100,000.00 │1,000   │          │
   │ Boeing           │Sto│37 3/8 *↓│    0.00 │            │37 3/8  │          │
   │ Gnarlywear, Inc. │Sto│13     *↑│    0.00 │            │13      │          │
   │ -Cash-           │   │         │          │ 2186705.00 │        │          │
   │                  │   │         │          │            │        │          │
   │                  │   │         │          │            │        │          │
   ├──────────────────┴───┴────────┴──────────┴────────────┴────────┴──────────┤
   │ Total Market Value                          2,445,175                      │
   └───────────────────────────────────────────────────────────────────────────┘
 Brokerage                           F8-Show Detail       F9-All Accounts
 Esc-Main Menu   Ctrl-B Buy  Ctrl-S Sell  Ctrl-N Reinvest  Ctrl-L Other Action
```

Figure 11-19:
The Portfolio
Update
Prices
screen.

To record the current market price for a security, highlight the security and
then enter the current price in the Market Price field.

After you update the market price for each security shown, choose View
Register from the View menu. Quicken displays a message, `OK to record
prices?`, and then shows what it thinks is the current date. If the date isn't
correct, fix it. Press Enter to remove the message and redisplay the register
screen. Quicken updates the total market value figure shown in the lower right
corner of the screen.

Some Quick Reminders

I'm sorry that this chapter has been so long. I have just a couple other things to tell you. You should find these tidbits helpful.

Adjusting your errors away

You can adjust the cash balance in a brokerage account and the shares balance in both mutual fund and brokerage accounts.

Oops, my brokerage cash balance is wrong

To adjust the cash balance in a brokerage account, select Adjust Balance from the Activities menu. From the Adjust Balance menu, choose the Cash Balance command.

Quicken lets you specify the correct cash balance and enter the date. Just fill in the fields and press Enter.

Quicken adds an adjustment transaction to the register to fix the cash balance. (If you add cash, Quicken uses the MiscInc action. If you subtract cash, Quicken uses the MiscExp action.)

Oops, my brokerage account shares are wrong

To adjust the shares balance for a security in a brokerage account, select Adjust Balance from the Activities menu. From the Adjust Balance menu, choose the Shares Balance command.

Quicken lets you specify the security, the correct shares balance, and the date as of which the figure you enter is correct. Fill in the fields and press Enter.

Quicken adds an adjustment transaction to the register to fix the shares balance. (Quicken uses the ShrsIn and ShrsOut actions.)

You can edit security names using the Security List. Choose the Security list command from the Shortcuts menu, highlight the security, and press Ctrl-E. Quicken displays a screen that you can use to change the security name.

Oops, my mutual fund shares are wrong

To adjust the shares balance for a mutual fund account, select Adjust Balance from the Activities menu.

Quicken lets you specify the correct shares balance and the date as of which the figure you enter is correct. Fill in the fields and press Enter. Quicken adds an adjustment transaction to the register to fix the shares balance for the mutual fund, using the ShrsIn and ShrsOut actions.

Reports

I just want to say one thing about Quicken reports as they relate to your investments: remember that they are there. If you need more information, see Chapter 5.

The Path Not Taken

Earlier in the chapter, I noted that there are two ways to track your investments. The register approach, which I describe fully, and the Portfolio approach.

If you yearn to use the Portfolio approach, read on. Although I won't go into detail, you should pick up everything you need to know.

Viewing a portfolio

With the portfolio approach, Quicken lets you look at your investments as a portfolio of securities. In other words, Quicken lumps all of a security's transactions together, and then it summarizes these transactions.

Figure 11-20 shows a Portfolio Details screen, which shows much of the same information I describe earlier in the chapter.

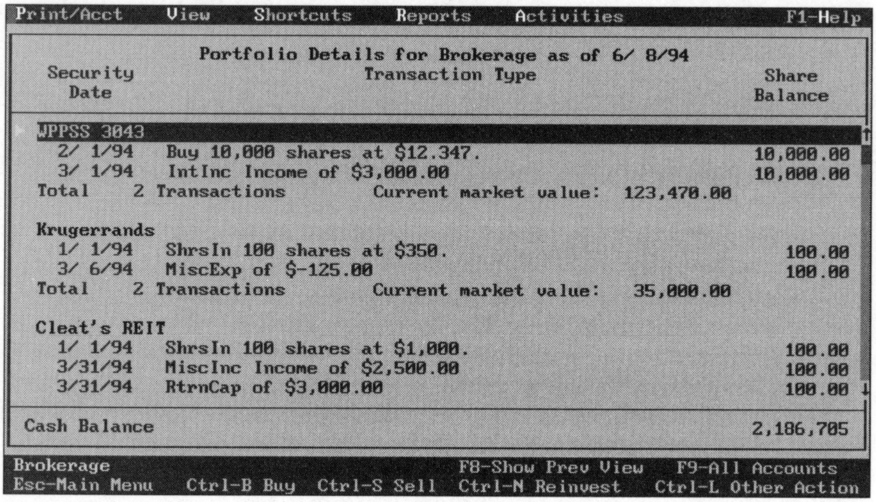

```
 Print/Acct    View     Shortcuts      Reports    Activities              F1-Help
┌──────────────────────────────────────────────────────────────────────────────┐
│                    Portfolio Details for Brokerage as of 6/ 8/94               │
│      Security                    Transaction Type                    Share     │
│      Date                                                            Balance    │
│                                                                                │
│ UPPSS 3043                                                                     │
│      2/ 1/94   Buy 10,000 shares at $12.347.                       10,000.00  │
│      3/ 1/94   IntInc Income of $3,000.00                          10,000.00  │
│   Total    2 Transactions          Current market value:  123,470.00          │
│                                                                                │
│   Krugerrands                                                                  │
│      1/ 1/94   ShrsIn 100 shares at $350.                             100.00  │
│      3/ 6/94   MiscExp of $-125.00                                    100.00  │
│   Total    2 Transactions          Current market value:   35,000.00          │
│                                                                                │
│   Cleat's REIT                                                                 │
│      1/ 1/94   ShrsIn 100 shares at $1,000.                           100.00  │
│      3/31/94   MiscInc Income of $2,500.00                            100.00  │
│      3/31/94   RtrnCap of $3,000.00                                   100.00  │
│                                                                                │
│ Cash Balance                                                        2,186,705  │
│                                                                                │
│ Brokerage                              F8-Show Prev View    F9-All Accounts    │
│ Esc-Main Menu   Ctrl-B Buy   Ctrl-S Sell  Ctrl-N Reinvest   Ctrl-L Other Action│
└──────────────────────────────────────────────────────────────────────────────┘
```

Figure 11-20: The Portfolio Details screen.

You don't have to view a portfolio at the detailed level shown in Figure 11-20. You also can use the **V**iew menu commands **H**oldings, **P**erformance, **V**aluation, Update Prices, **S**ummary, **G**ains, and **D**etail to slice, dice, and summarize the information in all kinds of different ways.

I could provide an extensive (and boring) description of all the nuances of these views. But I don't want to inundate you with largely useless and easily forgotten information. If you want, go ahead and fool around with the different views; you may find some of them helpful.

Recording transactions

So you want to use the Portfolio method to record transactions.

You need to display screens — let's call them *transaction screens* — that collect the same information that you normally enter into the investment register. Press Ctrl-B to display the transaction screen for buy transactions, Ctrl-S to display the transaction screen for sell transactions, and Ctrl-N to display the transaction screen for reinvestment transactions. (To record some other transaction, press Ctrl-L to display the complete list of investment actions. After you choose an action, Quicken displays a transaction screen that collects the necessary information.)

Quicken uses the information that you enter into a transaction screen to record a transaction into the investment account register. In effect, when you use a transaction screen, you get Quicken to record the transaction into the register. (By the way, you can see the investment register any time by choosing the View **R**egister command from the **V**iew menu. To flip back to the Portfolio Details screen, press Ctrl-R.)

If you want to edit or delete a portfolio transaction or security, first select it on the Portfolio Details screen. Then choose either the **E**dit Security/Trans command or the **D**elete Security/Trans command from the **S**hortcuts menu. (You also can edit the security or transaction from the Register screen, too.)

Portfolio tools

If you work with a portfolio view, you can use some other commands. For example, you can chart securities prices with the **G**raph Price History command from the **S**hortcuts menu. You can combine securities with the same stock symbol in a portfolio, using the **M**erge Sec Symbol command from the **V**iew menu.

If you're turned on by this portfolio view business, start noodling around with these other commands. They aren't difficult to use.

Part IV
Serious Business

In this part...

*I*f you use Quicken in a business, you'll find it helpful to get some information about how to use it for payroll, customer receivables, and vendor payables. Sure, you could learn these things by sitting down with your certified public accountant, having a cup of coffee, and paying about $100-an-hour.

Or you can read on, pretend we're chitchatting over coffee, and save the $100.

Chapter 12
Payroll

●●

In This Chapter
▶ Creating payroll categories and accounts
▶ Getting an Employer ID Number
▶ Finding social security, medicare, and federal income tax withholding information
▶ Calculating gross wages, payroll deductions, and net wages
▶ Recording payroll checks
▶ Making federal tax deposits
▶ Filing quarterly and annual payroll tax returns
▶ Producing W-2s and other annual wage statements
▶ Handling state payroll taxes

●●

*M*any businesses use Quicken. Many of these businesses have employees. Many employees want to be paid on a regular basis. Methinks, therefore, that many people in business may find this chapter about using Quicken to prepare employee payroll checks helpful.

Setting Up Payroll

To prepare payroll checks and summarize payroll information, you must set up some special accounts and categories, and you must prepare quarterly and annual returns.

You can set up the special payroll accounts and categories yourself — unfortunately, this work is terribly complicated. Because I'm basically a lazy person, I recommend telling Quicken to take care of these accounts and categories.

Preparing Quicken to handle payroll

Do the following to get Quicken ready for payroll processing:

1. Select Use Tutorials/Assistants from the Main Menu.

Quicken displays the Use Tutorials/Assistants menu shown in Figure 12-1.

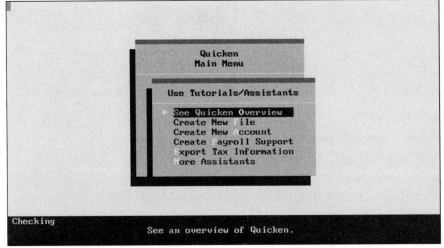

Figure 12-1:
The Use
Tutorials/
Assistants
menu.

2. Choose the Create Payroll Support command from the Use Tutorials/ Assistants menu.

3. Press Enter.

Quicken then asks you to enter your state's postal abbreviation.

4. Type the abbreviation for your state and then press Enter.

If you don't know your state's postal abbreviation, press Enter. Quicken lists the states and their abbreviations. Use the arrow keys to highlight your state and then press Enter.

You're done. Quicken now feverishly creates the liability accounts and categories that you need to track the wages you pay employees and the payroll taxes you withhold and owe. A *liability account* is a Quicken account that keeps track of some debt you owe — in this case, payroll tax money you owe the government.

QuickPay

Intuit provides a software program called QuickPay that works with Quicken to calculate gross wages, federal and state income taxes, and social security and Medicare taxes. I don't think that QuickPay is necessary (or even all that handy) if you have just one or two employees who are always paid the same amount. If your only employee is a nanny or a secretary who is paid a straight salary, for example, you won't save time by using QuickPay.

If you have a few employees, though, and they're paid an hourly rate and work different numbers of hours every week, I suggest buying QuickPay to simplify your financial life and your payroll bookkeeping. In this case, you should find QuickPay invaluable — certainly well worth the $50 or so that Intuit charges. And no, I don't earn a sales commission if you buy more software from Intuit.

Getting the tax stuff right

You need to do a couple other things to process payroll correctly.

Requesting (or demanding) an Employer ID Number

First, file a Request For Employer Identification Number form, or an SS-4, with the Internal Revenue Service (IRS). To get a copy of an SS-4, call the IRS and ask for one. Or call a friend who's an accountant. (See, there *is* a reason to invite people like me to your dinner parties.)

Although the IRS now lets you apply for and receive an Employer ID Number over the telephone (a very cool move by the IRS), you still need to fill out an SS-4 form so that you can answer the IRS's questions. (You also need to mail or fax the form to the IRS after your phone conversation.)

Withholding federal income, social security, and medicare taxes

Before you can handle federal income, social security, and medicare taxes, your employees must fill out W-4 forms, which tell you their filing status and how many personal exemptions they want to claim.

Guess where you get blank W-4 forms . . . that's right, from your friendly IRS agent.

You also need a *Circular E Employer's Tax Guide,* which tells you how much you should withhold in federal income, social security, and medicare taxes. You also can get this pamphlet by calling the IRS. (*Note:* There are additional federal and state forms you need to fill out to satisfy the government requirements for hiring employees.)

Paying Someone for a Job Well Done

After Quicken prepares the special accounts and categories and you collect the necessary tax information, you're ready to pay your employees.

Calculating gross wages

If Betty earns $14 an hour and she worked 40 hours this week, you owe her $560. If Joe's salary is $400 per week, you owe him $400. Pretty easy, huh?

All that deduction stuff

To figure out how much Big Brother says you must withhold, check the tables in the *Circular E Employer's Tax Guide*.

If Betty is single and claims just one personal exemption, for example, you would check the *Circular E* table shown in Figure 12-2. I've circled the amount ($89) that she must pay in federal income taxes.

SINGLE Persons–WEEKLY Payroll Period
(For Wages Paid After December 1990)

At least	But less than	0	1	2	3	4	5	6	7	8	9	10
$540	$550	$95	$83	$72	$60	$53	$47	$41	$35	$29	$22	$16
550	560	98	86	75	63	55	49	42	36	30	24	18
560	570	101	89	77	66	56	50	44	38	32	25	19
570	580	103	92	80	69	58	52	45	39	33	27	21
580	590	106	95	83	71	60	53	47	41	35	28	22
590	600	109	97	86	74	63	55	48	42	36	30	24
600	610	112	100	89	77	65	56	50	44	38	31	25
610	620	115	103	91	80	68	58	51	45	39	33	27
620	630	117	106	94	83	71	60	53	47	41	34	28
630	640	120	109	97	85	74	62	54	48	42	36	30
640	650	123	111	100	88	77	65	56	50	44	37	31
650	660	126	114	103	91	79	68	57	51	45	39	33
660	670	129	117	105	94	82	71	59	53	47	40	34
670	680	131	120	108	97	85	74	62	54	48	42	36
680	690	134	123	111	99	88	76	65	56	50	43	37
690	700	137	125	114	102	91	79	68	57	51	45	39
700	710	140	128	117	105	93	82	70	59	53	46	40
710	720	143	131	119	108	96	85	73	62	54	48	42
720	730	145	134	122	111	99	88	76	64	56	49	43
730	740	148	137	125	113	102	90	79	67	57	51	45
740	750	151	139	128	116	105	93	82	70	59	52	46
750	760	154	142	131	119	107	96	84	73	61	54	48
760	770	157	145	133	122	110	99	87	76	64	55	49
770	780	159	148	136	125	113	102	90	78	67	57	51
780	790	162	151	139	127	116	104	93	81	70	58	52
790	800	165	153	142	130	119	107	96	84	72	61	54
800	810	168	156	145	133	121	110	98	87	75	64	55
810	820	171	159	147	136	124	113	101	90	78	66	57
820	830	173	162	150	139	127	116	104	92	81	69	58
830	840	176	165	153	141	130	118	107	95	84	72	60
840	850	179	167	156	144	133	121	110	98	86	75	63
850	860	182	170	159	147	135	124	112	101	89	78	66
860	870	185	173	161	150	138	127	115	104	92	80	69
870	880	187	176	164	153	141	130	118	106	95	83	72
880	890	190	179	167	155	144	132	121	109	98	86	74
890	900	193	181	170	158	147	135	124	112	100	89	77
900	910	196	184	173	161	149	138	126	115	103	92	80
910	920	199	187	175	164	152	141	129	118	106	94	83
920	930	201	190	178	167	155	144	132	120	109	97	86
930	940	204	193	181	169	158	146	135	123	112	100	88
940	950	207	195	184	172	161	149	138	126	114	103	91
950	960	210	198	187	175	163	152	140	129	117	106	94
960	970	213	201	189	178	166	155	143	132	120	108	97
970	980	215	204	192	181	169	158	146	134	123	111	100
980	990	219	207	195	183	172	160	149	137	126	114	102
990	1,000	222	209	198	186	175	163	152	140	128	117	105
1,000	1,010	225	212	201	189	177	166	154	143	131	120	108
1,010	1,020	228	215	203	192	180	169	157	146	134	122	111
1,020	1,030	231	218	206	195	183	172	160	148	137	125	114
1,030	1,040	234	221	209	197	186	174	163	151	140	128	116
1,040	1,050	237	224	212	200	189	177	166	154	142	131	119
1,050	1,060	240	227	215	203	191	180	168	157	145	134	122
1,060	1,070	243	231	218	205	194	183	171	160	148	136	125
1,070	1,080	246	234	221	209	197	186	174	162	151	139	128
1,080	1,090	250	237	224	211	200	188	177	165	154	142	130
1,090	1,100	253	240	227	214	203	191	180	168	156	145	133
1,100	1,110	256	243	230	217	205	194	182	171	159	148	136
1,110	1,120	259	246	233	220	208	197	185	174	162	150	139
1,120	1,130	262	249	236	224	211	200	188	176	165	153	142
1,130	1,140	265	252	239	227	214	202	191	179	168	156	144
1,140	1,150	268	255	243	230	217	205	194	182	170	159	147
1,150	1,160	271	258	246	233	220	208	196	185	173	162	150
1,160	1,170	274	261	249	236	223	211	199	188	176	164	153
1,170	1,180	277	265	252	239	226	214	202	190	179	167	156
1,180	1,190	281	268	255	242	229	216	205	193	182	170	158

$1,190 and over — Use Table 1(a) for a **SINGLE** person on page 22. Also see the instructions on page 20.

Page 25

Figure 12-2: Betty's federal withholding.

And Joe? If his filing status is married filing jointly and he claims three personal exemptions, you would flip to the *Circular E* page shown in Figure 12-3. Again, I circled the amount you should withhold.

MARRIED Persons—WEEKLY Payroll Period
(For Wages Paid After December 1990)

At least	But less than	0	1	2	3	4	5	6	7	8	9	10
$0	$70	$0	$0	$0	$0	$0	$0	$0	$0	$0	$0	$0
70	75	1	0	0	0	0	0	0	0	0	0	0
75	80	1	0	0	0	0	0	0	0	0	0	0
80	85	2	0	0	0	0	0	0	0	0	0	0
85	90	3	0	0	0	0	0	0	0	0	0	0
90	95	4	0	0	0	0	0	0	0	0	0	0
95	100	4	0	0	0	0	0	0	0	0	0	0
100	105	5	0	0	0	0	0	0	0	0	0	0
105	110	6	0	0	0	0	0	0	0	0	0	0
110	115	7	0	0	0	0	0	0	0	0	0	0
115	120	7	1	0	0	0	0	0	0	0	0	0
120	125	8	2	0	0	0	0	0	0	0	0	0
125	130	9	3	0	0	0	0	0	0	0	0	0
130	135	10	3	0	0	0	0	0	0	0	0	0
135	140	10	4	0	0	0	0	0	0	0	0	0
140	145	11	5	0	0	0	0	0	0	0	0	0
145	150	12	6	0	0	0	0	0	0	0	0	0
150	155	13	6	0	0	0	0	0	0	0	0	0
155	160	13	7	1	0	0	0	0	0	0	0	0
160	165	14	8	2	0	0	0	0	0	0	0	0
165	170	15	9	2	0	0	0	0	0	0	0	0
170	175	16	9	3	0	0	0	0	0	0	0	0
175	180	16	10	4	0	0	0	0	0	0	0	0
180	185	17	11	5	0	0	0	0	0	0	0	0
185	190	18	12	5	0	0	0	0	0	0	0	0
190	195	19	12	6	0	0	0	0	0	0	0	0
195	200	19	13	7	1	0	0	0	0	0	0	0
200	210	21	14	8	2	0	0	0	0	0	0	0
210	220	22	16	10	3	0	0	0	0	0	0	0
220	230	24	17	11	5	0	0	0	0	0	0	0
230	240	25	19	13	6	0	0	0	0	0	0	0
240	250	27	20	14	8	2	0	0	0	0	0	0
250	260	28	22	16	9	3	0	0	0	0	0	0
260	270	30	23	17	11	5	0	0	0	0	0	0
270	280	31	25	19	12	6	0	0	0	0	0	0
280	290	33	26	20	14	8	2	0	0	0	0	0
290	300	34	28	22	15	9	3	0	0	0	0	0
300	310	36	29	23	17	11	5	0	0	0	0	0
310	320	37	31	25	18	12	6	0	0	0	0	0
320	330	39	32	26	20	14	8	1	0	0	0	0
330	340	40	34	28	21	15	9	3	0	0	0	0
340	350	42	35	29	23	17	11	4	0	0	0	0
350	360	43	37	31	24	18	12	6	0	0	0	0
360	370	45	38	32	26	20	14	7	1	0	0	0
370	380	46	40	34	27	21	15	9	3	0	0	0
380	390	48	41	35	29	23	17	10	4	0	0	0
390	400	49	43	37	30	24	18	12	6	0	0	0
400	410	51	44	38	32	26	20	13	7	1	0	0
410	420	52	46	40	33	27	21	15	9	2	0	0
420	430	54	47	41	35	29	23	16	10	4	0	0
430	440	55	49	43	36	30	24	18	12	5	0	0
440	450	57	50	44	38	32	26	19	13	7	1	0
450	460	58	52	46	39	33	27	21	15	8	2	0
460	470	60	53	47	41	35	29	22	16	10	4	0
470	480	61	55	49	42	36	30	24	18	11	5	0
480	490	63	56	50	44	38	32	25	19	13	7	0
490	500	64	58	52	45	39	33	27	21	14	8	2
500	510	66	59	53	47	41	35	28	22	16	10	3
510	520	67	61	55	48	42	36	30	24	17	11	5
520	530	69	62	56	50	44	38	31	25	19	13	6
530	540	70	64	58	51	45	39	33	27	20	14	8
540	550	72	65	59	53	47	41	34	28	22	16	9
550	560	73	67	61	54	48	42	36	30	23	17	11
560	570	75	68	62	56	50	44	37	31	25	19	12
570	580	76	70	64	57	51	45	39	33	26	20	14
580	590	78	71	65	59	53	47	40	34	28	22	15
590	600	79	73	67	60	54	48	42	36	29	23	17
600	610	81	74	68	62	56	50	43	37	31	25	18
610	620	82	76	70	63	57	51	45	39	32	26	20
620	630	84	77	71	65	59	53	46	40	34	28	21

(Continued on next page)

Figure 12-3:
Joe's tax
deduction.

Always use up-to-date information. Federal income tax withholding changes annually, so don't use the tables shown in Figures 12-2 and 12-3.

Figure social security and medicare taxes by multiplying the gross wage figure by a set percentage. Social security equals 6.2 percent of the gross wages up to a specified limit — roughly $60,000 in 1994. Medicare equals 1.45 percent of the gross wages up to a specified limit — roughly $130,000 in 1994. Be sure to check your faithful *Circular E* or call the local IRS office if you think these limits come into play for a particular employee. (By the time you read this book, though, medicare taxes may be calculated on *all* of a person's gross wages.)

Determining net wages

To determine net wages, subtract federal income tax, social security, and Medicare from the gross wages (see Table 12-1).

Table 12-1	Payday Calculations		
	Betty	*Joe*	*Explanation*
Gross Wages	$560.00	$400.00	Their pay
Withholding	$89.00	$32.00	From *Circular E*
Social Security	$34.72	$24.80	6.2% of gross wages
Medicare	$8.12	$5.80	1.45% of gross wages
Net Wages	$428.16	$337.40	Take-home pay

If Table 12-1 doesn't make sense to you, take another look at Figures 12-2 and 12-3 and then reread the previous sections about deductions. In the table, I try to show how Betty's and Joe's gross pay are nickel-and-dimed by the government.

Other taxes and deductions

If you understand how federal income, social security, and medicare taxes work, you shouldn't have a problem working with any other taxes.

State income tax withholding, for example, works like federal income tax withholding. (You need to get the state equivalent of *Circular E,* of course.)

In general, treat other taxes and amounts paid by the employee similarly. In fact, you only really have to worry about things that affect employees' gross pay for income taxes but not for social security taxes — such as 401(k) deductions and certain fringe benefits. If you need help dealing with these kinds of things, ask your accountant. (This stuff is just too difficult; there's no way for me to provide general answers that work for everyone. Sorry.)

Recording a payroll check

After you calculate the net wages, you're ready to record the check. This process is a little bit complicated, but stick with me, partner, and you should zip through it in no time.

If Betty and Joe are milling around your computer, asking "Gee, Boss, how much longer? I want to get to the bank before it closes," tell 'em to cool their heels for three minutes.

Suppose that you want to record the check by using the Register screen. (You record the check in the Write Checks screen in basically the same way. If you use the Write Checks screen, though, you're ready from the start to print the payroll check.) After you highlight the first empty field in the register, follow these steps:

1. **Enter the date of the payroll check in the Date field.**

2. **Enter the payroll check number in the Num field.**

3. **Type the employee's name in the Payee field.**

4. **Enter the net wages amount in the Payment field.**

5. **Press Ctrl-S to open the Split Transactions screen.**

6. **Enter the gross wages amount in the first field of the Split Transaction screen.**

   The category should be Payroll:Gross.

7. **Enter the amount withheld in social security taxes in the second field of the Split Transaction screen.**

   Instead of a category, use the liability account [Payroll-FICA]. The social security tax withheld should be 6.2 percent of the gross wages.

8. **Enter the amount withheld in medicare taxes in the third field of the Split Transaction screen.**

   Instead of a category, use the liability account [Payroll-MCARE]. The medicare tax withheld should be 1.45 percent of the employee's gross wages.

9. **Enter the amount of federal income taxes withheld in the fourth field of the Split Transaction screen.**

   Instead of a category, use the liability account [Payroll-FWH].

The Split Transaction screen shown in Figure 12-4 illustrates how Quicken records Joe's $400 gross wages, the taxes withheld, and his $337.40 net wages.

If you get extra split lines that shouldn't be there, you can delete them by pressing Ctrl-D.

10. (Optional) If you plan to print this check on a payroll check form that has a remittance advice or payroll stub, press PgDn three times.

Only the first 16 lines of the Split Transaction screen print on a payroll stub. If you use lines 17 and higher for the employer portions of the payroll tax, you won't confuse employees about employee versus employer payroll taxes. If you want to confuse your employees, of course, go ahead and enter all the payroll tax stuff together. Then, to be mean, hide when they come looking for you for an explanation. (I'm just joking about the hiding part.)

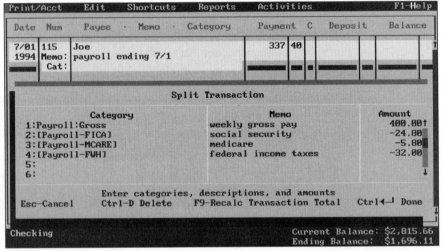

Figure 12-4:
The Split Transaction screen recording Joe's gross wages and $337.40 payroll check.

11. Enter the employer's matching share of social security in the next two empty fields of the Split Transaction screen.

If the employee pays $24.80 to social security, for example, use the first empty field to enter $24.80 of expense categorized to the Payroll:Comp FICA expense category. Then use the second empty field to record $24.80 of payroll FICA tax liability using the [Payroll-FICA] account.

12. Enter the employer's matching share of Medicare in the next two empty fields of the Split Transaction screen.

If the employee pays $5.80 to Medicare, for example, use the first empty field to enter $5.80 of expense categorized to the Payroll:Comp MCARE expense category. Then use the second empty field to record $5.80 of payroll FICA tax liability using the [Payroll-MCARE] account. (Refer to Figure 12-5 for this split transaction information.)

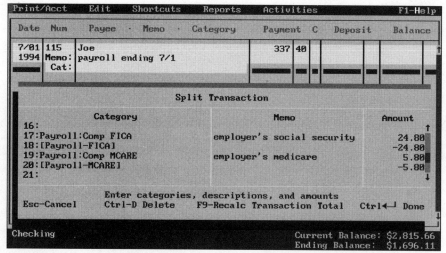

Figure 12-5: The employer's matching share of social security and medicare taxes.

The accounts that you use to show the payroll taxes withheld and owed are liability accounts. The balances of these accounts tell you how much you owe the government.

13. **If you have any other employer-paid payroll taxes, record them following in the next empty fields.**

    You can use this same basic approach to record federal and state unemployment taxes.

14. **Press Ctrl-Enter to close the Split Transaction screen.**

15. **To record the payroll check and related employer-paid payroll tax information, press Ctrl-Enter again.**

Making Tax Deposits

Make no mistake: Big Brother wants the tax money you withhold from an employee payroll check. Big Brother also wants the payroll taxes you owe — the matching social security and medicare taxes, the federal unemployment taxes, and so on.

Every so often, then, you need to pay Big Brother the taxes you owe.

This process is really simple. Just write a check payable to the Internal Revenue Service for the balances of your payroll tax liability accounts. If you made out only the one check to Joe, for example, your payroll liability accounts would show the balances listed in Table 12-2.

Table 12-2	What you owe Big Brother
Liability Account	*Balance*
Payroll-FICA	$49.60
Payroll-MCARE	$11.60
Payroll-FWH	$32.00
Total	$93.20

The balances in the Payroll-FICA and Payroll-MCARE accounts include both the employee's and the employer's taxes.

When you write a check for the $93.20 you owe (see Figure 12-6), you actually transfer the check amount to the payroll liability accounts rather than assign the check amount to a payroll tax category. In effect, to pay your payroll taxes, you transfer money from your checking account to the government.

The first time you see this kind of transfer, it might confuse you. Take a minute to think about this. After you write the check to the government, you neither have the money in your checking account nor owe the government money any longer. The checking account and the liability account then balance, and both need to be decreased. In Quicken, you decrease account balances by using an account transfer.

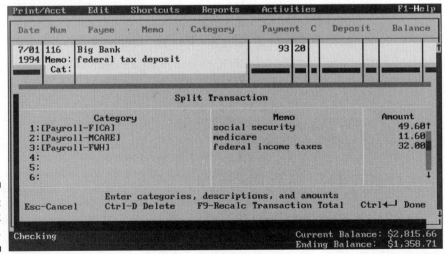

Figure 12-6:
The check to the IRS.

When do you make payroll tax deposits? It all depends on how much you owe. As I'm writing this, if you owe less than $500, you can wait until the end of the quarter. In this case, you make your deposit when you file your quarterly payroll tax return. This is called the De Minimis rule. I think the rule gets its name from the Congresswoman who created it, Dee Minimis. But, I'm not sure about this. It may also be because De Minimis is Latin for, basically, "itsy-bitsy."

If you owe $500 or more, you need to pay the money more quickly. How quickly depends on things like how much you've historically paid and how much you owe. There are several nuances to these rules, so consult a tax advisor. Or call the Internal Revenue Service.

To make a payroll tax deposit, just mail your check along with a federal tax deposit coupon (Form 8109) to a financial institution that's qualified as a federal tax depository or to the Federal Reserve bank that serves your area. Because you requested an Employer ID Number, the IRS should have sent you a book of coupons already. Make your check payable to the depository or the Federal Reserve.

Filing Quarterly Payroll Tax Returns

At the end of every quarter, you must file a quarterly payroll tax return. (By the way, I mean calendar quarters. You don't do file returns four times each Sunday afternoon as you and your couch-potato spouse watch football.)

If you own a business, for example, you need to file a Form 941 (Employee's Quarterly Federal Tax Return), which reveals how much you've paid in gross wages, withheld in federal taxes, and owe in payroll taxes. If you don't own a business but employ household employees — such as a nanny — you need to file a Form 942. Like Form 941, this form reveals how much you've paid in gross wages, withheld in federal taxes, and owe in payroll taxes (All these numbered forms make me feel like I'm watching a rerun of "Adam 12": *"One Adam 12, One Adam 12. . . . Do you copy? . . . We've got a 941 in progress. . . . Backup units on the way. . . . Officer requests assistance."*)

It's pretty darn easy to fill out these forms. You just need to know the gross wages totals.

To get the gross wages totals and the balances for each payroll tax liability account, print a Business Payroll report:

1. Display the Reports menu.

Choose the Create Reports command from the Main Menu, or select the **R**eports menu from the Register screen or Write Checks screen.

2. Choose the Business Reports command.

Quicken displays the Business Reports menu.

3. Choose the Payroll Report command.

Quicken displays the Payroll Report screen.

4. Choose the Print Report command from the File menu.

Quicken produces a report like the one shown in Figure 12-7.

Use the Payroll Report information to fill out your quarterly payroll tax return. Use either the 941 or the 942 to tell the IRS how much you paid, how much you withheld, how much you owe in social security and medicare taxes (combining both the employer's and the employee's), and which federal tax deposits you've made.

The Compensation to employee total should equal all your employees' gross wages; your employer payroll taxes are calculated based on this figure.

The company FICA and medicare contributions are the amounts that you've recorded to date for the employer social security and medicare taxes, so you need to double these figures to determine the actual social security and medicare taxes you owe.

The Total Transfers from the Payroll liability accounts represent the federal tax deposits you paid.

By the way, if your accountant fills out the 941 or 942, you didn't need to read this stuff. Accountants usually don't have any problem completing the quarterly payroll tax return. In fact — and I kid you not — they usually enjoy it.

Figure 12-7:
The Payroll
Report
screen.

```
                                          PAYROLL REPORT
                                       7/ 1/94 Through 9/30/94
  All Accounts                                                                           Page 1
  6/ 8/94
                                                                              OVERALL
                      Category Description        Joe          Big Bank         TOTAL

   INCOME/EXPENSE
     EXPENSES
       Payroll transaction:
         Company FICA contribution       24.80           0.00           24.80
         Company Medicare contrib         5.80           0.00            5.80
         Compensation to employee       400.00           0.00          400.00
                                        --------        --------       --------
       Total Payroll transaction        430.60           0.00          430.60

     TOTAL EXPENSES                      430.60           0.00          430.60
                                        --------        --------       --------

   TOTAL INCOME/EXPENSE                 -430.60           0.00         -430.60

   TRANSFERS
     TO Payroll-FICA                      0.00          -49.60          -49.60
     TO Payroll-FWH                       0.00          -32.00          -32.00
     TO Payroll-MCARE                     0.00          -11.60          -11.60
     FROM Payroll-FICA                   49.60           0.00           49.60
     FROM Payroll-FWH                    32.00           0.00           32.00
     FROM Payroll-MCARE                  11.60           0.00           11.60
                                        --------        --------       --------
   TOTAL TRANSFERS                       93.20          -93.20           0.00

   OVERALL TOTAL                        -337.40         -93.20         -430.60
                                        ========        ========       ========
```

Those Pesky Annual Returns and Wage Statements

At the end of the year, you need to file some annual returns — such as the 940 federal unemployment tax return — and the W-2 and W-3 wages statements.

The 940 annual return is darn easy if you've wrestled with 941 or 942 quarterly returns. The 940 works the same as those more difficult quarterly tax returns. You print the ol' Payroll report, enter a few numbers, and then write a check for the amount you owe.

To fill out the W-2s and the W-3 (which summarizes your W-2s), print the Payroll report. Then, carefully following directions, enter the gross wages, social security and medicare taxes withheld, and federal income taxes withheld in the appropriate blanks. If you have a little trouble, call the IRS. If you have a lot of trouble, splurge and pay someone else to fill out the forms for you. Any experienced bookkeeper can do it for you.

Don't worry if this payroll taxes business seems terribly complicated. Payroll accounting isn't easy for everyone. If you think numbers are your friend, though, you should have no trouble at all after you learn the ropes.

Doing the State Payroll Taxes Thing

I haven't talked about state payroll taxes, yet — at least not in any detail. I wish I could provide you with detailed, state-specific help. Unfortunately, doing so would make this chapter about 150 pages long and cause me to go stark, raving mad.

You will need to prepare any state unemployment annual summary before preparing the 940 because the 940 may require information from the state returns.

You still need to deal with state payroll taxes, though. Luckily, the basic mechanics are the same for federal and state payroll taxes. (Quicken does create a state withholding liability account: [Payroll-SWHWA] for the Payroll State WithHolding for WAshington, [Payroll-SWHCA] for Payroll State WithHolding for CAlifornia, and so on.) Employer-paid state unemployment taxes are similar to employer-paid federal taxes. Employee-paid state taxes work like employee-paid social security and medicare taxes.

If you understand how federal payroll taxes work in Quicken, you really shouldn't have a problem with state payroll taxes.

Hey, When Is Payday?

Quicken includes a **Calendar** command in the **Activities** menu. For the most part, I think the calendar is a blatant marketing feature — a bell or whistle that's used to raise the ante in the software poker game. (*Oh, a new financial planner? I'll raise you one calendar. There. Beat that.*) Nonetheless, the calendar can come in darn handy when doing payroll: it will notify you when payroll tasks need to be completed. Payday. Quarterly returns. Annual wage statements. You get the idea.

Remembering payday

Your employees, of course, will remember payday. And unless they are very timid, you can rely on them to remind you that they need to be paid. If you don't want to rely on them, however, you can schedule payroll transactions so that they appear on the calendar. Quicken tells you, "Betty and Joe want their money. Now." (Actually, Quicken is much more polite.)

To schedule a payroll transaction — such as an employee's weekly payroll check — here's what you do:

1. **Choose the Scheduled Transaction command from the Shortcuts menu.**

   Quicken displays the Scheduled Transaction List screen (see Figure 12-8).

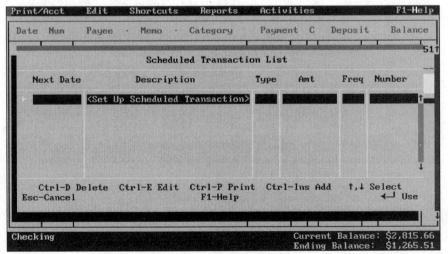

Figure 12-8:
The
Scheduled
Transaction
List screen.

2. Select <Set Up Scheduled Transaction>.

Here's a fun way to do this: go into the bathroom, take all your clothes off, put them on again inside out, come back to your desk, and then press Home and Enter. Yeah. Quicken displays the Set Up Scheduled Transaction screen shown in Figure 12-9.

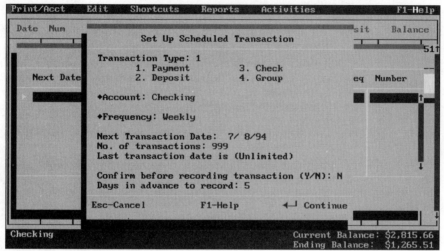

Figure 12-9:
The Set Up
Scheduled
Transaction
screen.

```
 Print/Acct    Edit    Shortcuts    Reports    Activities         F1-Help
  Date  Num  ░░░░░░░░░░░░░░░░░░░░░░░░░░░░░░░░░░░░░░░░░░░░░░░░sit    Balance
            ┌───────────────────────────────────────────────┐         51↑
            │            Set Up Scheduled Transaction        │
            │   Transaction Type: 1                          │
            │          1. Payment        3. Check            │
   Next Date│          2. Deposit        4. Group            │eq   Number
            │                                                │           ↑
          ► │   ◆Account: Checking                           │
            │                                                │
            │   ◆Frequency: Weekly                           │
            │                                                │
            │   Next Transaction Date:  7/ 8/94              │
            │   No. of transactions: 999                     │
            │   Last transaction date is (Unlimited)         │
            │                                                │
            │   Confirm before recording transaction (Y/N): N│
            │   Days in advance to record: 5                 │  ↓
            │                                                │
            │   Esc─Cancel         F1─Help       ◄─┘ Continue│
            └───────────────────────────────────────────────┘
  Checking                                Current Balance: $2,815.66
                                          Ending Balance:  $1,265.51
```

3. Move the cursor to the Transaction Type field and tell Quicken which kind of transaction you want to enter.

In the case of a payroll check, press either 1 for Payment (for a hand-written check) or 3 for Check (for a computer-printed check). You can set up other kinds of scheduled transactions, but I don't think you need to worry about them. Why make your life more complicated?

4. Tell Quicken where you want the transaction recorded.

After you move the cursor to the Account field, press Ctrl-L, and Quicken displays a list of accounts. Just highlight the account where you want Quicken to record the transaction and press Enter.

5. Indicate how often Quicken should record the transaction.

After you move the cursor to the Frequency field, press Ctrl-L. Quicken displays a list of frequencies: Weekly, Every two weeks, Twice a month, and so on. Highlight how often you want to record the transaction and press Enter. If you're setting up a weekly payroll check payment, for example, select Weekly.

6. Tell Quicken when to schedule the next transaction.

Move the cursor to the Next Transaction Date field and enter a date.

7. (Optional) Tell Quicken when to stop scheduling these transactions.

In the case of an employee's payroll check, you may not know a definite termination date. Shoot, Betty's been with you for years. And Joe? Well, he's got three young children. In the case of a regular transaction that has an end — lease payments, for example — you can enter the number of transactions in the No. of Transactions field. When there's no definite limit, type **999**.

8. Indicate whether you want Quicken to automatically record the transaction in the account's register.

If you want Quicken to record the transaction into the account's register without asking you first, move the cursor to the Confirm Before Recording Transaction field and press N. If you want Quicken to ask you to confirm that the scheduled transaction should be entered, move the cursor to the Confirm Before Recording Transaction field and press Y.

9. Indicate how many days in advance you want to be reminded.

Although the default is five days, I don't think that makes much sense for weekly payroll. Instead, you may want to be reminded the day before Betty and Joe are supposed to get their checks.

10. Press Enter.

Quicken displays the Scheduled Payment Transaction screen (see Figure 12-10).

11. Describe the payroll transaction.

Fill out the fields shown on-screen. When you're done, press F10.

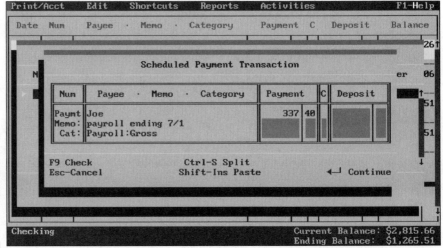

Figure 12-10:
The
Scheduled
Payment
Transaction
screen.

Here's a cool thing that happens if you've previously processed payroll for Betty: when you start typing **Betty** on the Scheduled Payment Transaction screen, QuickFill fills in all the fields with the payroll information from the last check you wrote to her.

OK, you're finished. From now on, Quicken automatically records the transaction for you at the appropriate time — the next scheduled date. Or if you said, "Check with me first," Quicken asks you to confirm the scheduled transaction before it actually enters the transaction in the register. Pretty cool, huh?

Reviewing the calendar

You can look at your scheduled transactions by checking the Scheduled Transactions List screen (see Figure 12-8). You also can look at the calendar to see when you have scheduled transactions. To view the calendar, choose the Calendar command from the Activities menu.

In a strange twist of fate, Figure 12-11 just happens to show the Calendar screen. Press PgUp and PgDn to move backward and forward a month at a time.

If you look closely at the Friday dates, you should see a letter T on each. This mark tells you that you have scheduled transactions on those dates.

Suppose that you can't remember what a particular scheduled transaction is. Further, suppose that Betty and Joe are too shy to tell you that it's payday. No problem. Select the date with the arrow keys or the mouse and then press Ctrl-J. Quicken displays the Scheduled Transaction List screen and highlights the transaction scheduled for the selected date.

Figure 12-11:
The Calendar screen.

```
 Print/Acct      Edit      Shortcuts      Reports      Activities               F1-Help

  Date   Num    Pay                                                    eposit    Balance
                              July - 1994
  7/01  115    Joe     Sun   Mon   Tue   Wed   Thur   Fri   Sat                 2,478 26
  1994  SPLIT  payr
        Cat:   Payr                                   1     2                   -----  --
  7/01  116    Big                                                              2,385 06
  1994  SPLIT  fede     3     4     5     6     7   T  8     9

  8/01  113    Mamm    10    11    12    13    14   T  15    16                  2,210 51
  1994  SPLIT  Acct
                       17    18    19    20    21   T  22    23    -----  --     1,265 51
  8/07  114    Casc
  1994  SPLIT  Augu    24    25    26    27    28   T  29    30

  7/01                 31          first day: Month   Year  Today
  1994                             last  day: montH   yeaR

               Ctrl-J Transactions              Ctrl-N Notes
                   PgUp,PgDn-Month          F9-Paste Date
               Esc-Cancel                   Ctrl-G Go to Date

 Checking                                              Balance:  $2,815.66
                                                Ending Balance:  $1,265.51
```

Calendar Notes is sort of cool

If you want to post a note on the calendar — reminding you to make a federal income tax deposit, for example — you can use Quicken's Calendar Notes feature.

To add notes to the calendar, press Ctrl-N while the Calendar screen is displayed. Or if the calendar isn't displayed, choose the Calendar Notes command from the Activities menu. Quicken displays a screen like the one shown in Figure 12-12. Highlight the date, press Enter, and begin typing. To alert you that Calendar Notes is present, Quickens puts the letter N on the day.

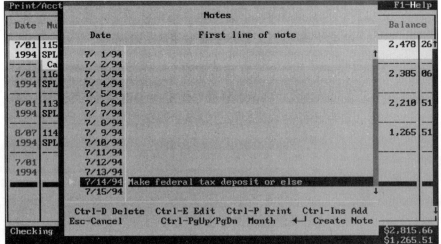

Figure 12-12: The Calendar Notes screen.

"Big deal," you say. "A lot of good it does me to create a Calendar Note. Now I have to remember to look at the calendar, right?"

Wrong. Quicken displays the note on-screen when you select your first Main Menu option on the day of a Calendar Note. Suppose, for example, that you enter a Calendar Note for July 14 that says, "Make federal tax deposit or else." When you first select a Main Menu option on July 14, you see a message box with

    Make federal tax deposit or else.

If you like what the calendar offers, go ahead and try some of the other control keys and commands. You know the most interesting and useful features, but there's always more to discover.

Chapter 13
Customer Receivables

· ·

In This Chapter

▶ Setting up an account to track customer receivables

▶ Recording customer invoices

▶ Recording customer payments

▶ Tracking what your customers owe

· ·

*Q*uicken isn't really designed to track the amounts clients and customers owe. If your list of receivables isn't enormous, however, you can jury-rig a reasonable system. In effect, you can use Quicken to keep a list of your customers' unpaid invoices.

Setting Up Shop

To get started, set up an Asset account specifically for tracking customer receivables. Follow these steps:

1. Display the Select Account To Use screen.

Choose the Select Account command from the Main Menu (see Figure 13-1).

2. Select <New Account>.

Press Home and then Enter. Quicken displays the Set Up New Account screen (see Figure 13-2), an old friend. Perhaps a friend you've seen too often. And they say familiarity breeds contempt.

3. Press 4 to indicate that you want to set up an Asset account.

4. Type a name for the account in the Name for This Account field.

I'd go with a name like **Acct Rec.** But one of the fun things about running your own business is that you get to make the decisions. Go for it.

5. Press Enter.

Quicken displays the Starting Balance and Description screen shown in Figure 13-3. ("Geez, Louise," you say to yourself. "Is there anybody new at this party?")

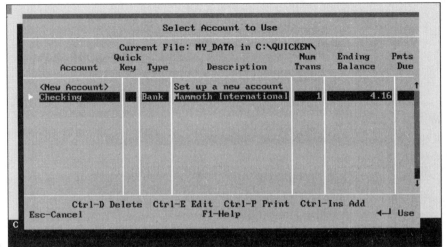

Figure 13-1:
The Select
Account to
Use screen.

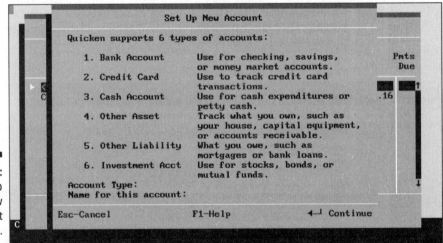

Figure 13-2:
The Set Up
New
Account
screen.

6. Enter the starting balance as zero.

To create the actual accounts receivable balance, you enter individual accounts receivable records. I describe this process later in the chapter.

7. Accept the default date.

You don't need to enter a date.

8. Type a description of the account.

How about something like **Accounts Receivable**?

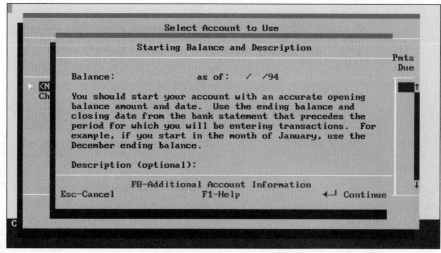

```
                    Select Account to Use
                                                              Pmts
                Starting Balance and Description              Due

          Balance:              as of:   /  /94

 <N       You should start your account with an accurate opening    T
 Ch       balance amount and date.  Use the ending balance and
          closing date from the bank statement that precedes the
          period for which you will be entering transactions.  For
          example, if you start in the month of January, use the
          December ending balance.

          Description (optional):

                   F8-Additional Account Information
          Esc-Cancel                 F1-Help             ◄┘ Continue

 C
```

Figure 13-3:
The Starting
Balance
and
Description
screen.

9. Press Enter.

Quicken displays the Select Account to Use screen again. Mysteriously, the screen now lists an additional account — the Accounts Receivable account you just created.

In Quicken, you work with one account at a time. Do you remember how to select an account? To tell Quicken which account you want to modify, display the Select Account to Use screen. Highlight the account you want and then press Enter. Quicken selects the account and displays the Register screen.

Recording Customer Invoices

When I was younger, I thought that you should use an Asset account to bill customers, measure sales with accrual-based accounting, and track customer invoices like a regular small-business accounting system.

But now I think that using Quicken only to keep a list of your unpaid customer invoices (and payments) is the easiest approach. To do more than that invites Rube Goldberg*esque* complexity. If you do want to do all that other stuff, you're really better off with a real small-business accounting system, such as Intuit's QuickBooks.

Quicken doesn't generate an invoice unless you twist its arm really hard and do a bunch of silly, unwieldy things. I assume, therefore, that you're generating invoices some other way — perhaps with a word processor or by manually filling out invoice forms.

When you bill a customer, just enter a transaction for the invoice amount in the your Accounts Receivable register:

1. **Enter the invoice date — the date you bill your customer — in the Date field.**

2. **Input the invoice number in the Ref field.**

   This number should match the number on the invoice you create.

3. **Type the customer name in the Payee field.**

Use the same customer name for every invoice. Be careful that you use the same spelling every time you type that customer's name. Of course, Quicken's QuickFill feature should help; after you type **Mowgli's Lawn Mower Repair** for one receivable, when you type **Mowg** in the future, Quicken assumes that you're entering another transaction for Mowgli's Lawn Mower Repair and fills in the Payee field. If you don't use the same name, you can't prepare a report that shows what a customer owes. You can't do so because Quicken summarizes A/R transactions by payee names. So, if you use several different payee names, Quicken uses each unique payee name as the basis for a summary total.

4. **Enter the invoice amount in the Increase field.**

5. **Press Ctrl-Enter to record the transaction.**

   Quicken asks you either to enter a category or confirm that you don't want to use a category. Because you don't want to use a category for accounts receivable, select the "Yes, that's right, I don't want to use a category" option.

Figure 13-4 shows a $750 invoice to Mowgli's Lawn Mower Repair. The ending balance, displayed in the lower right corner, is actually the sum of all the transactions in the register.

```
 Print/Acct    Edit    Shortcuts    Reports    Activities         F1-Help

  Date  Ref      Payee  ·  Memo  ·  Category   Decrease  C  Increase   Balance


                        ████ BEGINNING ████
  1/01         Opening Balance                                           0 00
  1994                          [Acct Rec]

  1/10  1      Mowgli's Lawn Mower Repair                      750 00   750 00
  1994  Memo:  for rebuilding engine
        Cat:
  1/10
  1994
                            ██ END ██


 Acct Rec                 (Alt+letter accesses menu)
 Esc-Main Menu       Ctrl◄┘  Record                   Ending Balance: $750.00
```

Figure 13-4:
An invoice in the Asset register.

Recording Customer Payments

When you work with customer payments in Quicken, you need to do two things.

First, you must record the customer check as a deposit to your bank account. At the same time, record the customer's payment in an income category. (If you have questions, refer to Chapter 4.)

Second, you must update your accounts receivable list to include the customer's payment. Follow these steps:

1. **Display the Accounts Receivable account in the Register screen.**

   Choose the Use Register command from the Main Menu.

2. **Display the Accounts Receivable account.**

   Select the Print/Acct menu by pressing Alt-A, choose the Select/Set Up Account command, highlight the Accounts Receivable account, and then press Enter.

3. **Select the invoice transaction that a customer has paid. Then press Ctrl-S.**

   Quicken displays the Split Transaction screen.

4. **Use the second and subsequent lines of the Split Transaction screen to describe the customer payments.**

   Refer to Figure 13-2 to see how this step is done. I stick in memo descriptions to describe the split line amounts.

5. **Adjust the invoice transaction total to agree with the split transaction lines and press F9.**

6. **Press Ctrl-Enter.**

   Quicken closes the Split Transaction dialog box.

7. **Indicate whether the entire invoice is paid.**

   When a customer completely pays the invoice, put an asterisk in the C (or cleared) column to mark the invoice as paid.

Figure 13-5 shows the first $750 invoice to Mowgli's Lawn Mower Repair paid and marked as cleared.

Figure 13-6 shows the register after you close the Split Transaction screen. Notice that the Increase field of the first invoice is blank, indicating that the unpaid balance is zero. Note also that I've gotten pretty crazy and entered some other invoices, too. (What can I say? It's my job.)

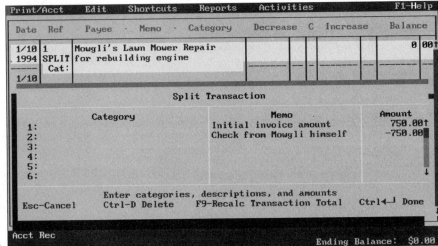

Figure 13-5:
Recording a
customer
payment
from
Mowgli's.

Figure 13-6:
The
Accounts
Receivable
register with
the first
invoice
marked as
paid.

Tracking What Your Customers Owe

To summarize what your customers owe, just print the A/R By Customer Business Report. The process is simple.

The A/R By Customer Report summarizes all uncleared transactions. To Quicken, the first Opening Balance transaction looks like a customer unless you mark it as cleared. Accordingly, either delete the Opening Balance transaction or mark it as cleared.

1. **Display the Reports menu.**

   Select Create Reports from the Main Menu.

2. **Select Business Reports to display the Business Reports menu.**

3. **Choose the A/R By Customer command from the Business Reports menu.**

   Quicken displays the A/R by Customer screen. It gives you the option of specifying a report title and of selecting the range of dates you want summarized in the report.

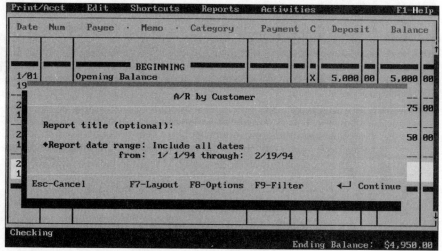

Figure 13-7:
The A/R by Customer screen.

4. **(Optional) Give a name to the A/R by Customer report.**

5. **Use the Report Date Range field to specify the period of time you want summarized in the report.**

   For example, current month, current quarter, current year, and so on.

6. **Press Enter.**

   Quicken displays the Select Accounts to Include screen, as shown in Figure 13-8.

7. **Select the accounts whose uncleared transactions should appear on the Accounts Receivable Report.**

   Initially, Quicken selects all Asset accounts. To unselect an Asset account that doesn't include customer accounts receivable information, highlight the account and press the spacebar.

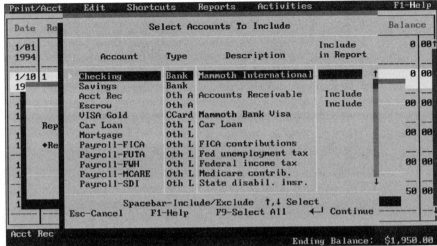

Figure 13-8:
The Select
Accounts To
Include
screen.

8. Press Enter.

Quicken produces a report that summarizes uncleared transactions by
payee name. Figure 13-9 shows an A/R By Customer Report based on the
three uncleared invoices shown in Figure 13-5.

| File/Print | Edit | Layout | Reports | Activities | | F1-Help |

A/R By Customer

1/ 1/94 Through 1/31/94
Acct Rec
6/ 9/94

Payee	1/94
Jasmine's Pantry	800.00
Mowgli's Lawn Mower Repair	750.00
Vernon's Truck Stop	400.00
OVERALL TOTAL	1,950.00

Acct Rec
Esc-Leave report

(Filtered)

Figure 13-9:
The A/R By
Customer
Report.

Agings

The standard A/R Report format isn't the only way to view customer accounts receivable information. You can also use Quicken's custom reporting features to produce *agings*. An *aging* is a report that summarizes the unpaid customer invoices by months using the invoice dates.

To produce an aging, make sure that the Accounts Receivable account is visible in the register. Then choose the **S**ummary command from the **R**eports **O**ther menu. Quicken displays a Create Summary Report screen that lets you specify a report title (such as A/R Aging), the dates of transactions you want to include (for example, through the current date), the fields (for example, Payee), and the column headings (the aging time period, such as months).

If you're going to use Quicken to track things such as accounts receivables, I think you may find it useful to noodle around with the **R**eport **O**ther menu's **S**ummary command. Isn't it great how Quicken gives you a really cool way to analyze your customer receivables?

The 5th Wave

By Rich Tennant

"WE OFFER A CREATIVE MIS ENVIRONMENT WORKING WITH STATE-OF-THE-ART PROCESSING AND COMMUNICATIONS EQUIPMENT; A COMPREHENSIVE BENEFITS PACKAGE, GENEROUS PROFIT SHARING, STOCK OPTIONS, AND, IF YOU'RE FEELING FUNKY AND NEED TO CHILL OUT AND RAP, WE CAN DO THAT TOO."

Chapter 14
Vendor Payables

· ·

In This Chapter

▶ Describing vendor payables
▶ Tracking vendor payables
▶ Using Billminder

· ·

*I*t's a snap using Quicken to track how much you owe to all the people and businesses you owe, or *vendors,* including the landlord, the office supplies store, and the guy with the bent nose and fedora.

If you've set up a bank account, you don't have to do anything special to begin tracking the amounts you know you have to pay. If you need to set up a bank account, see Chapters 1 and 2.

Describing Vendor Payables (a.k.a. Your Unpaid Bills)

You describe your vendor payables by writing checks (in the Write Checks screen) that pay your bills.

Don't print the checks, though. Quicken tracks these unprinted checks because they represent your unpaid vendor invoices.

I'm tempted to explain again how you fill in the blanks of the Write Checks screen — remember the first tenet in the computer book writer's code of honor: "When in doubt, describe in detail." But, as you may know, filling out the Write Checks screen is darn easy.

If you're not sure how the process works, be patient. After all, you're still getting your feet wet. Just flip back to Chapter 5. By the way, see Figure 14-1 for another look at the Write Checks screen.

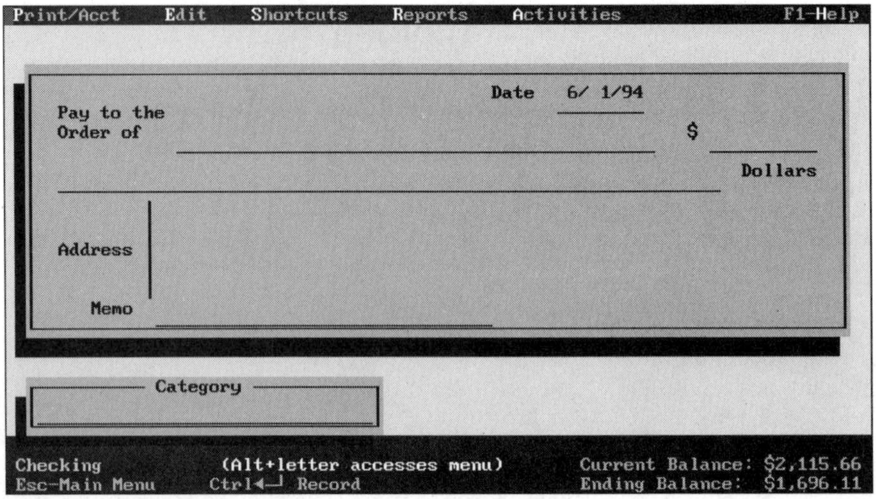

Figure 14-1:
The Write
Checks
screen.

Tracking Vendor Payables

When you want to know how much money you owe somebody, you can print a report that summarizes the unprinted checks by payee name. Pretty easy, huh?

To do so, print the A/P By Vendor business report. Here's a blow-by-blow account of the steps you need to follow:

1. Display the Reports menu.

To do so, choose Create Reports from the Main Menu.

2. Choose the Business Reports command.

Quicken, sensing that you mean business, displays the Business Reports menu.

3. Choose the A/P By Vendor command from the Business Reports menu.

Quicken displays the A/P (Unprinted Checks) by Vendor screen shown in Figure 14-2. Use this screen to enter a name for the report. You also can use this report to describe the range of dates covered by the report. To do so, use the Report data field.

4. Press Enter.

Quicken lists all the unprinted checks in your bank, cash, and credit card accounts. Figure 14-3 shows an example of this cute little report.

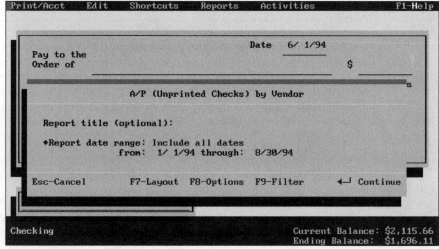

Figure 14-2:
The A/P
(Unprinted
Checks) by
Vendor
screen.

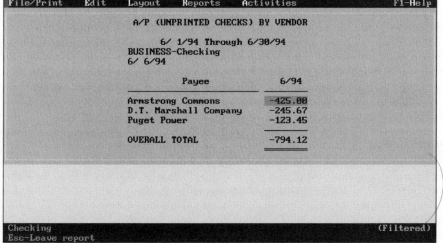

Figure 14-3:
The A/P
(Unprinted
Checks) by
Vendor
report.

A Minor Problem about How Quicken Handles Payables

One final point: Quicken counts an unprinted check as an expense only after you print it. Does this remark sound like much ado about nothing? Give me a minute to explain what it means.

How Quicken identifies an unprinted check

When you use the Write Checks screen to describe a check, Quicken records the check in the register, replacing the check number with asterisks. Whenever Quicken sees asterisks, it knows that the check is unprinted.

If you decide to get truly wild and crazy and use Quicken's electronic bill-paying feature, you should know that untransmitted payments show up in the register, too; Quicken replaces the check number with a series of greater than symbols (>>>>>). Whenever Quicken sees these symbols,

it knows that the check is an untransmitted electronic payment. Untransmitted payments don't appear on the A/P (Unprinted Checks) by Vendor report, however. Go figure.

So the people at CheckFree and Intuit don't sue me for saying that electronic payments are wild and crazy, let me say this, when I say "wild and crazy," I mean fun and adventurous. Like when you order Thai food and say, "Make that four stars, please." Or not wearing socks with your wing tips. You understand.

If you record a $1,000 check on December 31 but you don't print the check until January 1, for example, Quicken doesn't count the $1,000 as an expense for December. Instead, Quicken counts the $1,000 as an expense for January.

If you know something about cash-basis accounting versus accounting-basis accounting, you may say to yourself, "Hey, man, that's because Quicken uses cash-basis accounting." And you're right.

This subtle difference can cause confusion if you have worked with a regular full-featured accounting system that has an accounts payable module. You see, Quicken's payables aren't what a full-featured accounting system calls accounts payable. Full-featured accounting systems usually count the $1,000 check as an expense as soon as you enter it in the system.

Meet a New Friend Named Billminder

Let me introduce you to Billminder, a separate program in Quicken. Its job is simple but significant: it looks through your unprinted checks for any checks with dates falling on or before the current date. If Billminder finds any, it says, "Hey, dude! You have checks that you need to print." Or if you have overdue checks, it says, "Get the lead out, dude, the situation is getting gnarly." (I'm paraphrasing here.) You can tell Quicken to run the Billminder program every time you turn on your computer.

I think Billminder is way cool. Besides, it doesn't mind if you call it Bill.

Turning Bill on

To tell Bill you want it to remind you of the checks you need to print, do the following:

1. **Choose Set Preferences from the Main Menu.**

   Quicken displays the Set Preferences menu.

2. **Choose the Automatic Reminder Settings command from the Set Preferences menu.**

   Quicken displays the Automatic Reminder Settings screen, where it all happens. Figure 14-4 shows the Automatic Reminder Settings screen in all its splendor.

3. **Tell Bill the number of days in advance you want to know about unprinted checks.**

   Enter a value in the first field on-screen; you must input a number between 0 and 30.

   By the way, Bill also can remind you about reminder messages in the Investment register and scheduled transactions. (I talk a little bit about reminder messages in Chapter 11. Refer to Chapter 19 for information about scheduled transactions.)

4. **Turn Bill on.**

   Move the cursor to the Turn On Billminder field and press Y.

5. **Press Enter to save the instructions.**

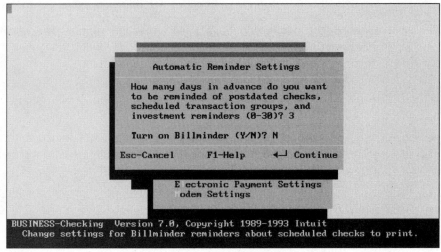

Figure 14-4:
The
Automatic
Reminder
Settings
screen.

Making Bill work

You don't need to do anything special to use Bill, as long as you turn off your computer at the end of the day.

If Bill is turned on, it looks at each unprinted check in your accounts every time you start your computer. If Bill sees a check you should know about, it displays an appropriate message.

If you don't turn your computer off at the end of the day, Bill doesn't work.

"So, Bill won't work unless I turn off the computer every day," you say. "What a snob."

Don't fret, Bill doesn't have a superiority complex. Nor does this quirk have anything to do with Bill's work ethic.

It all boils down to your AUTOEXEC.BAT file. As you may know, the AUTOEXEC.BAT file is a list of programs and commands you want your computer to run automatically every time it starts. In fact, the AUTOEXEC.BAT file gets its name from its function, AUTOmatically EXECute.

When you install Quicken, you add the Billminder program to the AUTOEXEC.BAT file. Every time you turn on your computer, the computer runs all the commands and programs listed in the AUTOEXEC.BAT file. Because Billminder is one of the programs listed in the AUTOEXEC.BAT file, it runs too.

When Billminder starts, it looks at your automatic reminder setting. If this indicates that you do want to be reminded, Billminder goes to work, looking through your registers for checks that need to be printed. If the reminder setting indicates you don't want to be reminded, Billminder quits without doing anything.

Part V
The Part of Tens

The 5th Wave — By Rich Tennant

In this part...

As a writing tool, laundry lists aren't something high school English teachers encourage. But you know what? The old laundry list format is pretty handy for certain sorts of information.

With this in mind (and, of course, deepest apologies to my high school English teacher, Mrs. O'Rourke), the next and final part, simply provides you with ten-item lists of information about Quicken: answers to ten commonly asked questions about Quicken, ten things every business owner using Quicken should know, ten things you should (or shouldn't) do if you are audited, and so forth.

Chapter 15
Ten Questions I'm Frequently Asked about Quicken

● ●

In This Chapter
▶ Does Quicken work for a corporation?
▶ Does Quicken work for a partnership?
▶ Can I use Quicken to track more than one business?
▶ What kind of business shouldn't use Quicken?
▶ Can I use Quicken retroactively?
▶ Can I do payroll with Quicken?
▶ Can I prepare invoices with Quicken?
▶ Can I import data from my old accounting system?
▶ What do you think of Quicken?

● ●

Does Quicken Work for a Corporation?

Sure. Simple question, simple answer.

But let me talk for a minute about what's unique about a corporation — at least from an accountant's perspective. A corporation needs to track its stockholders' equity, as well as its assets (like bank accounts and receivables) and liabilities (like mortgages and trade payables).

Stockholders' equity includes the money people originally pay for their stock, any earnings the corporation has retained, cumulative income for the current year, and some other stuff.

"Ugh," you say. Ugh is right. Accounting for the stockholders' equity is a mighty complicated process at times. So complicated, in fact, that Quicken can't track a corporation's stockholders' equity.

I'm not saying that a corporation can't use Quicken. I'm not saying that a corporation shouldn't use Quicken. Just remember that someone — probably your poor accountant — needs to do your stockholders' equity accounting periodically.

Fortunately, the financial information you collect with Quicken provides, in rough form, much of the information that your accountant needs.

Quicken doesn't exactly ignore a corporation's stockholders' equity. In an Account Balances report (like the Quicken Balance Sheet), the difference between total assets and total liabilities actually represents the total stockholders' equity. (Quicken labels this total Net Worth.) As long as the total assets and total liabilities figures are correct, you know the total stockholders' equity.

Does Quicken Work for a Partnership?

Sure it does. But a partnership that uses Quicken faces the same basic problem as a corporation that uses Quicken. A partnership needs to track what the partners have put into and taken out of the business.

Again, Quicken does calculate a net worth figure by subtracting total liabilities from total assets. And as long as the total assets and total liabilities figures are correct, you know the total partnership capital. But the partners need to keep track of what each partner puts into the business, earns as a partner in the business, and then takes out of the business.

Can I Use Quicken for More than One Business?

Yes, but be *very* careful. Make sure that you don't get the businesses' financial records mixed up.

Quicken has the capacity to work with more than one file; each file can be a separate set of financial records. Although you can't record automatic transfers between accounts in different files — you must record each side of the transaction separately — you can keep truly separate business records.

To create another file, choose the **S**elect/Set Up File command from the **F**ile Activities menu (which, in turn, appears in the Set **P**references menu, which, in turn, appears in the Main Menu). If you need help, refer to Chapter 7.

Separate bank accounts are usually a must. If you do keep financial records in Quicken for more than one business, you should set up separate bank accounts. In fact, my attorney tells me that you have to set up a separate corporate bank account for a corporation to be considered a truly separate legal entity. If you have questions, talk to your attorney.

What Kind of Business Shouldn't Use Quicken?

I can hear you say it now: "Quicken works for corporations (sort of), and it works for partnerships (sort of). Does that mean Quicken works for every kind of business?"

No. Quicken is a darn good product. In fact, for many small businesses, it's a great product. But Quicken is not right for every situation.

Take the following test to determine whether Quicken will work for your business. If you answer yes to two or three of these questions, you should consider moving up to a full-featured small-business accounting system.

1. **Do you regularly need to produce business forms other than checks?**

   If not, you're in good shape with Quicken, which produces checks easily. If you need the occasional invoice, I think you can create it easily in your computer. For example, I produce a handful of invoices a month with my word processor and never have any problems. If you produce a bunch of forms besides checks, however, you should consider switching to a different accounting system. If you like Quicken, take a look at QuickBooks, which you can use to create customized invoice forms.

2. **Do you need to track assets other than cash or investments?**

   Do you have a long list of customer receivables that you need to monitor? Or do you buy and resell inventory? If so, you may want to use an accounting system — QuickBooks, for example — that tracks these items easily.

3. **Are you having problems measuring your profits with cash-basis accounting?**

   I'm not going to get into a big, tangled discussion about cash-versus accrual-basis accounting. It wouldn't be any fun for you; it wouldn't be any fun for me. Nevertheless, you should know that if you can't accurately measure your business profits by using cash-basis accounting (which Quicken uses), you may be able to measure your business profit more accurately by using accrual-basis accounting. To do so, though, you must switch to an accounting system that supports accrual-basis accounting. By the way, to measure your profits the right way, you or your accountant needs to use — horror of horrors — double-entry bookkeeping.

If you use Quicken but have outgrown the checkbook-on-a-computer scene, look at QuickBooks. Don't worry, I don't get a kickback from Intuit. Here's the deal: QuickBooks looks and feels a lot like Quicken. Plus, it can use the data you've already collected with Quicken. Moving to QuickBooks from Quicken is only a bit more complicated than rolling off a log.

Can I Use Quicken Retroactively?

Sure. And this idea is better than it may seem at first.

It shouldn't take long to enter a year's worth of transactions in Quicken, as long as you're working from decent records. I bet you can get it done on a rainy Saturday afternoon. If you're a millionaire, you might need a couple afternoons. (If you're a millionaire, though, you can hire someone to do the work for you. Of course, maybe you're a millionaire because you won't hire other people to do the work for you.)

After you enter all the information in a Quicken register, you can monitor your spending, see what your income and outgo look like, and reconcile your bank accounts.

Can I Do Payroll with Quicken?

Yes. Refer to Chapter 12.

In fact, a handy payroll utility in Quicken called QuickPay can save you a great deal of time if you have a bunch of employees — or even just one hourly employee.

Can I Prepare Invoices with Quicken?

No. If you need to prepare a bunch of invoices each month, you should consider moving up to a full-featured small-business accounting system.

Can I Import Data from My Old Accounting System?

Yes. To do so, export the old system's data into a file that matches the Quicken Interchange Format, or QIF, specification. Then import this file into an empty Quicken file.

This process isn't for the timid or fainthearted. In my opinion, it also isn't for people who have better things to do with their time.

My advice? Go to a movie. Mow your lawn. Read a novel. Just forget all this importing business.

If you're switching to Quicken, I doubt that you've got zillions of transactions to enter. It probably makes sense, therefore, to switch programs at the beginning of your *fiscal,* or accounting, year. Then the asset and liability account balances are the only data you must load into Quicken. And you can do so easily when you set up the accounts.

What Do You Think of Quicken?

I think Quicken's great. So do others. Heck, Intuit sells about two million copies a year.

Why should you use Quicken? Here are the best reasons:

- ✔ You always know your bank account balances, so you never have to wonder whether you have enough money to pay a bill or charge a purchase.

- ✔ You can reconcile your account in two minutes. (I'm not joking. Two minutes. One hundred twenty seconds.)

- ✔ You can get a firm handle on what you're really making and spending.

- ✔ You can budget your spending and then track your spending against your budget.

- ✔ You can measure your business profits as often as you want by using cash-basis accounting.

- ✔ You can monitor your investments and measure their returns.

Real Auditors always do their best work between 1 and 5 a.m.

Chapter 16

Ten Tips for Bookkeepers Who Use Quicken

- -

In This Chapter

▶ How and why you cross-reference

▶ Why you shouldn't use a suspense account

▶ Why you should reconcile promptly

▶ What you should do at the end of every month

▶ What you should do at the end of every year

▶ How Quicken handles debits and credits

▶ How to convert to Quicken from some other system

▶ What to do if you're (unwittingly, of course) a party to income tax evasion

▶ What you should know about payroll taxes

- -

An amazing number of people use Quicken for small-business accounting: dentists, contractors, lawyers, and so on. And, not surprisingly, a great number of bookkeepers use Quicken.

If you're jumping up and down, waving your hands, saying, "I do, I do, I do," this chapter is for you. I tell you here what you need to know to make your use of Quicken smooth and sure.

Tricks for Learning Quicken if You're New on the Job

First, take a moment to feel good about your new job. Second, be thankful that you use Quicken and not one of the superpowerful-but-frightening complex accounting packages.

But enough schmoozing, already. Get to work.

Learning the Basics

If you're new to computers, you need to know a thing or two about them. Don't worry. This stuff isn't as difficult as you may think. (Remember that a bunch of anxious folk have gone before you.)

First, you need to know how to get the darn thing turned on and how to start Quicken.

Turning a computer on

Before you use the computer, you need to

1. **Find and flip on the computer's power switch (usually a big red switch).**

2. **Push a switch to turn on your monitor (the television-like screen).**

3. **Flip a switch to turn on the printer.**

Even if you're a little timid, go ahead and ask your boss how to turn the computer and its peripherals on. This won't be considered a stupid question. Different computers get turned on in different ways. For example, the computer and its peripherals may already be on and plugged into a fancy-schmancy extension cord called a *power strip* — but this power strip thing is turned off.

By the way, the word *peripherals* refers to things that work with the computer, such as the printer.

Starting Quicken

After you turn on the computer, you should see something on-screen, called the *DOS prompt*, that looks like this

```
C:\>
```

To start Quicken, just type **q** or **Q** at the DOS prompt (the case doesn't matter). Then press Enter.

By the way, if a Q doesn't start Quicken, ask your boss for help. Somebody has fooled around with the computer and mucked things up.

Learning Quicken

After you know how to turn on the computer and how to start Quicken, you're ready to rock. Give Part II of this book a quick read. Then carefully read those chapters in Part IV that apply to your daily work.

One last thing: Quicken is a lot easier than you think. Remember when you learned how to drive a car? Sure, it was confusing at first: all those gauges and meters . . . the tremendous power at your fingertips . . . traffic. After you gained some experience, though, you loosened your death grip on the wheel. Heck, you even started driving in the left lane.

Give yourself a little time. Before long you'll be zipping around Quicken, changing lanes three at a time.

Cross-Reference and File Source Documents

Let me shift gears. Be sure to cross-reference and file (neatly!) the source documents (checks, deposit slips, and so on) you use to enter transactions. I won't tell you how to set up a document filing system. There's a pretty good chance you can do so better than I — in fact, I usually use a crude, alphabetic scheme.

Check forms (the check source documents) are numbered, so that you can cross-reference checks simply by entering check numbers when recording a check transaction. But be sure to do the same for deposits and other withdrawals, too.

Cross-referencing enables you to answer any questions about a transaction that appears in a register. All you have to do is find the source document you used to enter the transaction.

Always Categorize

Always categorize a transaction. In an account transfer, specify the account to which an amount has been transferred.

A favorite but sloppy accounting trick is to assign funny transactions to a *suspense account.* Suspense accounts, though, often become financial landfills where you (and anyone else using Quicken) dump transactions you don't know what do to with.

Quickly, the suspense grows and grows. And pretty soon, it's a huge mess and no one has the energy to clean it up.

By the way, you can tell Quicken to remind you to enter a category every time you enter a transaction. Here's how to get this reminder:

1. **Choose Set Preferences from the Main Menu.**

   Quicken displays the Set Preferences menu.

2. **Choose the Transaction Settings command from the Set Preferences menu.**

   Quicken displays the Transactions Settings screen.

3. **Tell Quicken to warn you if a transaction has no category.**

   Move the cursor to the Warn If Transaction Has No Category field (the fourth field on the screen) and press Y.

4. **Press F10.**

   Quicken saves the change and returns to the Set Preferences menu.

5. **Press Esc.**

   Quicken returns to the Main Menu.

Reconcile Promptly

This subject is a pet peeve, so bear with me if I get a little huffy.

I think that you should always *reconcile*, or balance, a business's bank accounts within a day or two after you get the bank statement. You'll catch any errors you or the bank has made.

You'll also minimize the chance that you'll suffer financial losses from check forgery. Here's why: if a business or individual promptly alerts a bank about a check forgery, the bank rather than the business suffers the loss in most cases.

Reconciling in Quicken is fast and easy so there's no good excuse not to reconcile promptly. Chapter 6 describes how to reconcile accounts in Quicken.

Things You Should Do Every Month

In a business, everyone has some routine tasks: go through the In basket, return phone messages, and clean the coffee machine.

Here are six bookkeeping chores you should do at the end of every month:

1. **If the business uses a petty cash system, replenish the petty cash fund. Make sure that you have receipts for all withdrawals.**

2. **Reconcile the bank and credit card accounts.**

3. **If you're preparing payroll, be sure to remit any payroll tax deposit money owed.**

   Call the Internal Revenue Service for more information.

4. **Print a copy of each of the account registers for the month.**

   Set these copies aside as permanent financial records. Chapter 5 describes how to print reports, including the account registers.

5. **Print two copies of the monthly cash flow statement and the P&L statement.**

   Give one copy to the business's owner or manager. Put the other copy with the permanent financial records.

6. **If you haven't done so already during the month, back up the file containing the Quicken accounts to a floppy disk.**

   You can reuse the floppy disk every other month. Chapter 7 describes how to back up files.

Don't view the preceding list as all-inclusive. There may be other things you need to do. I'd hate for people to say, "Well, it doesn't appear on Nelson's list, so I don't have to do it." Yikes!

Things You Should Do Every Year

Here are the things I think you should do at the end of every year:

1. **Do all the usual month-end chores for the last month in the year.**

   See the list in the preceding section.

2. **Prepare and file any state and federal end-of-year payroll tax returns.**

   Businesses in the United States, for example, need to prepare the annual federal unemployment tax return (Form 940).

3. **Print two copies of the annual cash flow statement and the annual P&L statement.**

   Give one copy to the business's owner or manager. Put the other copy with the permanent financial records.

4. **If the business is a corporation, print a copy of the Business Balance Sheet report.**

   This report will help whoever prepares the corporate tax return.

5. **Back up the file containing the Quicken accounts to a floppy disk.**

   Store the floppy disk as a permanent archive copy.

6. **If the business's accounts are full — you notice that Quicken runs slower — use Quicken's Year End command to shrink the file.**

   Quicken creates a new version of the file, keeping only the current year's transactions (see Chapter 7).

Again, don't view the preceding list as all-inclusive. If you think of other things to do, do them.

About Debits and Credits (if You're Used to Them)

If you've worked with a regular small-business accounting system before, you may already miss those old friends, debit and credit. (Is it just me, or do *debit* and *credit* sound like the neighbor kid's pet frogs to you, too?)

Quicken is a single-entry accounting system and, as a result, doesn't really have debits and credits. Double-entry systems have debits and credits. (As you may know, the two entries in a double-entry system are your old friends: debit and credit. For every debit, you have equal credit.)

Quicken does supply a sort of chart of accounts, which you can use to describe accounting transactions. The Category and Account List screen (which you can usually display by pressing Ctrl-C) actually parallels a regular accounting system's chart of accounts.

Accordingly, when you record a transaction that increases or decreases one account, you record the offsetting debit or credit when you categorize or transfer the account.

Converting to Quicken

If you're converting to Quicken from a manual system or from another more complicated small-business accounting system, here are two important tips:

✔ Start using Quicken at the beginning of a year. The year's financial records are then in one place — the Quicken registers.

✔ If it's not the beginning of the year, go back and enter the year's transactions. Again, the year's financial records are then in one place — the Quicken registers. (Entering the year's transactions will take time if you have a lot to enter. In fact, you may want to postpone your conversion to Quicken.)

Income Tax Evasion

A nice fellow wandered into my office the other day and told me that he had inadvertently gotten entangled in his employer's income tax evasion. He didn't know what to do.

He had (unwittingly, he said) helped his employer file fraudulent income tax returns. Then, already sucked into the tar pit, he had lied to the IRS during an audit.

I didn't have anything good to tell him.

I never did get the fellow's name, so I'll just call him *Chump*. It really didn't make any financial sense for Chump to help his employer steal. Chump didn't get a share of the loot; he just helped his employer commit a felony. For free. (What a guy!)

Second, although Chump didn't receive (supposedly) any of the booty, he probably still is in serious trouble with the IRS. The criminal penalties can be enormous; prison, I understand, is not fun.

I'm not going to spend any more time talking about this. But I do have a piece of advice for you: Don't be a Chump.

Segregating Payroll Tax Money

While I'm on the subject of terrible things the IRS can do to you, let me touch on the problem of payroll tax deposits — the money you withhold from employee checks for federal income taxes, social security, and medicare.

If you have the authority to spend the money you withhold, don't — even if the company will go out of business. If you can't repay the payroll tax money, the IRS will go after the business owners and also after *you.*

It doesn't matter that you're just the bookkeeper; it doesn't matter whether you regularly attend church. The IRS doesn't take kindly to those who take what belongs to the IRS.

By the way, I should mention that the IRS is more lenient in cases where you don't have any authority to dip into the payroll tax money and the business owner or your boss does so. If this scenario rings bells with you, however, be darn careful not to get involved. And start looking for a new job.

Chapter 17
Ten Tips (More or Less) for Business Owners

In This Chapter

▶ Sign all your own checks

▶ Don't sign a check the wrong way

▶ Review canceled checks before your bookkeeper does

▶ How to pick a bookkeeper if you use Quicken

▶ Get smart about passwords

▶ Cash-basis accounting doesn't work for all businesses

▶ When to switch to accrual-basis accounting

▶ What to do if Quicken doesn't work for your business

▶ Keep things simple

*I*f you run a business and you use Quicken, you need to know some stuff. You can learn these things by sitting down with your certified public accountant over a cup of coffee at $100 an hour. Or you can read this chapter.

Sign All Your Own Checks

I have nothing against your bookkeeper. In a small business, however, it's just too darn easy for people — especially full-charge bookkeepers — to bamboozle you. By signing all the checks yourself, you keep your fingers on the pulse of your cash outflow.

Yeah, I know this can be a hassle. I know this means you can't easily spend three months in Hawaii. I know this means you have to wade through paperwork every time you sign a stack of checks.

By the way, if you're in a partnership, I think you should have at least a couple of the partners cosign checks.

Don't Sign a Check the Wrong Way

If you sign many checks, you may be tempted to use a John Hancock-like signature. Although this makes great sense if you're autographing baseballs, don't do it when you're signing checks. A wavy line with a cross and a couple of dots is really easy to forge.

Review Canceled Checks Before Your Bookkeeper Does

Be sure you review your canceled checks — before anybody else sees the monthly bank statement.

This chapter isn't about browbeating bookkeepers. But a business owner will discover whether someone is forging signatures on checks only by being the first to open the bank statement and then review each of the canceled check signatures.

If you don't do this, unscrupulous employees — especially bookkeepers who can update the bank account records — can forge your signature with impunity. And they won't get caught if they never overdraw the account.

Another thing: if you don't follow these procedures, *you* will probably eat the losses, not the bank.

How to Pick a Bookkeeper if You Use Quicken

Don't worry. You needn't request an FBI background check.

In fact, if you use Quicken, you don't need to hire people who are familiar with small-business accounting systems. Just find people who know how to keep a checkbook and work with a computer; you shouldn't have a problem getting them to understand Quicken.

Of course, you don't want someone who just fell off the turnip truck. But even if you do hire someone who rode into town this way, you're not going to have much trouble getting that person up to speed with Quicken.

When you hire someone, find someone who knows how to do payroll — not just the federal payroll tax stuff (see Chapter 15), but also the state payroll tax monkey business.

Get Smart about Passwords

In Chapter 8, I got all hot and bothered about passwords. Let me add here that I suggest you use a password to keep your financial records confidential if you use Quicken in a business and it's you who does the Quicken *thang* (especially if you have employees who know how to operate a PC and have access to the PC you use for Quicken).

Cash-Basis Accounting Doesn't Work for All Businesses

When you use Quicken, you employ an accounting convention called *cash-basis accounting* to measure your profits. When money comes in, you count it as revenue. When money goes out, you count it as expense.

Cash-basis accounting is fine when a business's cash inflows mirror its sales and its cash outflows mirror its expenses. This isn't the case, though, in many businesses. A single-family home contractor, for example, may have cash coming in (by borrowing from banks) but may not make any money. A pawn-shop owner who loans money at 22 percent may make scads of money even if cash pours out of the business daily. As a rule of thumb, when you're buying and selling inventory, accrual-basis accounting works better than cash-basis accounting.

So this isn't earthshaking. It's still something you should think about.

When to Switch to Accrual-Basis Accounting

If tracking cash flows doesn't indicate whether your business is making a profit, then you probably need to switch to accrual-basis accounting. Almost certainly you need to switch accounting systems.

What to Do if Quicken Doesn't Work for Your Business

Quicken is a great checkbook program. In fact, my friends at Microsoft won't like me saying this, but Quicken is probably the best checkbook program.

However, if Quicken doesn't seem to fit your needs — for example, you need accrual-basis accounting (see preceding section) — you may want one of the more complicated but also more powerful small-business accounting packages.

If you like using Quicken, look at QuickBooks. You also should look at other more powerful programs, such as full-featured DOS programs like DacEasy, Pacioli 2000, and Peachtree. Or if you want to look into the Microsoft Windows operating environment, take a peek at Microsoft Profit, M.Y.O.B. from Teleware, and the Peachtree Accounting for Windows packages.

I am amazed that PC accounting software remains so affordable. You can buy a great accounting package — one you can use to manage a $5 million or a $25 million business — for a few hundred bucks. This is truly one of the great bargains.

Keep Things Simple

Let me share one last comment about managing small-business financial affairs. *Keep things as simple as possible.* In fact, keep your business affairs simple enough that it's easy to tell whether you're making money and whether the business is healthy.

This may sound like strange advice, but as a CPA I've worked for some very bright people who built monstrously complex financial structures for their businesses, including complicated leasing arrangements, labyrinthine partnership and corporate structures, and sophisticated profit-sharing and cost-sharing arrangements with other businesses.

I can only offer anecdotal evidence, of course, but I strongly believe that these supersophisticated financial arrangements don't produce a profit when you consider all the costs. What's more, these supersophisticated arrangements almost always turn into management and record-keeping headaches.

Chapter 18
Ten Things You Should Do If You're Audited

● ●

In This Chapter

▶ Leave Quicken at home

▶ Print summary reports for tax deductions

▶ Collect all source documents

▶ Call a tax attorney if the agent is "special"

▶ Don't volunteer information

▶ Consider using a pinch hitter

▶ Understand everything on your return

▶ Be friendly

▶ Don't worry

▶ Don't lie

● ●

*B*ecause you may use Quicken to track things like your income tax deductions, I want to mention some of the things you shouldn't do if you get audited.

Leave Quicken at Home

Don't bring Quicken with you to an IRS audit, even if you're really proud of that new laptop.

Here's the problem: Quicken's reporting capabilities are incredibly powerful. If you've been using Quicken diligently, you own a rich database describing almost all your financial affairs. When you bring Quicken (and your Quicken file) to the IRS, you're spilling your financial guts.

Now I'm not one who recommends sneaking stuff by the IRS. But it is dumb to give an IRS agent the opportunity to go on a fishing expedition. Remember, the agent isn't going to be looking for additional deductions.

I know of a young, inexperienced CPA who took Quicken to an audit. After the IRS agent would ask a question, the CPA would proudly tap a few keys on the laptop, smile broadly, and then show the agent on screen, for example, all the individual entertainment expenses claimed by the taxpayer in question.

Funny thing, though, the IRS agent also saw some other things — such as money that should have been claimed as income, reporting requirements the taxpayer failed to meet, and obvious out-of-line deductions.

Print Summary Reports for Tax Deductions

Ol' Quicken can be your friend, though, if you're audited.

Before you go to the audit, find out what the IRS is questioning. Print a summary report of every questioned deduction: charitable giving, medical expenses, travel and entertainment, and so on. You'll have an easy-to-understand report explaining how you came up with every number the IRS wants to examine.

By the way, I know a very clever tax attorney who used Quicken in this manner. The audit lasted half an hour.

Collect All Source Documents

After you print a summary report of every questioned deduction, collect all the source documents — usually canceled checks — that prove or indicate a transaction in question.

For example, if you claim $600 in charitable giving, the report summarizing this deduction may show 12 $50 checks written to your church or the local United Way agency. To verify this report, find the 12 canceled checks.

Call a Tax Attorney if the Agent Is "Special"

An IRS *special agent* isn't an agent endorsed by Mr. Rogers. IRS special agents investigate criminal tax code violations. If a special agent is auditing your return, you're in a heap of trouble. So get a tax attorney.

In my mind, being audited by a special agent is like being arrested for murder. Call me a scaredy cat, but I'd want legal representation even if I were innocent.

Don't Volunteer Information

Loose lips sink ships. Don't volunteer any information — even if it seems innocuous. Just answer the questions you're asked.

Again, I'm not suggesting that you lie. The agent is looking for income you forgot or deductions you overstated. The more information you provide, the more likely you'll reveal something damaging.

For example, if you offhandedly tell the agent about your other business — where you knit socks for golf clubs — you may wind up debating whether that cute little business is really a business (and not a hobby) and whether knitting golf socks entitles you to deduct those country club dues and green fees.

Consider Using a Pinch Hitter

I don't think an audit should terrify you. And I'm someone who scares easily: dinner parties where I don't know anyone, stormy nights when the neighborhood seems particularly deserted, driving on bald tires. You get the idea. Nonetheless, if you used a paid-preparer, think about sending that person in your place.

You pay for this service, of course. But it may help if the person who prepared your return does the talking.

Understand Everything on Your Return

Be sure that you understand everything on your return. You won't help yourself if you tell an agent that you don't have a clue about some number on your return.

Be Friendly

Be nice to the IRS. Remember, the agents actually work for you. In fact, the more taxes that the agents collect from people who owe the federal government, the less the rest of us have to pay. (An article in *Money* magazine a few years ago suggested that we end up paying several hundred dollars more a year in income taxes because so many people cheat.)

Don't Worry

If you've been honest and careful, you've got nothing to worry about. Sure, maybe you made a mistake. Maybe the agent will find the mistake. And maybe you'll have to pay some additional taxes.

If you haven't been honest and careful, I offer my condolences. Sorry.

Don't Lie

Don't lie; it may be perjury. You could go to jail and share a cell with someone named Skull-crusher.

You get the picture. And it's not pretty.

So don't lie.

Chapter 19

Ten Things I Blew Off
(and My Excuses)

In This Chapter

▶ Using Checkfree to make electronic payments

▶ Exporting tax information

▶ Handling memorized transactions

▶ Working with command line parameters

▶ Printing custom reports

▶ Meeting Quicken's assistants

▶ Adjusting Quicken's printer settings

▶ Adjusting Quicken's transaction settings

▶ Adjusting Quicken's check and reports settings

▶ Using Saving Goals Accounts

▶ What to do when you still need to know

I want to end this book with a confession. In my haste to make things as easy as possible for you, I left out some things — some subjects I never talk about, some features I just gloss over . . . you get the idea.

Nevertheless, a big part of understanding something is knowing (at least roughly) what you don't know. So here's a list of the features I don't cover, the topics I wimp out on, and the things you can do if your inquiring mind wants or needs to know.

Electronic Payments with Checkfree

Checkfree enables you to pay your bills electronically.

First, enter the bills that you want to pay like you enter a check in the Write Checks screen. If you need to write a $52 check to the electric company, for example, you fill out the Write Checks screen with this information.

Then you connect to the Checkfree service — through a modem — and send the payment information, including the date the bill should be paid. The Checkfree people look through their records and find everyone who's supposed to pay the same electric company on the same day. They then send the electric company one big check and a list of the people whose payments are included in the big check. A day or two later, the Checkfree people deduct what you owed from your checking account.

"Steve, buddy," you say, "this Checkfree thing sounds pretty cool. Why don't you cover it someplace?"

Well, while some people love Checkfree, I think it's a little complicated for a new Quicken user to handle right away. And it costs several dollars a month. And you need a modem. And you need to give Quicken a bunch of rather technical information so that it can use your modem to successfully connect to the Checkfree computer. What's more, some businesses may not accept the one big check approach.

Exporting Tax Information

You can export tax deduction information to a third-party income tax preparation program like Turbotax or TaxCut. But, frankly, I don't think this process is worth your time.

For one thing, you don't pull that many numbers from the Quicken registers anyway. When you complete a business tax return, for example, you only pull two or three dozen category totals. (You import the category totals into TurboTax — nothing else.) And a personal return probably needs only half a dozen categories, maybe fewer. I think that it's really easier just to pull these totals from a Quicken report.

Memorized Transactions and Memorized Transaction Groups

Quicken lets you memorize transactions by adding them to a list; you can recall them later.

I describe how you use memorized transactions as part of splitting loan payments between principal reductions and interest expense in Chapter 10. You also can use memorized transactions, however, for other simpler transactions that I don't describe. But I don't tell you about this function because it's really just a quick way to copy and reuse old transactions.

There's no doubt about it: memorized transactions are cool. With Quicken's QuickFill, though, you really don't need to use them unless you're working with loan payments. Remember, QuickFill automatically recalls old transactions for you. (See Chapter 4 to refresh your memory about QuickFill.)

Command Line Parameters

Usually, you start Quicken by pressing Q at the DOS prompt. By typing more information, though, you can tell Quicken to do something else, such as select a certain file or load a specific account.

If this option piques your interest, check the documentation or pick up one of those monstrous Quicken tutorials. But, honestly, don't you have better things to do with your time?

Custom Reports

Quicken enables you to print a report that organizes register information any way you want. In general, you do so by using the Transaction, Summary, Budget, Account Balances, or Comparison Reports commands from the Reports menu.

Quicken's Assistants

Quicken has several assistants that help you through the program's more complicated tasks: creating a new file or account, setting up payroll, exporting income tax information, amortizing loans, and keeping investment records.

I don't describe any of the assistants per se. I figure that being your little assistant is my job.

The Printer Settings Command

If you've explored Quicken's menus, you may have stumbled onto the **P**rinter Settings command, which appears both in the Set **P**references menu (which you access from the Main Menu) and the Change Printer **S**tyles submenu (which you get to from the **P**rint/Acct menu).

If you fool around with this command, you should find some tricky ways to print things, depending on your printer. You may be able to use compressed type, for example.

True, this command is sort of cool. I just don't think it's as important as the other stuff I talk about.

The Transaction Settings Command

The Transaction Settings command, which appears in the Set **P**references menu, lets you make changes to the way Quicken operates — you can tell Quicken to remind you to include a category, for example. (Actually, I mention this trick in Chapter 16.)

I don't talk about the other transaction settings because there's no compelling reason you should use them. Most of the transaction settings are pretty self-explanatory, though. And the way Quicken sets things up are best for, like, 99.9% of the population anyway.

The Check & Reports Settings Command

As you can guess, the Check & Reports Settings command tweaks the Write Checks screen and alters the way Quicken prints reports.

Again, I don't talk about these settings because there's no superimportant reason for you to use them.

Savings Goals Accounts

Quicken lets you set up a special type of asset account called a savings goal account. You use a savings goal account to earmark money in an account — like your checking account — for some purpose. A vacation. Holiday gifts. A moped. Well, you get the idea.

But I didn't spend time talking about the Savings Goal account. Sure, it's a neat little trick, but there's an easier way to keep track of money you've set aside or earmarked for some purpose. In fact — and if this isn't a coincidence — I describe how to do this in the next chapter.

If You're Not Impressed with My Excuses

If my excuses don't satisfy you, check the Quicken user guide for more information on these commands.

You also may send me a letter in care of the publisher. I'm not looking for criticism; I just want to do right by you. If you think that a topic should have been left in or a section could have been left out, I'm the sort of guy who wants to know. (What's more, if you make a really compelling point, I'll make the change to the next version of the book.)

Chapter 20
Ten Quicken Magic Tricks (More or Less)

In This Chapter
▶ Recording checks that you cash
▶ Showing that you've set aside a portion of an account balance
▶ Splitting with percentages
▶ Date field editing tricks
▶ Tracking petty cash and mad money
▶ Understanding the power of DOS

This is your lucky day. In this chapter, I violate the magician's credo ("Never reveal your secrets") — at least as it applies to Quicken. Here are some tricks that I think will help you work with Quicken.

Recording Checks That You Cash

This process isn't as easy as it sounds. Normally, you deposit a check in your bank account and then simply categorize the increase, such as Gross Sales (if you're using Quicken in a business and the check is from a customer) or Salary (if you're using Quicken at home and the check is from your employer).

What do you do if you cash the check? Do you just endorse the sucker and tell the teller to give you the cash? Hmmm. . . .

Actually, recording this kind of check isn't that hard to do. Just use the Split Transaction screen to show both the income category and the way you plan to use the money. If you cash a $1,000 check and plan to use all $1,000 as spending money, you could enter a positive $1,000 in the Salary category and a negative $1,000 in the Entertain category, for example. Figure 20-1 shows this trick. (You'll notice that I haven't asked why you need $1,000 in cash. Sure, I'm interested in how you're going to spend all that money. But it's none of my business.)

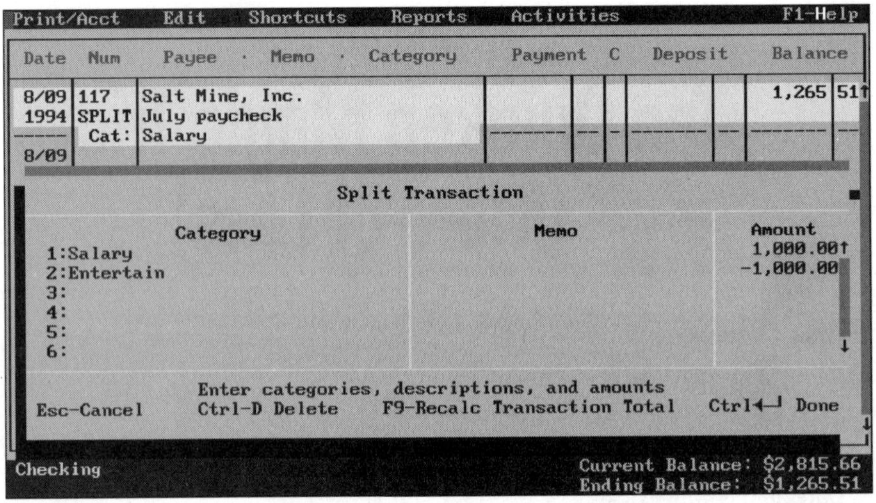

```
 Print/Acct    Edit    Shortcuts    Reports    Activities              F1-Help

 Date   Num    Payee  ·  Memo  ·  Category    Payment   C   Deposit    Balance

 8/09  117    Salt Mine, Inc.                                          1,265 51↑
 1994  SPLIT  July paycheck
 ----  Cat:  Salary                                        ---------  --- --
 8/09

                          Split Transaction                                 ■

                Category                        Memo              Amount
        1:Salary                                                 1,000.00↑
        2:Entertain                                             -1,000.00
        3:
        4:
        5:
        6:                                                              ↓

                 Enter categories, descriptions, and amounts
     Esc-Cancel      Ctrl-D Delete    F9-Recalc Transaction Total    Ctrl◄─┘ Done

 Checking                                       Current Balance: $2,815.66
                                                Ending Balance:  $1,265.51
```

Figure 20-1:
A zero-
amount
transaction.

Note that the transaction shown in Figure 20-1 produces a transaction that equals zero. Don't worry: this is correct, because cashing the check doesn't affect your checking account balance. By filling out the Split Transaction screen as I do in Figure 20-1, however, you end up recording both the $1,000 income and the $1,000 expense. Pretty cool, huh?

Indicating That Money in an Account Is Set Aside

Suppose that you're saving money for some future expenditure. For example, maybe you're saving money for a special trip or purchase. Or perhaps you're a small-business owner saving money to make your next quarterly estimated tax payment.

If you leave the cash that you accumulate in your regular checking account, how can you show that you've already earmarked a portion of the cash?

You can enter a postdated transaction for the amount that you've allocated. Quicken calculates two balances for an account: a current balance and an ending balance. The current balance is the balance as of the current date — in other words, the balance that includes all the transactions made on or before the current date. The ending balance is the current balance adjusted for any postdated transactions.

Figure 20-2 shows an account register with a $500 postdated transaction for estimated taxes. The current balance doesn't include the postdated transaction; the ending balance does.

```
  Print/Acct    Edit    Shortcuts     Reports    Activities             F1-Help

   Date  Num    Payee  ·  Memo  ·  Category    Payment  C   Deposit    Balance

   7/07  114   Cascade Mortgage Company        945 00              1,440 06↑
   1994  SPLIT August mortgage→[Mortgage]

   7/31  117   Salt Mine, Inc.                                     1,440 06
   1994  SPLIT July paycheck    Salary

   8/01  113   Mammoth National                174 55              1,265 51
   1994  SPLIT Acct# 1234567    [Car Loan]
        =====  ============================    ====== == = ======= == ======= ==
   9/15        Internal Revenue Service        500 00                765 51
   1994  Memo: estimated tax payment
         Cat: Tax:Fed
   8/01
   1994                       END



  Checking              (Alt+letter accesses menu)     Current Balance: $1,265.51
  Esc-Main Menu     Ctrl←┘ Record                       Ending Balance: $  765.51
```

Figure 20-2:
An account
register with
a postdated
transaction.

If you turn on Billminder and you set the check number to ****, Quicken even
reminds you when it's time to pay. (Refer to Chapter 14 for a description of
Billminder.)

Splitting with Percentages

If you use the Split Transaction screen to split a payment or deposit among
categories, you can enter percentages in the Split Transaction screen's
Amount field.

Suppose that you enter a $1,000 check: if you enter **75%** in the first Split
Transaction Amount field, Quicken calculates 75 percent of $1,000, or $750.
Then Quicken replaces 75% with $750.

Date Field Editing Magic

I mention elsewhere that you can use the + and – keys to edit dates: when the
cursor is on a Date field, pressing + adds a day to the date and pressing –
subtracts a day from the date.

This trick may be the only date field editing magic you need. If you're a little
more adventurous, however, try the tricks listed in Table 20-1.

Table 20-1	Date Field Editing Tricks
Press	**Date Changes To**
T	Current date
M	First day of this month or preceding month (If it's already the first day of the month, pressing M changes the date to the first day of the preceding month)
H	Last day of this month or preceding month
Y	First day of this year or preceding year
R	Last day of this year or preceding year

You also can use Quicken's calendar to enter a date. First, move the cursor to the Date field. Next, display the Calendar screen by choosing the Calendar command from the **Activities** menu. Then highlight the date you want and press F9. Quicken enters the date in the selected Date field.

If you think that you might like to use these tricks, go ahead and try them out now. Just move the cursor to the nearest Date field and go crazy.

It may help you to remember that *M* and *H* are the first and last letters in *month* and that *Y* and *R* are the first and last letters in *year.*

OK, so this trick may not be as good (or as useful) as making someone disappear. But I think it's still kind of neat.

Tracking Petty Cash and Mad Money

You can track a business's petty cash or your personal cash by using a special Quicken cash account — you set up a cash account and then enter the increases and decreases in the cash account's register.

Adding a cash account

To set up a cash account, you follow roughly the same steps as you do to add a bank account. Here's how to set up a cash account:

1. **Choose the Select Account command from the Main Menu.**

   Quicken displays the Select Account to Use screen. I've shown this screen a zillion times already, so I won't show it again.

2. **Select the <New Account> option from the Select Account to Use screen.**

   Press Home and Enter. Quicken displays the Set Up New Account screen. I've shown this screen a bunch of times, too. You don't really want to see it again, do you?

3. **Press 3 to indicate that you want to set up a cash account.**

4. **Name the account.**

   Type a name in the Name for This Account field.

5. **Press Enter.**

   Quicken displays the Starting Balance and Description screen. Another familiar friend — I mean, screen.

6. **Enter the cash balance that you hold.**

   Move the cursor to the Balance field and enter the balance value.

7. **Enter the account balance date.**

   Type the two-digit month number, the two-digit day number, and the two-digit year number in the Date field. (You probably want the current date.)

8. **Enter a description for the account.**

   Enter whatever you want: petty cash, mad money, slush fund, or so on.

9. **Press Enter.**

   Quicken redisplays the Select Account to Use screen. The screen now lists an additional account — the cash account you just created.

Tracking cash inflows and outflows

Quicken doesn't get much simpler. To record your cash inflows and outflows, use the Register screen. To display this screen for the cash account, for example, just select the cash account from the Select Account to Use screen. Quicken displays the cash account version of the register, as shown in Figure 20-3.

Remember that you can display the Select Account to Use screen by choosing the Select Account command from the Main Menu or by choosing the Select Account command from the **P**rint/Acct menu (which is listed in both the Register screen and Write Checks screen menus).

As Figure 20-3 shows, you record money that you spend by filling in the Date, Payee, and Decrease fields. To record money that you receive, fill in the Date, Payee, and Increase fields. To indicate your reasons for receiving and spending the cash, use the Category and Memo fields.

Print/Acct	Edit	Shortcuts	Reports	Activities		F1-Help

Date	Ref	Payee · Memo · Category	Spend		Receive	Balance
		▬▬▬ BEGINNING ▬▬▬				
7/01 1994		Opening Balance [Mad Money]			50 00	50 00
7/10 1994		Lunch at Chez Mac the usual Groceries	3 56			46 44
7/11 1994		U-Park-it-n-U-Risk-it parking Auto	4 00			42 44
7/20 1994	Memo: Cat:	Sam's Market lottery tickets Invest Exp	10 00			32 44
7/20 1994						
		▬▬▬ END ▬▬▬				

Mad Money   (Alt+letter accesses menu)
Esc-Main Menu   Ctrl◄─┘ Record   Ending Balance: $32.44

Figure 20-3: The cash account version of the register.

The Power of DOS

One final trick: use the Use **DOS** command in the Activities menu to return to the DOS prompt without actually exiting Quicken. As a result, you can issue DOS commands, such as "Format a disk," "Copy that file," or "Do my laundry," from within Quicken.

When you choose the Use **DOS** command, it's very important to remember that you haven't exited Quicken. Don't turn off your computer just because you see the DOS prompt. You need to return to Quicken, exit it, and then do whatever you do to turn off your computer. (You probably just flip the big red switch.)

What's that? Oh, yes. To return to Quicken after choosing the Use **DOS** command, type **exit** at the DOS prompt.

Appendix A:
How to Install Quicken in Eleven Easy Steps If You're Really Busy

● ●

*I*f you haven't already installed Quicken, get it over with right now and follow these steps:

1. **Turn on your PC.**

2. **Get the Quicken floppy disks.**

   Find the Quicken package, rip it open, and then take out the floppy disks. (The floppy disks are those plastic 5.25-inch or 3.5-inch squares in the package.)

3. **Insert the first floppy disk.**

   Stick the floppy disk that's labeled "Install Disk — Disk 1 of 2" into your floppy drive slot. If you have a choice, try to stick it into the top floppy drive. The top drive is named A; the bottom drive is named B. Not very original, eh? You would have thought the folks at Microsoft could have come up with something a little more original, like Alberta or Babbitt.

4. **Start the Install program.**

   If you stuck the Install Disk 1 floppy disk into the top slot, type `a:install` at the `C:>` prompt, which should already be displayed. If you stuck the Install Disk 1 floppy disk into the bottom slot, type `b:install` at the `C:>` prompt. You should hear the whirling and grinding of the floppy disk drive and see a screen that asks you if you have a color monitor or not (see Figure A-1).

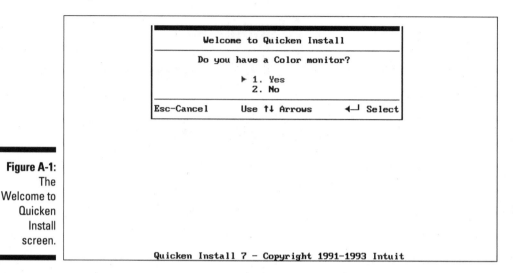

Figure A-1:
The
Welcome to
Quicken
Install
screen.

5. Answer the "Yo! Dude! Do you have a color monitor?" question.

How? Use the up and down arrow keys to highlight either the Yes or No
answer. Then press Enter. If your keyboard doesn't have an Enter key,
press the key labeled Return. What happens next is pretty exciting.
Quicken displays the Choose Install method screen (see Figure A-2).

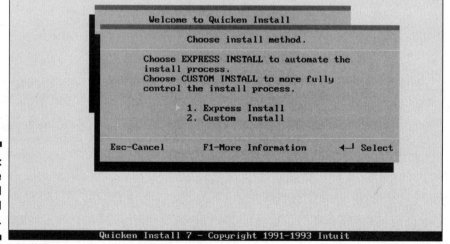

Figure A-2:
The Choose
Install
Method
screen.

6. Highlight Custom Install method.

Using the up and down arrow keys, highlight the Custom Install method
and then press Enter. Quicken displays the Drive and Directory screen
(see Figure A-3).

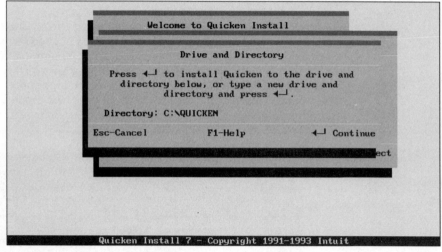

7. Press Enter.

This tells Quicken to accept the suggestion that you put the Quicken files in a directory named, cleverly, Quicken. Quicken displays the Choose a Printer screen (see Figure A-4).

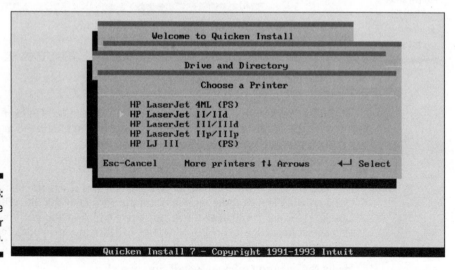

8. Select your printer.

Look at your printer (if you have one) and then use the up- and down-arrow keys to move the little triangle shown on your screen until it rests next to the name of your printer; then press Enter. You probably know this, but the up- and down-arrow keys show little arrows on their keytops. (If you're using a Hewlett-Packard Laserjet II, for example, press the down arrow a bunch of times until the little triangle rests next to the printer description HP Laserjet II.) Quicken displays the Use Billminder screen (see Figure A-5).

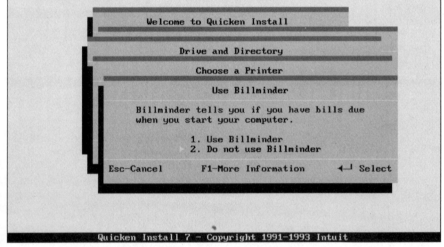

Welcome to Quicken Install

Drive and Directory

Choose a Printer

Use Billminder

Billminder tells you if you have bills due
when you start your computer.

1. Use Billminder
2. Do not use Billminder

Esc-Cancel   F1-More Information   ↵ Select

Quicken Install 7 – Copyright 1991–1993 Intuit

Figure A-5:
The Use
Billminder
screen.

9. Press Enter.

This tells Quicken that you don't want to use Billminder. Quicken next displays the Confirm Settings screen, which I haven't included as a Figure because you don't need to do anything with it.

10. Press Enter (yes, again).

Quicken removes the Confirm Settings screen and starts the installation. Quicken will display some messages on the screen — like "Installing Quicken" — and you'll hear the floppy drive whirling and grinding. You'll also see some other messages that give you little nuggets of Quicken knowledge. Go ahead and read these if you want.

11. Insert the second Quicken Install floppy disk.

After your computer's floppy disk works for a bit, you'll see a message that asks you to insert the second floppy disk. Just do it. Then press Enter. You'll see more messages about installing Quicken and still more messages with nuggets of knowledge. Eventually, you'll see the Installation Complete screen. Figure A-6 shows this screen. Now press Enter to return to the DOS prompt.

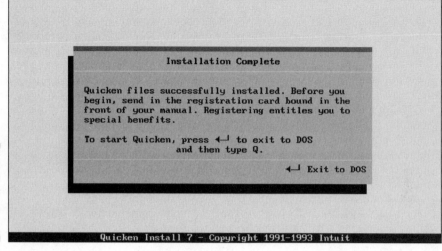

Figure A-6:
The
Installation
Complete
screen

Appendix B
Glossary of Business and Financial Terms

1-2-3

The Lotus 1-2-3 spreadsheet program.

940 Payroll Tax Form

The annual federal unemployment tax return. There's also a 940EZ version that is supposed to be EZier to fill out.

941 Payroll Tax Form

The quarterly federal payroll tax form that tells the IRS what federal employee payroll taxes (social security and medicare) you've collected and remitted.

942 Payroll Tax Form

The quarterly payroll tax form that tells the IRS what domestic employee payroll taxes you've collected and remitted. (Use the 942, for example, if you employ a nanny and you want to be the U.S. Attorney General someday.)

Account

In Quicken, a list of the increases and decreases in an asset's value or in a liability's balance.

Account Balance

The value of asset or the outstanding principal owed for a liability. For example, the value of a checking account is the cash value of the account; the balance of a mortgage liability is the principal you still owe.

Account Transfer

An amount you move from one account (such as a checking account) to another (such as a savings account).

Account Type

Quicken provides several versions, or types, of accounts: four for keeping records of the things you own and two for keeping records of the amounts you owe.

- Bank accounts — for tracking checking and savings accounts
- Cash accounts — for tracking the cash in your pocket or wallet
- Investment accounts — for tracking mutual funds and brokerage accounts
- Other asset accounts — for tracking anything else you own
- Credit card accounts — for tracking your plastic
- Other liability accounts — for tracking everything else you owe

Accounts Payable

In a business, the amounts you owe your trade creditors — your landlord, the office supplies store, the distributor from whom you purchase your inventory, and so on. People who prefer monosyllabic speech often refer to accounts payable as A/P.

Accounts Receivable

In a business, the amounts your customers or clients owe you. People who prefer monosyllabic speech often refer to accounts receivable as A/R.

Amortization

The itsy-bitsy principal payments you make over the course of repaying a loan. Eventually, these principal reductions pay off the loan.

ASCII

An acronym standing for American Standard Code for Information Interchange. A standard for saving information so that most programs can read it. People usually use the term to refer to files — in other words, ASCII files — that contain just regular old text: letters, numbers, symbols from the keyboard, and so on.

Backing Up

Making a copy. If something terrible happens — fire, hard disk failure, thermo-nuclear exchange — you still have a copy on floppy disk.

Balancing an Account

The steps you take to explain the difference between what your records show as a balance and what the bank's records (statement) show. Also referred to as "reconciling an account."

Billminder

A program that comes with Quicken. When asked by you, Billminder looks through your postdated checks whenever you start your computer. If there's a check that needs to be paid, Billminder tells you.

Bookkeeper

Someone who keeps the "books," or financial records.

Brokerage Account

An account specifically set up to track a brokerage account you use to invest in securities. Unlike a mutual fund account, a brokerage account includes a cash element.

Budget

A plan that says how you plan to make and spend money.

Capital Accounts

The money a sole proprietor leaves in or contributes to the sole proprietorship. Also the money a partner leaves in or contributes to a partnership.

Capital Gain

What you earn by selling an investment for more than you paid.

Capital Loss

What you lose by selling an investment for less than you paid.

Category

In Quicken, how you summarize income and outgo. For example, you might use a category such as "Wages" to summarize your payroll check deposits. And you might use categories such as "Housing," "Food," and "Fun" to summarize your checks.

Category List

The list of categories you can use. While setting up the first account in a file, Quicken suggests category lists for home users and for business users.

Certified Public Accountant

Someone who's taken a bunch of undergraduate or graduate accounting courses, passed a rather challenging two-and-a-half day test, and worked for at least a year or two under a CPA doing things like auditing, tax planning and preparation, or consulting.

Chart

A picture that shows numbers. In Quicken, you can produce pie charts, bar charts, line charts, and so on.

Check Form

The preprinted form you use to provide payment instructions to your bank: "OK, Mammoth National, pay Joe Shmoe $32 from my account, 00704-844." Theoretically, you could use just about anything as a check form — a piece of paper, a block of wood, and so on. In fact, rumor has it that someone once used a scrap of cowhide. It's easier for your poor bank, though, if you use check forms that follow the usual style and provide OCR characters along the form's bottom edge.

Check Date

The date you write your payment instructions, or check. Technically, the check date is the date on which your payment instructions to the bank become valid.

Circular E

Instructions from the Internal Revenue Service to employers. This publication tells how much federal income tax to withhold and other stuff like that. Call the IRS and request a copy if you need one.

Cleared

When a check or deposit has been received by the bank. An *uncleared* transaction hasn't been received by the bank.

Click

The process of pointing to something on a screen with a mouse and then pressing the mouse's left button. Occasional secondary usage refers to a snobbish group of adolescents.

Commands

What you use to tell Quicken what it should do. For example, "Quicken, I command thee to print a report."

Controller

A business's chief accountant — and usually the brunt of most accountant jokes. Also known as a *comptroller*.

Corporation

A legal business entity created by state law, owned by shareholders, and managed by directors and officers. As a business entity, a corporation has unique advantages and some disadvantages. Ask your attorney for more information.

Credit Card Accounts

An account specifically set up to track credit card charges, payments, and balances.

Cursor

Someone who uses vulgar language habitually. Also the little blinking line or square (mouse pointer) that shows where what you type will go.

Deleted Transaction

A transaction that Quicken has removed from the register. *See also **Voided Transaction.***

Directory

Basically, a drawer (like a filing cabinet drawer) that DOS uses to organize your hard disk.

Disk

The thingamajig in your computer on which DOS stores your programs (like Quicken) and your data files (like the Quicken file for your financial records). A hard disk (inside your computer) can store a great deal of information; floppy disks (5¼-inch or 3½-inch), which can be removed, store less data than a hard disk.

DOS

An acronym standing for Microsoft's Disk Operating System. Quicken uses DOS to handle the hardware (things like the screen, the keyboard, and so on). Because this book is about financial stuff, I should mention that DOS is one reason why Bill Gates became America's richest man.

Double-Click

Two clicks of the mouse in quick succession.

Exit

To shut down, terminate, or stop a program.

Field

Where bunnies hop around. Also input blanks on a screen.

File

Where data is stored. Your Quicken financial records, for example, are stored in a file.

File Assistant

A clever program within a program that asks a few questions and then sets up a new Quicken file. You almost certainly used the File Assistant when you set up Quicken.

Filename

The name of a DOS file in which Quicken stores data. Actually, what Quicken calls a filename is actually the name used for several files.

Financial Wizards

People who believe that they know so much about the world of finance it is actually their duty to share their expertise.

Find

A tremendous bargain, as in "At $22,000, the five-bedroom house was a real find." In Quicken, also an Edit menu command that you can use to locate transactions. *See also **Search Criteria.***

Formatting

Hey, this is too complicated for a book like this, isn't it? Let's just say that formatting means doing some things to a disk so that you can write files to that disk.

Graphics Adapter Cards

A chunk of circuitry inside your computer that Quicken and other programs need to draw pictures on your monitor. The acronyms EGA, VGA, CGA, and SVGA all refer to graphics adapter cards. But you really shouldn't have to worry about this stuff. Heck, you really don't need to know the difference between an EGA and the PTA (as in Harper Valley — get it?). Also needed for playing neat computer games.

Help

A program's on-line documentation — which can almost always be accessed by pressing F1. Also a verbalized cry for assistance.

IntelliCharge

A credit card especially for Quicken users that lets you receive your monthly statement on disk or through a modem. As a result, you need not enter your monthly credit card charges.

Internal Rate of Return

An investment's profit expressed as a percentage of the investment. If you go down to the bank and buy a certificate of deposit earning 7 percent interest, for example, 7 percent is the CD's internal rate of return. I don't want to give you the heebie-jeebies, but internal rates of return can get really complicated really fast.

Liability Accounts

An account specifically set up for tracking loans, payments, the principal and interest portions of these payments, and the outstanding balance.

Memo

A brief description of a transaction. Because you also give the payee and category for a transaction, it usually makes sense to use the Memo field to record some other bit of information about a check or deposit.

Menu

In Quicken, a list of commands. In a restaurant, a list of food and drinks you can order from the kitchen.

Menu Bar

Although it sounds like a place where menus go after work for a drink, a menu bar is a horizontally arranged row, or bar, of menus.

Missing Check

A gap in the check numbers. For example, if your register shows a check 101 and a check 103, check 102 is a missing check.

Mouse

A furry little rodent. Also a pointing device you can use to select menu commands and fields.

Mutual Fund Account

An account specifically set up to track a mutual fund investment.

Partnership

A business entity that combines two or more former friends. In general, each partner is liable for the partnership's entire debts.

Password

A word you have to give Quicken before Quicken will give you access to a file. The original password, "Open sesame," was used by Ali Baba.

Payee

The person to whom a check is made payable. (If you write a check to me, Steve Nelson, for example, I'm the payee.) In Quicken, however, you can fill in a payee field for deposits and for account transfers.

Power User

Someone who's spent far more time than is healthy fooling around with a computer. Power users are good people to have as friends, though, because they can often solve your worst technical nightmares. However, note that most people who describe themselves as power users aren't.

Register

The list of increases and decreases in an account balance. Quicken displays a register in a window that looks remarkably similar to a crummy old paper register — your checkbook. To print a copy of the register you see on your screen, press Ctrl-P and then Enter.

Report

An on-screen or printed summary of financial information from one or more registers.

Restore

Replace the current version of a file with the backup version. You may want to do this after a fire, hard disk failure, or thermonuclear exchange. *See also* **Backing Up.**

QIF

An acronym standing for Quicken Interchange Format. Basically, QIF is a set of rules that prescribes how an ASCII file must look if you want Quicken to read it. If you're a clever sort, you can import category lists and even transactions from ASCII files that follow the QIF rules.

Quicken

The name of the checkbook-on-a-computer program that this book is about. You didn't really need to look this up, did you?

QuickFill

A clever little feature. If Quicken can guess what you're going to type next in a field, it'll type, or QuickFill, the field for you. QuickFill types in transactions, payee names, and category names.

QuickPay

An extra program you can buy from Intuit, the maker of Quicken, to make payroll a snap.

QuickZoom

A clever big feature. If you have a question about a figure on an on-screen report, highlight the figure and choose QuickZoom from the File/Print menu. Quicken then lists all the individual transactions that go together to make the figure.

Scroll Bars

The vertical bars along the window's right edge and the horizontal bars along the window's bottom edge. Use them to scroll, or page, through your view of something that's too big to fit on one page.

Search Criteria

A description of the transaction you want to locate. *See also **Find.***

Sole Proprietor

A business that's owned by just one person and that doesn't have a separate legal identity. In general, businesses are sole proprietorships, partnerships, or corporations.

Spacebar

An intergalactic cocktail lounge. Also the big long key on your keyboard that produces a blank space.

Split Transactions

A transaction assigned to more than one category or transferred to more than one account. A split check transaction, for example, might show a $50 check to the grocery store paying for both groceries and automobile expenses.

Stockholders' Equity

The money that shareholders have contributed to a corporation or allowed to be retained in the corporation. You can't track stockholders' equity with Quicken.

Subcategory

A category within a category. For example, the suggested Quicken home categories list breaks down utilities spending into a Gas and Electric subcategory and a Water subcategory.

Tax Deduction

For an individual, an amount that can be deducted from total income (such as alimony or Individual Retirement Account contributions) or used as an itemized deduction and deducted from adjusted gross income (such as home mortgage interest or charitable contributions). For a business, any amount that represents an ordinary and necessary business expense.

Transposition

Flip-flopped numbers — for example, 23.45 entered as **24.35** (the 3 and 4 are flip-flopped as a 4 and 3). These common little mistakes have caused many bookkeepers and accountants to go insane.

Techno-Geek

Someone who believes that fooling around with a computer is more fun than anything else in the world.

Voided Transaction

A transaction that Quicken has marked as void (using the Payee field), marked as cleared, and set to zero. Void transactions appear in a register, but because they are set to zero, they don't affect the account balance. *See also **Deleted Transaction.***

W-2 and W-3

A W-2 is the annual wages statement you use to tell employees what they made and to tell the IRS what your employees made. When you send in a stack of W-2s to the IRS, you also fill out a W-3 form that summarizes all your individual W-2s. W-2s and W-3s aren't much fun, but they're not hard to fill out.

X

What Quicken uses in the C (or cleared) column to show that a transaction has cleared the bank and been processed by you in a monthly reconciliation.

Zen Buddhism

A Chinese and Japanese religion that says enlightenment comes from things like meditation, self-contemplation, and intuition — not from faith, devotion, or material things. I don't really know very much about Zen Buddhism. I did need a Z entry for the glossary, though.

Index

Note: All references shown in italics denote illustrations

• *Symbols* •

' (apostrophe), address field block on Write Checks screen, 71
* (asterisk) in the C column, 95–96, 153
***** number appears as (five asterisks) on check register screens, 78
$ (dollar) Amount field, Brokerage Account Register screen, 194–195
$ (dollar) Amount field, Investment Register screen, 184
$ (dollar) Amount field, Write Checks screen, 70
>>>>> (greater than) symbols, Register screen, 238
" (quotation mark), address field block on Write Checks screen, 71
? (question mark) string statements containing, 67
~ (tilde) string statements containing, 67
.. (two periods) string statements containing 67

• *A* •

account, 283
    balance, 284
    balance and postdated transactions, 272
    balance and unprinted checks, 237–238
    transfer, 109, 284
    type, 284
Account field, 185, 188, 190, 221
accounting
    accrual-basis, 245, 259
    cash-basis, 259
    corporate, 243–244
    double entry systems, 254
    invoices, 246
    multiple businesses, 244–245
    other DOS and Windows software, 260
    partnership, 244
    payroll, 246
    payroll tax money, 255–256
    QuickBooks software, 245–246
    retroactive records, 246
    setting money aside, 272
    single-entry systems, 254
    small business, 245–246
accounts
    additional bank, 23–26
    balancing, 91–102
    brokerage, 191–201
    cash, 274–275
    cash management/money market brokerage account, 194
    category identification, 60
    credit card, 144–147
    debit card, 157
    debts, 159–174
    description, 26
    finding, 51
    liability, 159–174
    loan, 130
    mortgage escrow, 168–171
    mortgage escrow as an asset account, 170–172
    mutual fund investment, 176–191
    naming, 25
    payable, 284
    payroll, 207–209
    payroll liability, 213–215
    personal cash, 274–275
    petty cash, 274–275
    receivable, 225–227, 284
    receivables account, 225–227
    reconciliation troubleshooting strategy, 252
    reconciling bank, 91–102
    savings goals, 269
    selecting correct, 69
    setting up a up bank, 10–14
    starting balance, 12, 26
    suspense, 251–252

tracking, 23

transactions, 109

transfers, 58, 109, 284

Accounts Receivable account, 225–*228*

Accounts Receivable register, clearing paid invoices on an account, *230*

Account Type field, Set Up New File screen, 144

accrual-basis accounting, 245, 259

Action field, 182, 185, 188, 194

Activities menu

Adjust Balance command, 202

Calculator command, 121

Calendar command, 56, 220

Calendar Notes command, 224

Financial Planning option, 124, 127, 130, 134, 138

Reconcile command, 92

Reconcile/Pay Credit Card Bill command, 151

Set Up Budgets screen, 41–42

Update Account Balance command, 172

Update Prices command, 201

Use Dos command, 105

Write Checks command, 70

Additional Account Information screen, Investment Account Type and Description screen, 179

Additional Prepayment field, Use Amortize Transaction, 167

Additions to Each Year field, Investment Planning calculator, 125

Add/Remove Shares action list, Investment Register screen, 183, 191

Add/Remove Shares actions, 182–183, 191, 195–196

Address field, Write Checks screen, 70–71

add shares, brokerage account, 195

Adjust Balance command, Activities menu, 202

Adjust Balance menu, 202

Adjustment Date field, Update Account Balance screen, 172

After-Tax Income fields, Retirement Planning calculator, 136

Age at Retirement field, Retirement Planning calculator, 136

aging, report, 233

alignment, check print outs, 74

Alt keys, activating commands with, 5, 15

Amortization, 285

amortization, loan, 161–168

Amount field, using percentages with a split transaction, 273

Annual Income After Taxes field, Retirement Planning calculator, 135

Annual Interest Rate field, 128, 163

Annual Yield field, 125, 138

A/P by Vendor command, Business Reports menu, 236

A/P by Vendor report

payables, 236

Quicken's Business, 85

APR, using to calculate loan refinancing costs, 132

A/P (Unprinted Checks) by Vendor report, 237

Untransmitted payments, 238

A/P (Unprinted Checks) by Vendor screen, 237

A/R by Customer report, Quicken's Business, 85, 230–232

arguments, search, 67

ASCII, 285

ASCII files, exporting, 87

As of Date field, Set Up New Accounts screen, 160

As of field, Starting Balance and Description screen, 146

Asset register, Accounts Receivable account, *228*

Asset register screen, *228*

audits, preparation for, 261–264

AutoCreate All command, Edit menu for Set Up Budget Screen, 44–46

AutoCreate Row command, Edit menu for Set Up Budget Screen, 44–46

AUTOEXEC.BAT file, 240

Automatically Create Budget screen, 44–46

Automatic Reminder Settings command, Set Preferences menu, 239

Automatic Reminder Settings screen, 239

automatic reminder, data back-up, 114–115

• B •

backing up, 285

backing-up data, 103–106, 114–115

Back Up File command, Print/Acct menu, 104

Backup Reminder Frequency screen, 114–115

balance
    account balance with unprinted checks in an account, 237–238
    account reconciliation, 91–102
    adjust loan account, 172–173
    adjust to correct cash, 202
    adjust to correct mutual fund shares, 202
    adjust to correct shares, 202
    effect of postdated transactions, 272–273
    starting, 12, 54

Balance field, 26, 145–146, 160

Balance Sheet report, Quicken's Business, 85

balancing an account, 285

Balloon at Payment Number field, Loan Calculator screen, 128–129

Balloon Payment screen, Set Amortization Information screen, 165

bank account, set up, 10–14

Bank Account register, recording a loan payment, 167–168

Bank Acct field, Make Credit Card Payment screen, 156

Bank Statement Ending Balance field, Reconcile Register with Bank Statement screen, 93

Bank Statement Opening Balance field, Reconcile Register with Bank Statement screen, 93

basis, tracking for investments, 177

Billminder, 238–240, 285
    check number set at ****, 273
    installation instructions, *280*
    postdated checks, 273
    reminder transactions in the investment register, 191

bookkeeping, 252–254

bookkeeper, 285

Borrowed or Lent field, Set Amortization Information screen, 164

brokerage account, 286
    buying securities, 197
    cash management/money market account, 194
    dividends, 198
    interest income, 199
    margin interest (MargInt) action, 199
    miscellaneous expenses, 200
    miscellaneous income, 198
    mutual funds investments, 196
    Portfolio Update Prices screen, *201*
    return of capital, 200–201
    sample buy and sell transactions in Brokerage Account Register screen, *197*
    selling securities, *197*
    setting up, 192–201
    updating securities prices, 201

Brokerage Account Register screen
    adding shares, 195
    recording cash going into a brokerage account, *195*
    sample transactions, *199*
    Shares Out (ShrsOut) action, 196
    Transfer Cash option, List of Actions, 194

budget, 286

Budget and Actual option, View Graphs menu, 88

budgets
    automatically increase/decrease amounts in, 45
    business, 38
    entering amounts with Fill Columns command, 44
    entering amounts manually, 42–44
    home, 38
    income change adjustments, 39–41
    menu commands, 46–48
    personal, 38
    planning with information from spending habit survey by Robert Morris & Associates, 38–39
    setting up, 41–46

business
    predefined categories, 26, 29–30
    Quicken's reports, 85

businesses, accounting for multiple, 244–245

Business Reports command, Business Reports menu, 218

Business Reports menu, A/P by Vendor command, 236

buttons, Print, Create Graph screen, 89

Buy Shares (BuyX) action, Investment Register screen action options, 185

Buy Transactions screen, Portfolio Details screen, 204

• C •

calculation
  example of Loan calculator, *129*
  examples of ten-key, 123
calculator
  clear key, 122
  Esc to remove from view, 124
Calculator command, Activities menu, 121
calculators
  College Planning, 137–140
  Investment Planning, 124–126, *125*
  Loan, 127–130
  mouse commands, 124
  Refinance, 130–133
  Retirement Planning, 133–137
  ten-key functions, 121–124
Calculator screen, ten-key, *121–122*
Calendar command, Activities menu, 56, 220
Calendar Notes command, Activities menu, 224
Calendar Notes screen, *224*
Calendar screen
  entering date into date field from, 274
  payroll scheduling notes and transactions, *223–224*
capital accounts, 286
capital gain, 286
Capital Gains (dDistr) action, Investment Register screen, 188
Capital Gains (dDistr) action, Llong-term capital Ggains & Transfer distribution (CGLongX), Investment Register screen, 188

Capital Gains (dDistr) action, Sshort-term capital Ggains Ddistr & Transfer distribution (CGShortX), Investment Register screen, 188

capital gains distributions, Brokerage Account Register screen, 198

Capital Gains report, Quicken's Investment, 84

capital loss, 286

capital, return of, brokerage account, 200–201

case sensitivity, search statements, 67

cash account
  Register screen version, *276*
  setting up, 274–275
Cash Balance command, Adjust Balance menu, 202
cash-basis accounting, 259
Cash Flow command, Home Reports menu, 81
Cash Flow Report, on-screen sample, *82*
Cash Flow report
  Quicken's Business, 85
  Quicken's Home, 84
Cash Flow Report screen, *82*
Cash In (XIn) option, Transfer Cash options, 194
cash management/money market account, brokerage account, 194
Cash Out (XOut) option, Transfer Cash options, 195
categories
  account identification in Category field, 60
  budgeting for average spending, 45
  change definition of, 34
  create new, 32–34
  defining, 31
  delete, 34
  finding names, 53
  Itemized Home report, 84
  naming, 22, 33
  predefined business, 26, 29–30
  predefined home, 26–29
  reminder to enter, 252
  split, 61–63
  subcategories, 30–31
  suspense account use, 251–252
  tax deductions, 31
  uses, 22

Warn If Transaction Has No Category field, Transactions Settings screen, 252
Categorize Transfer List, New Category option, 32–33
Categorize/Transfer List option
    Edit menu, 190
    Shortcuts menu, 32, 71
category, 286
Category for Adjustment field, Update Account Balance screen, 172
Category field
    Cat field on Transaction to Find screen, 66
    Credit Card Statement Information screen, 152
    deposits, 56
    Reconcile Register with Bank Statement screen, 93
    Register screen, 53, 59, 148–149
    Write Check screen, 71
category list, 287
Category and Transfer List screen, 32–33, 53, 57
    Edit Category screen, 34–35
Cat field, category field on Transaction to Find screen, 66
Certified Public Accountant, 287
CGLong (long term capital gains) action, Brokerage Account Register screen, 198
CGShort (short term capital gains) action, Brokerage Account Register screen, 198
Change Color Schemes menu, Screen Colors command, 116
changing, passwords, 119
characters
    searching for an unknown, 67
    searching for a string of, 67
    use of symbols in filenames, 110
Charge field, Register screen, 148
Charges, Cash Advances field, Credit Card Statement Information screen, 152
chart, 287
charts, data summary, 89
Check & Reports Settings command, Write Checks screen, 269

check date, 287
check form, 287
Checkfree, electronic payments, 266
checklist
    monthly bookkeeping, 252–253
    yearly bookkeeping, 253–254
checks
    account balance with unprinted checks in an account, 237–238
    alignment on printer, 74–75
    changes to existing, 54–55
    clearing from bank account, 96
    corrections, 54, 72
    deleting, 72
    enter transactions on Register screen, 51–67
    forms leaders, 74
    forms selection, 23
    loading into printer, 72
    number appears as ***** (five asterisks), 78
    postdated, 272–273
    printing, 72–78
    printing a sample, 74
    recording, 59, 72
    recording cashed, 271–272
    register sample, 79
    reprinting, 77–78
    reviewing cancelled, 258
    sample of completed, 71
    signing, 257–258
    sort options for reports, 80
    unprinted, 78
    verifying uncleared, 97
    void, 64, 72, 78
    Write Checks screen, 70–73
Choose Install Method screen, 278
Choose a Printer screen, 279–280
Circular E, 288
Circular E Employer's Tax Guide, payroll, 209
classes, transaction tags, 35
cleared, 288
    checks/deposits, 95–96
    loan payment transactions, Set Amortization Information screen, 165
    paid invoices in Accounts Receivable register, 229–230
clear key, calculator, 122

click, 288
double, 289
College Planning calculator, 137–140, *138*
sample data, *139*
College Planning command, Financial
Planning menu, 138
color
monitor selection, 278
screen settings, 115–117
command line parameters, 267
commands, 288
Adjust Balance, Activities menu, 202
A/P by Vendor, Business Reports
menu, 236
AutoCreate All, Edit menu for Set Up
Budget screen, 44–46
AutoCreate Row, Edit menu for Set
Up Budget screen, 44–46
Automatic Reminder Settings, Set
Preferences menu, 239
Back Up File, File Activities com-
mand on Main Menu, 104
Back Up File, Print/Acct menu, 104
Budget Edit, 47–48
Budget File, 47
Budget Layout, 47
Business Reports, Business Reports
menu, 218
Calculator, Activities menu, 121
Calendar, Activities menu, 56, 220
Calendar Notes, Activities menu, 224
Cash Balance, Adjust Balance menu,
202
Cash Flow, Home Reports menu, 81
Check & Reports Settings, Write
Checks screen, 269
College Planning, Financial Planning
menu, 138
Copy Transaction, Shortcuts menu, 55
Create Payroll Support, Use Tutori-
als/Assistants menu, 208
Create Reports, Main Menu, 231
Ctrl-P to print checks with Write
Checks screen displayed, 73
Delete Security/Trans, Shortcuts
menu, 204
Delete Transaction, Edit menu for
Register screen, 63–64

Delete Transaction, Edit menu for
Write Checks screen, 72
DOS, 276
Edit Budget Subcats, 48
Edit Budget Transfers, 48
Edit Clear Budget, 47
Edit Inflate/Deflate Budget, 47
Edit menu, 88
Edit Security/Trans, Shortcuts menu,
204
Edit Two Weeks, budget option, 47
Exit Quicken, Main Menu, 20
File Activities, Main Menu, 106, 109,
112
File Backup Budgets, 47
File Load Budget, 47
File Print Budgets, 47
File Restore Budgets, 47
File Save Budget As, 47
Fill Columns, Edit menu for Set Up
Budget screen, 44
Fill Right, Edit menu for Set Up
Budget screen, 45
Find, Edit menu for Register screen, 65
Full Page Adj, Vertical Check Adjust-
ment screen, 74–75
Go To Date, Edit menu for Register
screen, 65
Go To Transfer, Edit menu for
Register screen, 60
Graph Price History, Shortcuts
menu, 204
Higher/Lower, Vertical Check
Adjustment screen, 74–75
Include All Dates on reports, 81
Investment Planning, Financial
Planning menu, 124
Layout Hide Cents, budget option, 48
Layout menu, budget option, 88
Layout Months, budget option, 48
Layout Quarters, budget option, 48
Layout Years, 48
Loan Calculator, Financial Planning
menu, 127
Memorize Reports, File/Print menu,
86–87
Memorize Transaction, Shortcuts
menu, 55

Merge Sec Symbol, View menu, 204
mouse, 5, 16, 43–44, 124
Partial Page Adj, Vertical Check Adjustment screen, 75
Password Settings, Set Preferences menu, *118*–119
Payroll Report, Business Reports menu, 218
Percent View by Expense Total, budget option, 48
Percent View by Income Total, budget option, 48
Percent View by Respective Total, budget option, 48
Percent View Normal View, budget option, 48
Print Checks, Print/Acct menu, 73
Printer Settings, Main Menu, 268
Print Register, Print/Acct menu, 78–80
Print Report, File/Print menu, 83, 218
QuickReport, Reports menu, 86
QuickZoom, File/Print menu, 87
Reconcile, Activities menu, 92
Reconcile/Pay Credit Card Bill, 151
Record Transaction, Edit menu, 149, 184
Redo Last Report, Reports menu, 87
Refinance Calculator, Financial Planning menu, 130
Restore File, File Activities menu, 106–108
Retirement Planning, Financial Planning menu, 134
Scheduled Transaction, Shortcuts menu, 220
Screen Colors, Screen Settings menu, 115–116
Screen Settings, 116–117
Security List, Shortcut menu, 192
Select Account, Main Menu, 24, 26, 69, 147
Select/Set File, File Activities menu, 109
Select/Set Up Account, Print/Acct menu, 229
Set Backup Frequency, File Activities screen, 114
Set Preferences, Main Menu, 115, 118
Set Up Budgets, 41–42

Shares Balance, Adjust Balance menu, 202
Split Transaction, Edit menu for Register screen, 61
Split Transaction, Edit menu for Write Checks screen, 71
Summary, Reports Other menu, 233
Transaction Settings, Set Preferences menu, 252, 268
Update Account Balance, 172
Update Prices, Activities menu, 201
Use DOS, Activities menu, 105, 276
Use Register, Main Menu, 10, 41, 51, 78, 229
Use Tutorials/Assistants, 207
View Graph menu, 88–89
View menu, Portfolio Details screen, 204
View Register, 181
View Register, View menu, 204
Void Transaction, Edit menu for Register screen, 63–64, 72, 77–78
Write Checks, Activities or Main menu, 70
Write/Print Checks, Main Menu, 16, 41
Year End, File Activities menu, 112
Comm/Fee field, Investment Register screen, 185–186, 189
computer basics, 250
Confirm Before Recording Transaction field, Scheduled Transaction List screen, 222
Confirm Password screen, 118–119
Confirm Settings screen, 280
contribution period, Investment Planning calculator choices, 126
controller (comptroller), 288
conventions
    Alt key combinations, 5
    mouse commands, 5
    typeface styles, 5
conversion to Quicken, from a manual system, 254–255
copy, payee name to address field block, 71
Copy all Transactions to File Field, Start New Year screen, 112–*113*
copying, totals from previous year into next year's budget, 44–45

Copy Transaction command, Shortcuts menu, 55

corporate accounting, 243–244

corporation, 288

corrections, credit card entries, 149

Create Graph screen, 89

Create Opening Share Balance screen, *181*

Create Payroll Support command, Use Tutorials/Assistants menu, 208

Create Reports command, Main Menu, 231

Create Report screen, Reports menu, 82, 86

Create Reports menu, Main Menu, 81

Create Summary Report screen, Reports Other menu, 233

credit card accounts, 289

Credit Card Register, reconciliation version of, *153*

Credit Card Register screen, 152

credit cards, 143–144

    automatic check writing to pay statement, 156

    corrections, 149

    Credit Card Register Reconciliation screen sample, *154*

    hand written check payments, 156–157

    IntelliCharge and Quicken Visa, 157–158

    recording payments made from checking account, *150*

    recording payments when reconciling account, 151

    Register screen transaction sample, *149*

    setting up account, 144–147

    transactions, 148–151

Credit Card Statement Information screen, *151*–157

cross-referencing, source documents, 251

Current Age field, Retirement Planning calculator, 135

current balance, 272

Current Balance field, Set Amortization Information screen, 164

Current Payment field, Refinance Calculator screen, 131

Current Tax Rate field, Retirement Planning calculator, 135

Current Tuition (annual) field, College Planning calculator, 138

cursor, 289

customer invoices, Accounts Receivable account, 227–228

customer payments, Accounts Receivable account, 229

customization

    automatic backup reminders, 114–115

    passwords, 117–119

    reports, 86–88, 267

    screen color settings, 115–117

cutoff point date field, Start New Year screen, 112–113

• *D* •

DacEasy, accounting system software, 260

data

    automatic backup reminders, 114–115

    backing-up, 103–106

    excluding from a search, 67

    restoring from back-ups, 106–108

    saving, 20

    searching for, 65–67

data entry, Write Checks screen, 16–19

date, account starting, 13

Date field

    Investment Register screen, 182, 185

    Register screen, 13, 52, 56, 58, 148

    Starting Balance and Description screen, 26

    Write Checks screen, 70

date fields

    editing tricks, 53, 273–274

    entering date from Calendar screen, 274

Date of First Payment field, Set Amortization Information screen, 165

debit cards, setting up account, 157

defining, categories, 31

delete

    checks from Write Checks screen, 72

    transactions from register, 63

deleted transaction, 289

Delete Security/Trans command, Shortcuts menu, 204

Delete Transaction command
   Edit menu, Register screen, 63–64
   Edit menu, Write Checks screen, 72
Deposit field, Register screen, 56, 58
deposits
   changing, 58
   clearing from bank account, 95–96
   recording, 56–58
   sort options for reports, 80
   splitting, 63
   verifying uncleared, 97
Description field, 26, 146, 160
directory, 289
   install program, 279
disk, 289
disks, formatting for DOS, 105
display, 10-key calculator from Register
      or Write Checks screen, 121
Display field, Set Up Security screen, 193
Display Mode field, Set Up Mutual Fund
      Security screen, 180
Div action, Brokerage Account Register
      screen, 198
Dividend (DivX) action, Investment
      Register screen action options, 188
dividends, brokerage account, 198
DivX action, Brokerage Account Regis-
      ter screen, 198
documents, filing source, 251
DOS, 289
   Use DOS command, 276
double-click, 289
double entry, accounting systems, 254
drive, install program, 279
Drive and Directory screen, 279

● _E_ ●

Edit Budget Subcats command, 48
Edit Budget Transfers command, 48
Edit Category screen, Category and
      Transfer List screen, 34–_35_
Edit Clear Budget command, 47
Edit Inflate/Deflate Budget command, 47
editing, date field tricks, 273–274

Edit menu
   Categorize/Transfer option, 190
   commands, 88
   Delete Transaction command, 63–64
   Find command, 65
   Go To Date command, 65
   Go To Transfer command, 60
   Record Transaction command, 149, 184
   Set Up Budget screen, 44–46
   Split Transaction command, 61, 71
   Void Transaction command, 63–64,
      72, 77–78
Edit Security/Trans command, Short-
      cuts menu, 204
Edit Two Weeks command, Edit Budget
      menu, 47
EGA/VGA 43 Line-Display, Screen
      Settings commands, 116
electronic payments, Checkfree, 266
Employer Identification Number form
      request (SS-4) for payroll, IRS, 209
employer-paid federal payroll taxes,
      payroll, 214–215
employer-paid state payroll taxes,
      payroll, 219
ending balance, 272
End key, register, 65
enter, transactions in checkbook, 51
Enter Check Number screen, 74–77, _75_
Enter Name For File field, Set Up New
      File screen, 109
erase, field, 18
Esc key, 16
escrow account component
   as an account transfer in a Split
      Transaction, _170_
   as an expense category in a Split
      Transaction, 169–170
Estimated Annual Income ($ Per Share)
      field, Set Up Mutual Fund Security
      screen, 180
Estimated annual income ($ per share)
      field, Set Up Security screen, 193
exit, 289
exit Quicken, 20
export, formats supported, 87
exporting, tax information, 266

field(s), 289
    change information in a, 18
    erase, 18
    moving cursor to another, 18
    naming, 17
file, 289
File Activities command, Main Menu,
    106, 109, 112
File Activities menu, 106–109, 112
File Activities screen, Set Backup
    Frequency command, 114
File Assistant, 289
    setting up payroll account, 207–209
File Backup Budgets command, Budget
    File menu, 47
File Load Budget command, Budget File
    menu, 47
filename, 290
filenames, Quicken's references to, 111
File Password option, Password
    Settings screen, 118
File Print Budgets command, Budget
    File menu, 47
File/Print menu
    Memorize Reports, 86–87
    QuickZoom command, 87
File Restore Budgets command, Budget
    File menu, 47
files
    AUTOEXEC.BAT, 240
    controlling size, 111–114
    naming, 109
    passwords, 117–119
    setting up multiple, 109
    shrinking, 111–114
File Save Budget As command, Budget
    File menu, 47
Fill Columns command, Edit menu for
    Set Up Budget screen, 44
Fill Right command, Edit menu for Set
    Up Budget screen, 45
Finance Charges field, Credit Card
    Statement Information screen, 152
Financial Planning menu
    College Planning command, 138
    Investment Planning command, 124
    Loan Calculator command, 127

    Refinance Calculator command, 130
    Retirement Planning command, 134
Financial Planning option, Activities
    menu, 124, 127, 130, 134, 138
financial wizards, 290
find, 291
Find command, Edit menu for Register
    screen, 65
Form 940 (Annual Federal Tax Returns),
    payroll, 219, 283
Form 941 (Quarterly Federal Tax
    Returns), payroll, 217–218, 283
Form 942 (Quarterly Federal Tax
    Returns), payroll, 217–218, 283
formatting, 105, 291
Forms Leader (Ink Jet Only) field, Print
    Checks screen, 74
Forms Leader (Y/N) field, Print Checks
    screen, 74
For tax reporting purposes, is this a
    Tax-Deferred Account (Y/N) field,
    Investment Account Type and
    Description screen, 178
Frequency field, Set Up Scheduled
    Transaction, 221
Full Page Adj command, Vertical Check
    Adjustment screen, 74–75
function keys
    Ctrl-F1 for alphabetic list of Help
      topics, 19
    Ctrl-F7 for related Qcard information
      with Standard Categories screen, 11
    Ctrl-F8 to shrink/unshrink Qcard
      message with Standard Catego-
      ries screen, 11
    Ctrl-F9 to Show/Hide Qcards with
      Standard Categories screen, 11
    Ctrl-F10 to complete from Reconcile
      Register and Bank Statement
      screen entries, 97
    Ctrl-F10 to quit Credit Card State-
      ment Reconciliation Register
      screen, 154
    F1 to access Help screens, 291
    F2 for Print/Acct pull-down menu on
      Register screen, 13
    F3 for Edit pull-down menu on
      Register screen, 13

F4 for Shortcuts pull-down menu on Register screen, 13

F5 for Reports pull-down menu on Register screen, 13

F6 for Activities pull-down menu on Register screen, 13

F7 to display Balloon Payment screen from the Set Amortization Information screen, 165

F7 to display the Set Amortization Information screen from Loan Calculator, 163

F7 to display Vertical Check Adjustment screen, 74–75

F7 to set up loan account from Loan calculator, 130

F7 to toggle between contribution period choices in Investment Planning calculator, 126

F8 to calculate a loan figure other than regular payment on Loan Calculator, 129–130

F8 to display the Additional Account Information Screen from Investment Account Type and Description screen, 179

F8 to display Memorized Transaction Address screen from Set Amortization Information screen, 165

F8 to record additional account information on the Starting Balance and Description screen, 146

F8 to record additional data on liability account, 161

F8 to toggle between college planning variables to calculate a particular variable on College Planning calculator, 140

F8 to toggle between financial variables on Investment Planning calculator, 126

F8 to toggle between financial variables on Retirement Planning calculator, 137

F9 to display an on-screen amortization schedule from Set Amortization Information screen, 165

F9 to display a schedule of contributions/withdrawals/year-end retirement savings (or balances) on Retirement Planning calculator, 137

F9 to display Start Printing on Partial Page screen from Enter Check Number screen, 76–77

F9 to display year-to-year calculations on College Planning calculator, 140

F9 to paste calculations from Calculator screen into Register or Write screens, 123

F9 to print a sample check from Print Checks screen, 74

F9 to produce an on-screen schedule for a portfolio contribution plan from the Investment Planning calculator, 126

F9 to toggle between percent view and amount view on Norm View screen, 48

F9 to toggle between two-lines-per-transaction and one-line-per-transaction views of Register screen, 94–95

F9 to verify totals on Split Transaction screen, 63

F10 and Enter to record credit card charge, 149

F10 to complete reconciliation entries on Reconcile Register with Bank Statement screen, 94

F10 to complete Scheduled Payment Transaction screen entry, 222

F10 to display on-screen version of report from Create Report screen, 82

F10 to proceed with reconciliation from Reconciliation Is Not Complete message box, 156

F10 to record adjustment to balance in Update Account Balance screen, 173

F10 to record initial purchase of mutual fund shares on Investment Register screen, 184

F10 to record loan payment in register, 167

F10 to return to Enter Check Number screen from Start Printing on Partial page screen, 76

F10 to return to Enter Check Number screen from Vertical Check Adjustment Screen, 75

F10 to save changes, 35

F10 to save changes on Transactions Settings screen, 252

• *G* •

Goal field
  Set Up Mutual Fund Security screen, 180
  Set Up Security screen, 193
goals, investment, 180
Go To Date command, Edit menu for Register screen, 65
Go To Transfer command, Edit menu on Register screen, 60
graph commands, View Graphs menu, 88–89
graphics adapter cards, 291
Graph Price History command, Short-cuts menu, 204
graphs
  Income and Expense, 88
  monthly income and expense totals bar graph, 90
greater than (>>>>>) symbols, Register screen, 238
gross wage calculation, payroll, 209

• *H* •

Hand-written check (Y/N) field, Make Credit Card Payment screen, 156
hardware requirements, IntelliCharge option, 158
Help, 290
Help screens, 19, *20*
Higher/Lower command, Vertical Check Adjustment screen, 74–*75*
home
  budgets, 38
  predefined categories, 26–29
  Quicken's reports, 84
Home key, register, 65
hot keys, 14–15

• *I* •

icons, special, 6
importing, Quicken Interchange Format (QIF), 247
Impound/Escrow Amount field, Refinance Calculator screen, 131
Include All Dates command, reports, 81
income changes, 39–41
income and expense, bar graph, 90
Income and Expense, graph, 88
Income and Expense option, View Graph Menu, 88
Income, Expense, Or Subcategory field, Set Up Category screen, 34
income taxes, evasion, 255
Increase field, Asset register screen, 228
Inflate Payments field, Retirement Planning calculator, 135
Inflate Payments Yearly (Y/N) field, 125, 139
ink jet printers, check printing, 74
Insert key, 19
install
  Billminder, 280
  Confirm Settings screen, 280
  method selection, 278
  printer choices, *279*
  Quicken software on hard disk, 277–281
  registration instructions, *281*
Installation Complete screen, *281*
IntelliCharge, 291
  Quicken Visa credit card, 157–158
IntelliCharge (Y/N) field, Starting Balance and Description screen, 146
Interest Category field, Set Amortization Information screen, 164
Interest Earned field, Reconcile Register with Bank Statement screen, 94
Interest Earned Transaction Date field, Reconcile Register with Bank Statement screen, 94

Interest field, Refinance Calculator screen, 132
interest income, brokerage account, 199
internal rate of return, 292
Int Inc (Interest Income) action, Brokerage Account Register screen, 199
Investment Account Type and Description screen, Set Up New Account screen, *178*
Investment Income report, Quicken's, 84
Investment option, View Graphs menu, 88
Investment Performance report, Quicken's, 84
Investment Planning calculator, 124–126, *125*
Investment Planning command, Financial Planning menu, 124
Investment Planning screen, sample investment plan calculation, *127*
Investment Register screen, *182–184*
   Buy Shares (BuyX) action, 185
   Capital Gains (dDistr) action, 188
   Dividend (DivX) action, 188
   List of Accounts, 185
   Other Transactions option, List of Investment actions, 191
   purchase of additional mutual fund shares, 186
   recording a dividends reinvestment, 187
   recording a long-term capital gains distribution, *189*
   recording the sale of mutual fund shares, 190
   recording stock splits, 191
   reinvesting dividends or capital gains, 186–187
   remove shares from account without affecting portfolio value, 190–191
   selling a mutual fund investment, 189–190
   Sell Shares action (SellX), 189
   Sshort-term capital Ggains Ddistr & Transfer distribution (CGShortX), Capital Gains (dDistr) action, 188
investments
   goals, 180
   mutual funds, 176–191
   Portfolio Details screen, *203*–204

Quicken's reports, 84
record keeping, 175–177
setting up a mutual fund account, 177–184
tax-deferred, 176
tracking the *basis,* 177
Investment Transactions report, Quicken's, 84
invoices, 227–228, *246*
IRS, Employer Identification Number form request (SS-4) for payroll, 209
IRS special agent, audit and legal representation, 263
Is this a mutual fund (Y/N), Investment Account Type and Description screen, 178
Itemized Categories report, Quicken's Home, 84

• J •

Job/Project report, Quicken's Business, 85

• K •

keyboard commands
   + and - keys to edit dates, 273
   = to total tape on ten-key calculator, 122
   Alt-A to display Print/Acct menu from Register screen, 229
   Alt-E to display Edit menu from Set Up Budget Screen, 44
   Alt keys, 15
   Alt-S to display Shortcuts screen from Register or Write Checks screens, 32
   Alt to activate menu bar, 15
   arrow keys, 16
   A to print all checks from Print Checks screen, 73
   C to clear calculator, 122
   Ctrl-Backspace to erase a single character in a field, 66
   Ctrl+Backspace key to erase field, 18
   Ctrl-B to search backwards for a transaction, 66

Ctrl-C to display Category and Transfer list screen from Reconcile Register with Bank Statement screen, 93–94

Ctrl-C to display Category and Transfer List screen from Register screen, 148

Ctrl-C to display Category and Transfer list screen from Write Checks screen, 71

Ctrl-C to display list of accounts from Investment Register screen, 190

Ctrl-C to see list of accounts from Make Credit Card Payment screen, 156

Ctrl-C to display Category and Transfer List screen from Register screen, 53, 57

Ctrl-D to delete, 34

Ctrl-D to delete data from all fields in Transaction to Find screen, 66

Ctrl-D to delete entire check from Write Checks screen, 72

Ctrl-Enter to record credit card charge, 149

Ctrl-Enter to return to Starting Balance and Description screen from Additional Account Information screen, 146

Ctrl-C to display list of accounts from the Investment Register screen, 185

Ctrl-C to display list of categories from Update Account Balance screen, 173

Ctrl-D to delete extra split lines on Split Transaction screen, 213

Ctrl-D to erase all field entries in Investment Planning calculator, 126

Ctrl-Enter to record adjustment on Update Account Balance screen, 173

Ctrl-Enter to record the dividend or distribution action on the Investment Register screen, 188

Ctrl-Enter to record initial purchase of mutual fund shares on Investment Register screen, 184

Ctrl-Enter to record a reinvestment transaction on the Investment Register screen, 187

Ctrl-E to display Edit Category screen from Category and Transfer List screen, 34

Ctrl-E to edit security names from Shortcuts menu, 202

Ctrl-J to display Scheduled Transaction List from Calendar screen, 223

Ctrl-L display a list of investment actions from Investment Register screen, 182

Ctrl-L for list of display choices from Set Up Mutual Fund Security screen, 180

Ctrl-L to access list of common report date ranges from Reports menu, 81

Ctrl-L to display a list of accounts from Action field for Set Up Scheduled Transaction screen, 221

Ctrl-L to display list of frequencies from Frequency field for Set Up Scheduled Transaction screen, 221

Ctrl-L to display list of investment actions from the Investment Register screen, 186

Ctrl-L to display list of investment actions from Investment Register screen, 191

Ctrl-L to display a list of investment actions from the Investment Register screen Action field, 185

Ctrl-L to display a list of investment actions on the Investment Register screen, 188

Ctrl-L to display list of investment goals, 180

Ctrl-L to display list of investment types from Set Up Security screen, 193

Ctrl-M to save custom report specifications, 86

Ctrl-N to add notes to calendar from Calendar screen, 224

Ctrl-N to search forward for a transaction, 66

Ctrl-O to display 10-key calculator from Register or Write Checks screen, 121

Ctrl-P+Enter to print a college planning calculation schedule, 140

Ctrl-P+Enter to print an on-screen portfolio contribution schedule from Investment Planning calculator, 126

Ctrl-P+Enter to print retirement planning contributions/withdrawals/year-end retirement savings (or balances) schedule, 137

Ctrl-P to print an on-screen report, 83

Ctrl-P to print a graph, 89

Ctrl-P to print on-screen amortization schedule, 165

Ctrl-P to print register from Register screen, 78

Ctrl-S to choose Split Transaction command from Edit menu for Register screen, 61

Ctrl-S to choose Split Transaction command on Write Checks screen, 71

Ctrl-S to display Split Transaction dialog box, 165

Ctrl-T to display Memorized Transaction List screen, 167

Ctrl-V to void a check with Register screen displayed, 72

Ctrl-X to choose Go To Transfer command from Edit menu on Register screen, 60

Ctrl-Z to zoom in on a report figure, 87

Enter to total tape on ten-key calculator, 122

Esc to remove calculator from view, 124

Esc to unchoose a command, 16

hot keys, 14–15

H to change date field to last day of month or preceding month, 274

M to change date field to first day of month or preceding month, 274

R to change date field to last day of this year or preceding year, 274

screen scrolling, 43–44

spacebar to mark cleared checks on Credit Card Register Reconciliation screen, 153

S to print selected checks from Print Checks screen, 73

T to edit current date in date field, 274

Y to change date field to first day of this year or preceding year, 274

keys
  Esc, 20
  Insert, 19
  PgDn, 19
  PgUp, 19

• *L* •

laser printer, check printing, 73, 76

Layout Hide Cents command, budget layout option, 48

Layout menu commands, budget layout option, 88

Layout Months command, budget layout option, 48

Layout Quarters command, budget layout option, 48

Layout Years command, budget layout option, 48

learning curve, Quicken's, 249–251, 258–259

Leave Reconciliation (Your Work Will Be Saved) option, Reconciliation Is Not Complete message box, 98–99, 155

legal representation, audit by an IRS special agent, 263

liability account, setting up memorized loan payment transaction, 162–168

Liability account option, Set Up New Account screen, 160

liability accounts, 292
  payroll records, 213–*218*
  transactions, 162–171

List of Accounts, Investment Register, 185, 190

List of Actions, Brokerage Account Register screen, 194

List of Investment Actions
  Investment Register Screen action
    options, 182–*183*
  Other Transactions option, Broker-
    age Account Register screen, 200
List of Investment Goals, Investment
    Register, 180, 193
List of investment types, Set Up New
    Type, 193
List of investment types, Set Up
    Security screen, 193
Llong-term capital Ggains & Transfer
    distribution (CGLongX), Capital
    Gains (dDistr) action, Investment
    Register screen, 188
loan account
  amortization, 161–168
  cleared payment transactions, 165
  recording payments, 167–168
  setting up, 130
loan accounts, balance adjustments,
    172–173
Loan Amount field, Set Amortization
    Information screen, 164
Loan calculator, 127–130
Loan Calculator command, Financial
    Planning menu, 127
Loan Calculator screen, *128*–130
loans, sample payment transaction, *168*
long-term capital gains (CGLong),
    Brokerage Account Register
    screen, 198

• *M* •

Main Menu, *9*
  Create Reports command, 231
  Create Reports menu, 81
  File Activities command, 106, 109, 112
  Printer Settings command, 268
  Select Account command, 24, 26, 69,
    147
  Set Preferences command, 115, 118
  Use Register command, 10, 41, 51,
    78, 229
  Use Tutorials/Assistants command,
    207
  View Graphs menu, 88

Write/Print Checks command, 16, 32,
    41, 70
Make Credit Card Payment screen,
    156–157
manual system, conversion to Quicken,
    254–255
MargInt (Margin Interest) action,
    Brokerage Account Register
    screen, 199
Market Price field, Portfolio Update
    Prices screen, 201
measuring profits, 260
memo, 292
Memo field
  Investment Register screen, 184
  Register screen, 53, 56, 59, 66, 148
  Set Amortization Information
    screen, 164
  Write Check screen, 71
Memorized Transaction address screen,
    Set Amortization Information
    screen, 165
Memorized Transaction Groups, 267
Memorized Transaction List screen,
    162–168, 167
Memorized Transactions, 267
Memorize Reports command, File/Print
    menu, 86–87
Memorize Transaction command,
    Shortcuts menu, 55
menu, 292
  activation alternatives, 13
Menu Access, Screen Settings
    commands, 117
menu bar, 292
  activating with Alt key, 15
menus
  Adjust Balance, 202
  Business Reports, 236
  Change Color Schemes, 118
  Create Reports menu, Main Menu, 81
  File Activities, 106–109, 112
  File/Print, 86–87
  Financial Planning, 124, 127, 130, 134,
    138
  Print/Acct, 26, 73, 78–80, 104, 229
  Reports, 81, 86–87, 233
  Set Preferences, 115, *118*–119, 239,
    252, 268

View, 181, 201, 204
See also Activities menu, Edit menu,
Main Menu, Shortcuts menu
Merge Sec Symbol command, View
menu, 204
messages
add new category name to category
list, 53–54
"Budget Has Been Modified," 47
Check Register does not balance
with Bank Statement, 98
File Copied Successfully, Use old file
or file for new year?, 113
Leave Reconciliation (Your Work
Will Be Saved) option,
Reconciliation is Not Complete
message box, 98–99, *155*
OK to Delete Transaction, 63–*64*
OK to record transaction, 54
Proceed to Next Reconciliation Step
option, Reconciliation is Not
Complete message box, 99, 156
Reconciliation is Not Complete, *98*
method selection, install, 278
Microsoft Profit, accounting system
software for Windows, 260
miscellaneous payroll taxes and
deductions, 212
MiscExp (Miscellaneous Expense)
action, Brokerage Account
Register screen, 200
MiscExp option, Other Transactions
option, Investment Action List,
200
MiscInc (Miscellaneous Income) action,
Other Transactions option, List of
Investment actions, Investment
Register screen, 200
missing check, 292
Missing Check report
Quicken's Business, 85
Quicken's Home, 84
monitor, color selection, 278
Monitor Display, Screen Settings
commands, 116
Monthly Budget report, Quicken's
Home, 84
mortgage, escrow accounts, 168–172

Mortgage Closing Costs field, Refinance
Calculator screen, 132
Mortgage Points field, Refinance
Calculator screen, 132
mouse, 293
mouse commands
calculators, 124
choose/unchoose, 5, 16
screen scrolling, 43–44
mutual fund account, 293
mutual fund investment account
purchasing shares by reinvesting
dividends or capital gains, 186
purchasing shares by writing a
check, 185–*186*
recording a prior share purchase, *184*
setting up, 176–184
mutual funds investments, brokerage
account, 196
M.Y.O.B. from Teleware, accounting
system software for Windows, 260

• *N* •

940 payroll tax form, 283
941 payroll tax form, 283
942 payroll tax form, 283
Name field, Set Up Mutual Fund Security
screen, 179
Name for This Account field, Set Up
New Account screen, 144, 160,
178, 225
naming
accounts, 12, 25
categories, 22
fields, 17
files, 109
naming account, 12
net wage calculations, payroll, *212*
Net Worth option, View Graph Menu, 88
Net Worth report, Quicken's Home, 84
<New Account option>, Select Account
to Use screen, 24, 144, 160, 177
New Category option, Categorize
Transfer List screen, 32–33
New Security item, Security List screen, 192
Next Transaction Date field, Set Up
Scheduled Transaction screen, 221

No Goal option, List of Investment Goals, 180, 193
No. of Transactions field, Set Up Scheduled Transaction screen, 222
Number of Additional Copies (Laser Only) field, Print Checks Screen, 73
Number of Years Enrolled field, College Planning calculator, 138
Number of Years field, Investment Planning calculator, 125
Num field, Register screen, 53, 56, 58, 66

• O •

1-2-3 disk files, exporting, 87
   Lotus, 283
on-screen reports, 82–83
Other Income field, Retirement Planning calculator, 136
Other option, Reports menu, 86
Other Transactions option, MiscExp (miscellaneous expense) action, List of Investment actions, Investment Register screen, 200
Other Transactions option, MiscInc (Miscellaneous Income) action, List of Investment Actions, Investment Register screen, 200
Other Transactions option, RtnCap (return of capital), List of Investment Actions, Investment Register screen, 201
Other Transactions option, StkSplit (stock split) action, List of Investment actions, Investment Register screen, 191

• P •

P&L Statement report, Quicken's Business, 85
Pacioli 2000, accounting system software, 260
parameters, command line, 267
Partial Page Adj command, Vertical Check Adjustment screen, 75
partnership, 293

partnership accounting, 244
password, 293
   changing, 119
   files, 117–119
   removing, 119
   transaction, 119
   using, 259
Password Settings command, Set Preferences menu, 118–119
Password Settings screen, File Password option, 118
paste, calculations from Calculator screen into Register or Write screens, 123
payables
   A/P by Vendor business report, 236
   unpaid vendor, 235–237
   vendor, 235–240
payday schedule, payroll, 220–224
payee, 293
   address field on Write Checks screen, 70–71
Payee field
   Register screen, 53, 56, 58, 66, 148
   Set Amortization Information screen, 164
   Write Checks screen, 70
Payment field
   Register screen, 53, 66
   transfers to other bank accounts, 58
payments
   Accounts Receivable account, 229
   Checkfree electronic, 266
   loan accounts, 167–168
   Untransmitted, A/P (Unprinted Checks) by Vendor report, 238
Payments Made field, Set Amortization Information screen, 165
payroll
   accounting, 246
   automatic recording of paycheck transaction in account's register, 222
   Business Payroll report, 217–218
   Calendar screen notations and transactions, 223–224
   checks with remittance advice or payroll stubs, 214
   Circular E Employer's Tax Guide, 209

Employer Identification Number form request (SS-4) from IRS, 209
employer-paid federal payroll taxes, 214–215
employer-paid state taxes, 219
Form 940 (Annual Federal Tax Return), 219
Form 941 (Quarterly Federal Tax Returns), 217–218
Form 942 (Quarterly Federal Tax Returns), 217–218
gross wage calculation, 209
liability account entries, 216–218
miscellaneous taxes and deductions, 212
net wage calculations, 212
payday reminder, 222
payday schedule, 220–224
Payroll:Comp FICA expense, 214
Payroll:Comp MCARE expense, 214
Payroll-FICA liability account, 213–14
Payroll-FWH liability account, 213
Payroll-MCARE liability account, 213–214
Payroll-SWHXX liability account, 219
QuickFill, 223
QuickPay software by Intuit, 208
recording checks on Split Transactions screen, 213–215
sample federal tax deposit check, 216
sample of federal withholding schedule for married employee, 211
sample of federal withholding schedule for single employee, 210
scheduling payday, 220–222
setting up account with File Assistant, 207–209
Split Transaction screen with sample employer matching share of payroll taxes, 215
Split Transaction screen with sample of payroll check, 214
state payroll taxes, 219
tax deposits, 215–218
tax money accounting, 255–256
tax withholding, 209
Total Transfers from Payroll liability accounts, 218
W-2 and W-3 wage statements, 219

W-4 forms, 209
withholding calculations and schedules, 210–212
Payroll report, Quicken's Business, 85
Payroll Report command, Business Reports menu, 218
Payroll Report screen, Print Report command, 218
Pay to the Order of field, Write Checks screen, 70
Peachtree, accounting system software, 260
Peachtree Accounting for Windows, accounting system software for Windows, 260
percents, using with a split transaction in the Amount field, 273
Percent View by Expense Total command, budget view option, 48
Percent View by Income Total command, budget view option, 48
Percent View by Respective Total command, budget view option, 48
Percent View Normal View command, budget view option, 48
Periods Per Year field, 128, 163
personal, 26–29, 38, 84
Portfolio Details screen, 181–182, 203–204
View menu commands, 204
portfolio transactions, deleting securities, 204
Portfolio Update Prices screen, 201
Portfolio Value report, Quicken's Investment, 84
postdated transactions, account balance, 272
power user, 293
Predicted Inflation field, 125, 138
Predicted Inflation Rate field, Retirement Planning calculator, 136
Present Savings field, 134, 138
Present Value field, Investment Planning calculator, 124
Price field, Investment Register screen, 183
Principal Account field, Set Amortization Information screen, 164
Principal field
Loan Calculator screen, 128
Refinance Calculator screen, 131

print
    portfolio contribution schedule from
        Investment Planning calculator, 126
    Reconciliation report from Print
        Report screen, 97
Print/Acct menu
    Back Up File command, 104
    Print Checks command, 73
    Print Register command, 78–80
    Select/Set Up Account, 26
    Select/Set Up Account command, 229
Print All/Selected Checks field, Print
    Checks screen, 73
Print button, Create Graph screen, 89
Print Checks command, Print/Acct
    menu, 73
Print Checks screen, 73–77
printers
    ink jet, 74
    installation choices, 279
    laser, 73, 76
    loading checks, 72
    report print settings, 80
Printer Settings command, Main Menu,
    268
printing
    check register, 78–80
    checks, 72–78
    reports, 80–83
    reprinting checks, 77
    sample check, 74
Print One Transaction Per Line field,
    Print Register screen, 80
Print Register command, Print/Acct
    menu, 78–80
Print Register screen, 78–80
Print Report command
    File Print menu, 83
    Payroll Report screen, 218
Print Report screen, *83*
    exporting reports, 87
Print to field, Print Checks screen, 73
Print Transactions From/To fields, Print
    Register screen, 80
Print Transaction Splits field, Print
    Register screen, 80
problems, balancing your checkbook,
    99–102
Proceed to Next Reconciliation Step
    option, Reconciliation Is Not
    Complete message box, 99, 156
profits, measuring, 260

• Q •

Qcards, pop-up messages, 11
QIF (Quicken Interchange format), 294
    importing files, 247
q or Q at DOS prompt, start Quicken, 9
QuickBooks, small business accounting
    software, 227, 245–246
Quicken, 294
    install software on hard disk, 277–281
    learning curve, 249–251
    standard reports, 83–85
    starting, 250
Quicken's
    File Assistant, 289
    Tutorials/Assistants, 207–*208*, 268
Quicken Visa credit card, IntelliCharge,
    157–158
QuickFill, 55, 294
    payroll, 223
QuickPay, payroll software by Intuit,
    208, 246, 295
QuickReport command, Reports
    menu, 86
QuickReport screen, *86*
QuickZoom, 295
QuickZoom command, File/Print
    menu, 87
quotation mark ("), address field block
    on Write Checks screen, 71

• R •

Recall Transaction option, Shortcuts
    menu, 162
Reconcile command, Activities
    menu, 92
Reconcile/Pay Credit Card Bill com-
    mand, Activities menu, 151
Reconcile Register with Bank Statement
    screen, *92–94*
reconciliation

problems balancing your checkbook, 99–102
version of register, *95*
Reconciliation Is Not Complete message box
    Leave Reconciliation (Your Work Will Be Saved) option, 98–99, 155
    Proceed to Next Reconciliation Step option, 99, 156
Reconciliation report, Print Report screen, 97
reconciling
    accounts, 252
    bank account, 91–102
    credit card statements, 151–157
Record Additional Account Information, Starting Balance and Description screen, 146
records
    cashed checks, 271–272
    entering retroactive transaction, 246
    source documents, 251, 262
Record Transaction command, Edit menu, 149, 184
Redo Last Report command, Reports menu, 87
Refinance Calculator, 130–133, *131*
Refinance Calculator command, Financial Planning menu, 130
Refinance Calculator screen, 130–133
register, 294
    one-line-per transaction on Register screen, 94–*96*
    printing, 78–80
    print out of check, *79*
    Reconciliation, *97*
    reconciliation version of, *95*
    scrolling, 64–65
    title, 80
    two-lines-per transaction on Register screen, 94–*95*
Register screen, 51–67, *52*, 147
    Asset Account version for mortgage escrow account, *171*
    cash account version, *276*
    commands for, 60–61, 63–65, 72, 77–78
    credit card version, *147*
    Edit menu, 60–61, 63–65, 72, 78
    enter checks on, 51–67

function keys for, 13
greater than (>>>>>) symbols, 238
keyboard commands for, 53, 57, 60–61, 78
Print Account menu, *15*
Reports menu, 81
sample credit card transaction, *149*
Set Up Budgets screen, 41–*42*
Register View, Screen Settings commands, 117
registration instructions, *281*
Regular Payment field
    Loan Calculator screen, 128–129
    Set Amortization Information screen, 163
reinvesting dividends or capital gains, Investment Register screen, 186–187
Reinvestment Transactions screen, Portfolio Details screen, 204
Remember icon, 6
reminders
    account starting balance, 54
    care in selecting accounts, 227
    changing deposit transactions, 57–58
    correcting transfer transaction errors, 59
    to delete extra split lines on Split Transaction screen use Ctrl-D, 213
    how to remember date editing commands, 274
    interest expense deductions, 160
    reconciling bank statements, 54
    registration, 281
    using + and - keys to edit dates, 273
    ways to display the Select Account to Use screen, 275
reminder transactions in the investment register, Billminder, 191
remove shares, brokerage account, 196
removing, passwords, 119
report, 294
reports
    aging, 233
    A/P (Unprinted Checks) by Vendor, *237*
    custom, 267
    customizing, 86–88
    date range, 81–82
    exporting, 87

Include All Dates command, 81
memorize, 86–87
on-screen, 82–83
preparing documentation for an
    audit, 262
printer settings, 80
printing, 80–83
Quicken's Business, 85
Quicken's Home, 84
Quicken's Investment, 84
Quicken's Other option, 86–87
Reconciliation, Print Report screen, 97
titles for, 81
zoom in on figure for explanation, 87
Reports menu, *81*
    Create Report screen, 86
    Home Reports, 81
    Other option, 86
    QuickReport command, 86
    Redo Last Report command, 87
    Register screen menu bar, 81
    Write Checks screen menu bar, 81
Reports Other menu
    Create Summary Report screen, 233
    Summary command, 233
reprinting, checks, 77–78
restore, 294
Restore File command, File Activities
    menu, 106–108
restoring files
    data from back-ups, 106–108
    manually from records, 108
Retirement Planning calculator,
    133–137, *134*
Retirement Planning command, Finan-
    cial Planning menu, 134
return of capital, brokerage account,
    200–201
RtnCap (return of capital), Other
    Transactions option, List of
    Actions, Investment Register
    screen, 201

• S •

Save Changes to Budget option, Auto-
    matically Create Budget screen, 46

saving
    custom report specifications, 86
    data, 20
savings goals account, 269
Scheduled Payment Transaction screen,
    222
Scheduled Transaction command,
    Shortcuts menu, 220
Scheduled Transaction List screen, *220*
Scheduled Payment Transaction List
    screen, *221*
Screen Colors command, Screen
    Settings menu, 115–116
Screen Graphics, Screen Settings
    commands, 117
Screen Patterns, Screen Settings
    commands, 116
screens
    Additional Account Information,
        Investment Account Type and
        Description screen, 179
    A/P (Unprinted Checks) by Vendor,
        237
    Asset register, *228*
    Automatically Create Budget, 44–*46*
    Automatic Reminder Settings, *239*
    Backup Reminder Frequency,
        114–115
    Balloon Payment, 165
    Buy Transactions, Portfolio Details
        screen, 204
    Calculator, 121–122
    *Cale*ndar, 223–224, 274
    Calendar Notes, *224*
    Cash Flow Report, *82*
    Category and Transfer List, 32–*33*, 53
    check register showing recorded
        entries, *54, 57, 59*
    Choose Install Method, *278*
    Choose a Printer, *279*–280
    Confirm Password, 118–119
    Confirm Settings, 280
    Create Graph, 89
    Create Opening Share Balance, *181*
    Create Report, 82, 86
    Create Summary Report, 233
    Credit Card Register, 152
    Credit Card Statement Information,
        151–157

Drive and Directory, *279*
Edit Category, 34–*35*
Enter Check Number, 74–77, *75*
Help, 19, *20*
Help screen information about Quicken's Main Menu, *20*
Installation Complete, *281*
Investment Account Type and Description, 178–179
Investment Planning, *127*
Investment Register, *182–184*
Loan Calculator, *128*–130
Make Credit Card Payment, 156–157
Memorized Transaction address, Set Amortization Information screen, 165
Memorized Transaction List, *162*–168, *167*
Password Settings, 118
Payroll Report, 218
Portfolio Details, 181–*182*, *203*–204
Portfolio Update Prices, *201*
Print Checks, *73*–77
Print Register, 78–80
Print Report, Report menu, *83*, 87
QuickReport, *86*
Reconcile Register with Bank Statement, *92*–94
Refinance Calculator, 130–133
Reinvestment Transactions, Portfolio Details screen, 204
Scheduled Payment Transaction, 222
Scheduled Transaction List, *220*
scrolling with keyboard, 43–44
scrolling with mouse, 43–44
Security List, 192
Select Accounts to Include, A/R by Customer Report, 231–*232*
Select Account to Use, *13*, 24, *24*, 69, 91, 147
Select Account to Use, <New Account> option, 24, 144, 160, 177
Select Amortized Payment Type, *166*
Select Backup Drive, 104
Select Checks to Print, 74–*75*
Select Drive to Restore From, 106–*107*
Select File to Restore, *107*–108
Select/Set Up New File, 109–111, *110*

Sell Transactions, Portfolio Details screen, 204
Set Amortization Information, 163–166
Set Up Budget, 41–46, *42–43*
Set Up Category, 32–*33*
Set Up Mutual Fund Security, *179*–180
Set Up New Account, *11*, *25*, 144–147, 225
Set Up New File, 109–111, *110*
Set Up Password, *118*
Set Up Scheduled Transaction, *221*
Set Up Security, 192
Shortcuts menu, 32
Specific Credit Limit, 146
Split Transaction, *61*–63, 71, 273
Split Transaction with sample loan payment data, *166*
Standard Categories, *10*
Standard Categories, Set Up New File screen, 110–111
Starting Balance and Description, *12*, *25*, *146*, *161*
Start New Year, 112–*113*
Start Printing on Partial Page, *76*–77
ten-key Calculator, *122*
Transactions Settings, 252
Transaction to Find, *65*
Update Account Balance, *172*–173
Use Amortize Transaction, *167*–168
Use Billminder, *280*
Vertical Check Adjustment, 74–*76*
Welcome to Quicken Install, *278*
Write Checks, *17*, 32, 70–73, *70*
Year End, *112–113*
screens. *See also* Register screen
Screen Settings commands, 116–117
Screen Settings menu, *115*–116
    Screen Colors command,
scroll bars, 295
scrolling, register, 64–65
search
    excluding data from a, 67
    Find command, Edit menu for register screen, 65
    finding transactions, 65
    special characters, 67

specifying an unknown character, 67
specifying a character string, 67
statements containing a ? (question
    mark)), 67
statements containing a ~ (tilde), 67
statements containing .. (two
    periods), 67
search criteria, 295
securities
    deleting from Portfolio Details
        screen, 204
    updating prices for brokerage
        account, 201
Security field, Investment Register
    screen, 183, 188
Security List command, Shortcut menu,
    192
Security List screen, 192–194
    New Security item, 192
    Set Up Security screen, 192
Select Account command, Main Menu,
    24, 26, 69, 147
Select Accounts to Include screen, A/R
    by Customer Report, 231–232
Select Account to Use screen, 13, 24, 69,
    91, 147, 226
    <New Account> option, 24, 144–145,
        160, 225
Select Amortized Payment Type
    screen, 166
Select Backup Drive screen, 104
Select Checks to Print screen, 74–75
Select Drive to Restore From screen,
    106–107
Select File to Restore screen, 107–108
Select Screen Settings, Set Preferences
    menu, 115
Select/Set File command, File Activities
    menu, 109
Select/Set Up Account command, Print/
    Acct menu, 229
Select/Set Up New File screen, 109–111,
    110
    Set Up New File option, 109
Sell Shares action (SellX), Investment
    Register screen action options,
    189
Sell Transactions screen, Portfolio
    Details screen, 204

Service Charge field, Reconcile Register
    with Bank Statement screen, 93
Service Charge Transaction Date field,
    Reconcile Register with Bank
    Statement screen, 94
Set Amortization Information screen,
    163–166
Set Backup Frequency command, File
    Activities screen, 114
Set File Location field, Set Up New File
    screen, 110
Set Preferences command, Main Menu,
    115, 118
Set Preferences menu
    Automatic Reminder Settings
        command, 239
    Password Settings command,
        118–119
    Select Screen Settings, 115
    Transaction Settings command, 252,
        268
setting up
    Accounts Receivable account,
        225–227
    additional accounts, 23–26
    additional files, 109–111
    bank account, 10–14
    brokerage account, 192–201
    cash account, 274–275
    credit card account, 144–147
    debit card account, 157
    loan account, 130
    memorized loan payment transac-
        tion, 162–168
    mortgage escrow account as an
        asset account, 170–172
    multiple files, 109
    mutual funds investment account,
        176–184
    payroll accounts, 207–209
Set Up Budgets command, Activities
    menu on Set Up Budgets screen,
    41–42
Set Up Budgets screen
    Activities menu, 41–42
    Edit menu, 44–46
    Register screen, 41–42
    Write/Print Checks screen, 41
Set Up Category screen, 32–33

Set Up Mutual Fund Security screen, *179*–180
Set Up New Account screen, *11*, *25*, 144–147, *145*, *226*
   Liability account option, 160
   Name for This Account field, 144
   <New Account> option, 160
   Other Asset option, 225
Set Up New File screen, 109–111
   Standard Categories screen, 110–111
Set Up New Goal option, List of Investment Goals, 180, 193
Set Up New Type option, List of investment types, 193
Set Up Password screen, Set Preferences menu, *118*
Set Up Scheduled Transaction option, Scheduled Transaction List screen, 220
Set Up Security screen, 193
   Security List screen, 192
Shares Balance command, Adjust Balance menu, 202
Shares field, Investment Register screen, 184
Shares In (ShrsIn) action, Add/Remove Shares actions, 182–183, 195–*196*
Shares Out (ShrsOut) action, Add/Remove Shares actions, 182–183, 191, 196
Shortcuts menu
   Categorize and Transfer List command, 53
   Categorize/Transfer option, 32, 53, 57, 72
   Copy Transaction command, 55
   Delete Security/Trans command, 204
   Edit Security/Trans command, 204
   Graph Price History command, 204
   Memorize Transaction command, 55
   Register screen, 32
   Scheduled Transaction command, 220
   Security List command, 192
   Transfer option, 185
   Write Checks screen, 32
short term capital gains (CGShort), Brokerage Account Register screen, 198
shrinking files, 111–114

ShrsIn action, Add/Remove Shares actions, 182–*183*, 195–*196*
ShrsOut action, Add/Remove Shares actions, 182–*183*, 191, 196
single-entry, accounting systems, 254
small business accounting, 245–246
software
   DacEasy accounting system, 260
   install Quicken on hard disk, 277–281
   Microsoft Profit accounting system for Windows, 260
   M.Y.O.B. accounting system for Windows from Teleware, 260
   Pacioli 2000 accounting system, 260
   Peachtree accounting system, 260
   Peachtree Accounting for Windows, 260
   QuickBooks, 227
   QuickBooks accounting system, 245–246
   QuickPay by Intuit, 208, 246
sole proprietor, 295
Sort By Check Number field, Print Register screen, 80
source documents
   audit preparation, 262
   cross-referencing, 251
   filing, 251
spacebar, 295
special agent, audit by an IRS, 263
Specific Credit Limit screen, 146
split categories, 61–63
splitting, transfers, 63
Split Transaction command
   Edit menu, Register screen, 61
   Edit menu, Write Checks screen, 71
split transactions, 296
Split Transactions screen, 61–63, *61–62*, 71
   payroll check recording, 213–215
   recording a customer payment, 229–*230*
   sample loan payment data, 166
   using percentages in the Amount field, 273
SS-4 (Employer Identification Number form request) for payroll, IRS, 209
Standard Categories screen, *10*
   Set Up New File screen, 110–111
starting balance, 12

Starting Balance and Description
    screen, *161*
    Set Up New Accounts screen, *12, 25,*
        145–*146*, 160, 225, *227*
starting Quicken, 250
Start New Year screen, 112–*113*
Start Printing on Partial Page screen,
    76–77
start Quicken, q or Q at DOS prompt, 9
Statement Ending Date field, 93, 152
Statement Open Date field, 152
Statement Opening Date field, 93
StkSplit (stock splits) action, Invest-
    ment Register screen, 191
stockholders' equity, 296
string, searching for a character, 67
subcategories, 30–31
subcategory, 296
Summary command, Reports Other
    menu, 233
surveys, Robert Morris & Associates on
    business spending habits, 38
suspense account, categories, 251–252
Symbol field, 179, 193

• T •

tax, evasion of income, 255
tax deduction, 296
tax deductions
    categories, 31
    tracking, 22
tax deposits, payroll, 215–218
tax information, exporting, 266
Tax-related field, Set Up Category
    screen, 34
Tax Schedule field, Set Up Category
    screen, 34
Tax Schedule report, Quicken's
    Home, 84
Tax Sheltered (Y/N) field, Retirement
    Planning calculator, 134–135
Tax Summary report, Quicken's Home,
    84
tax withholding, payroll, 209
Technical sidebars, 3

Technical stuff
    determining corporation's
        stockholder's equity, 244
    ensuring that Billminder works
        properly, 240
    exiting Quicken, 20
    field names, 17
    icon, 6
    IntelliCharge hardware require-
        ments, 158
    Investment Planning calculator
        assumptions, 125
    keeping investment records, 181
    menu activation alternatives, 13
    Quicken references to filenames, 111
    Quicken's identification of unprinted
        checks, 238
    Retirement Planning calculator
        assumptions, 135
    search statements, 67
    total verification options for split
        transactions, 63
    when to set up new accounts, 247
techno-geek, 296
ten-key calculator, 121–124
Tip icon, 6
Tips
    accessing the back Up File command
        from Main Menu, 104
    actions ending with an "X" indicate
        cash movement, 198
    additional payroll software available
        from Intuit, QuickPay for book-
        keeping records, 208
    backing up files, 108
    Category field entries in transfer
        transactions, 60
    changing date in date fields, 53
    check forms, 23
    choosing correct distribution action
        for investment records, 188
    classes, 45
    completing optional information
        fields, 178
    copy payee name to address block, 71
    correcting errors on Transaction to
        Find screen, 66
    correcting mistakes in credit card
        entries, 149

displaying the Register screen through Activities menu, 52
displaying the Set Amortization Information screen while using Loan calculator, 163
display Select Account to Use screen, 24
editing securities names, 202
estimating taxes on income changes, 40
exporting to a tax schedule, 34
extra check copies for accounts payable files, 74
filenames, 110
finding category names, 53
fitting more information on the Register screen, 153
generating customer invoices, 227
graph report formatting, 89
handling mutual funds investments in a brokerage account, 196
list all outstanding accounts with A/R By Customer Report, 230
looking for transposed numbers in an unreconciled account, 101
making a permanent copy of a portfolio contribution plan from the Investment Planning calculator, 126
Print Checks command location, 73
Print Register command location, 73
Qcards, 11
recording investment actions, 186
refinancing strategy, 131
report printing, 81
reviewing old files, 114
scrolling to view reports on-screen, 83
selecting from the category names list, 148
selecting a liability account, 161
split categories for a check, 71
starting balance date, 14
storing additional information on liability accounts, 161
toggling between percent view and amount view on Normal View screen, 48
using liability accounts for withheld payroll taxes, 215

using spending habit survey by Robert Morris & Associates for budget planning, 38–39
titles, reports, 81
total, Checks to Print, 62
totals, rounding budget, 45
Total Transfers from Payroll liability accounts, Payroll Report, *218*
Total Years field
    Loan Calculator screen, 128
    Set Amortization Information screen, 164
tracking
    accounts, 23
    tax deductions, 22
training
    computer basics, 250
    learning curve, 249–251
    learning curves, 258–259
transaction
    account balance adjustments, 172–173
    account register with a postdated, *273*
    account transfers, 58–60, 109
    automatic recording of paycheck in account's register, 222
    categorizing entries, 251
    checks, 51–54
    class tags, 35
    copied, 55
    credit card, 148–151
    debit card accounts, 157
    delete from register, 63
    deposits, 56–58
    entering, 51
    escrow account disbursements, 171
    find, 65–66
    liability accounts, 162–171
    memorized, 55
    passwords, 119
    postdated, 272
    Register screen views, 94–*95*
    a sample loan payment, *168*
    sample of a zero amount, *272*
    sort options for reports, 80
    split, 61–63
Transaction to Find screen, 65–66

Transaction Settings command, Set
    Preferences menu, 252, 268
Transactions Settings screen, 252
Transaction Type field, Set Up
    Scheduled Transaction screen, 221
Transfer Cash option, List of Actions,
    Brokerage Account Register
    screen, 194
Transfer Cash options, Cash In (XIn)
    option, 194
Transfer option, Shortcuts menu, 185
transfers
    account, 58–60
    correcting an error, 60
    sort options for reports, 80
    splitting, 63
    transactions and multiple files, 109
Transfers In field, Investment Account
    Type and Description screen, 179
Transfers Out field, Investment Account
    Type and Description screen, 179
transposition, 296
troubleshooting
    balancing your checkbook, 99–102
    Q at C:/> doesn't start Quicken, 250
    reconciliation of credit card account
    does not equal zero, 155–156
Turn on Billminder field, Automatic
    Reminder Settings screen, 239
Tutorials/Assistants, Quicken's,
    207–*208*, 268
Type of Checks to Print On field, Print
    Checks screen, 73
Type field, Set Up Security screen, 193

• *U* •

Untransmitted payments, A/P
    (Unprinted Checks) by Vendor
    report, 238
Update Account Balance command,
    Activities menu, 172
Update Account Balance screen,
    172–173
Update Prices command, Activities
    menu, 201

Update This Account's Balance To field,
    Update Account Balance screen, 172
US/Canadian Loan (U/C) field
    Loan Calculator screen, 128
    Refinance Calculator screen, 131
    Set Amortization Information
    screen, 164
Use Amortize Transaction screen,
    167–168
Use Billminder screen, *280*
    installation instructions, 280
Use DOS command, Activities menu, 105
Use File for New Year option, File
    Copied Successfully message
    box, 113
Use Memorized Transaction field,
    Update Account Balance
    screen, 173
Use Old File option, File Copied
    Successfully message box, 113
Use Register command, Main Menu,
    10, 41, 51, 78, 229
Use Tutorials/Assistants command,
    Main Menu, 207
Use Tutorials/Assistants menu, *208*
    Create Payroll Support command,
    208

• *V* •

vendor payables, 235–240
verifying, uncleared checks/deposits, 97
Vertical Check Adjustment screen, 74–*76*
View Graphs menu, options, 88
View menu
    commands, Portfolio Details screen, 204
    Merge Sec Symbol command, 204
    View Register, 201
    View Register command, 181, 204
View Register, View menu, 201
View Register command, View menu,
    181, 204
views
    one-line-per transaction on Register
    screen, 94–95
    two-lines-per transaction on Register
    screen, 94–*95*

void, checks, 64, 72, 78
voided transaction, 297
Void Transaction command, Edit menu,
    Register screen, 63–64, 72, 78

• W •

W-2 and W-3 forms, 297
W-2 and W-3 wage statements, payroll, 219
W-4 forms, payroll, 209
wage calculations, payroll, 209–212
Warn If Transaction Has No Category
    field, Transactions Settings
    screen, 252
Warning icon, 6
Warnings
    backing up before shrinking files, 112
    editing transactions, 64
    keeping bank accounts for multiple
        businesses, 245
    recording initial mutual fund secu-
        rity purchases, 180
    restoring current files with back-up
        version, 108
    restoring data from back-up files, 106
    scheduling payroll tax deposits, 217
    tax withholding information
        up-dates, 211
    use of names on customer invoices,
        228
    using APR to calculate loan refinanc-
        ing costs, 132
    verifying name of active account, 69
Warning sidebars, 3
Welcome to Quicken Install screen, *278*
Withdrawal Until Age field, Retirement
    Planning calculator, 136
withholding calculations and schedules,
    payroll, *210–212*
Write Checks screen, 16–19, *17*, 32,
    70–73, *236–238*
    Check & Reports Settings command,
        269
    keyboard commands for, 71

Reports menu, 81
Shortcuts menu, 32
Write/Print Checks command, Main
    Menu, 16, 32, 41, 70
Write/Print Checks screen, Set Up
    Budgets screen, 41–*42*

• X •

X, 297
Xfer field, Investment Register screen,
    185, 190

• Y •

Year End Action field, Start New Year,
    112–*113*
Year End command, File Activities
    menu, 112
Year End screen, *112–113*
Yearly Payments field
    College Planning calculator, 139
    Retirement Planning calculator, 135
Years field, Refinance Calculator
    screen, 132
Years Until Enrollment field, College
    Planning calculator, 138

• Z •

Zen Buddhism, 297
zero amount transactions, *272*
zoom, report figure explanation, 87

Notes

Notes

Notes

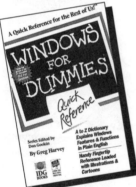

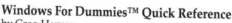

Order Form

Order Center: (800) 762-2974 (8 a.m.-5 p.m., PST, weekdays) or (415) 312-0650

For Fastest Service: Photocopy This Order Form and FAX it to : (415) 358-1260

Quantity	ISBN	Title	Price	Total

Shipping & Handling Charges

Subtotal	U.S.	Canada & International	International Air Mail
Up to $20.00	Add $3.00	Add $4.00	Add $10.00
$20.01-40.00	$4.00	$5.00	$20.00
$40.01-60.00	$5.00	$6.00	$25.00
$60.01-80.00	$6.00	$8.00	$35.00
Over $80.00	$7.00	$10.00	$50.00

In U.S. and Canada, shipping is UPS ground or equivalent.
For Rush shipping call (800) 762-2974.

Subtotal _____

CA residents add applicable sales tax _____

IN residents add 5% sales tax _____

Canadian residents add 7% GST tax _____

Shipping _____

TOTAL _____

Ship to:

Name _____

Company_____

Address_____

City/State/Zip _____

Daytime Phone _____

Payment: ❑ Check to IDG Books (US Funds Only) ❑ Visa ❑ MasterCard ❑ American Express

Card # _____ Exp. _____ Signature _____

Please send this order form to: IDG Books, 155 Bovet Road, Suite 310, San Mateo, CA 94402.
Allow up to 3 weeks for delivery. Thank you!

BOBFD

IDG BOOKS WORLDWIDE REGISTRATION CARD

RETURN THIS REGISTRATION CARD FOR FREE CATALOG

Title of this book: Quicken For DOS For Dummies

My overall rating of this book: ☐ Very good [1] ☐ Good [2] ☐ Satisfactory [3] ☐ Fair [4] ☐ Poor [5]

How I first heard about this book:

☐ Found in bookstore; name: [6] _____

☐ Advertisement: [8] _____

☐ Word of mouth; heard about book from friend, co-worker, etc.: [10]

☐ Book review: [7] _____

☐ Catalog: [9] _____

☐ Other: [11] _____

What I liked most about this book:

_____

_____

What I would change, add, delete, etc., in future editions of this book:

_____

_____

_____

Other comments:

_____

Number of computer books I purchase in a year: ☐ 1 [12] ☐ 2-5 [13] ☐ 6-10 [14] ☐ More than 10 [15]

I would characterize my computer skills as: ☐ Beginner [16] ☐ Intermediate [17] ☐ Advanced [18] ☐ Professional [19]

I use ☐ DOS [20] ☐ Windows [21] ☐ OS/2 [22] ☐ Unix [23] ☐ Macintosh [24] ☐ Other: [25]_____
(please specify)

I would be interested in new books on the following subjects:
(please check all that apply, and use the spaces provided to identify specific software)

☐ Word processing: [26] _____

☐ Data bases: [28] _____

☐ File Utilities: [30] _____

☐ Networking: [32] _____

☐ Other: [34] _____

☐ Spreadsheets: [27] _____

☐ Desktop publishing: [29] _____

☐ Money management: [31] _____

☐ Programming languages: [33] _____

I use a PC at (please check all that apply): ☐ home [35] ☐ work [36] ☐ school [37] ☐ other: [38] _____

The disks I prefer to use are ☐ 5.25 [39] ☐ 3.5 [40] ☐ other: [41]_____

I have a CD ROM: ☐ yes [42] ☐ no [43]

I plan to buy or upgrade computer hardware this year: ☐ yes [44] ☐ no [45]

I plan to buy or upgrade computer software this year: ☐ yes [46] ☐ no [47]

Name: _____ **Business title:** [48] _____ **Type of Business:** [49] _____

Address (☐ home [50] ☐ work [51]/**Company name:** _____ **)**

Street/Suite# _____

City [52]/**State** [53]/**Zipcode** [54]: _____ **Country** [55] _____

☐ **I liked this book!** You may quote me by name in future
IDG Books Worldwide promotional materials.

My daytime phone number is _____

IDG BOOKS

THE WORLD OF
COMPUTER
KNOWLEDGE

❏ **YES!**

Please keep me informed about IDG's World of Computer Knowledge. Send me the latest IDG Books catalog.